JEFF COOPER

The Soul and the Spirit

2nd Edition

My Father's Story
by
Lindy Cooper Wisdom

*"With regard to excellence, it is not enough to know,
but we must try to have and use it."*

– ARISTOTLE

For my dad.

ISBN 0-9621342-6-0

DESIGNED BY APEX PRINTING CORPORATION
PHOENIX, ARIZONA
PRINTED IN THE UNITED STATES

PUBLISHED BY GUNSITE ACADEMY, INC.
2900 W. GUNSITE ROAD
PAULDEN, ARIZONA 86334

CONTENTS

Introduction

My father is not an ordinary man. He is a writer, teacher, philosopher and thinker with a large following. The deep respect people have for him and the high esteem in which they hold him has become apparent to me slowly over the years. Only now, in my own middle age, do I begin to see his character as unique and to realize that both he and the depth of his appeal are remarkable.

Some months ago, I had the privilege of accompanying my parents and eight others on a month-long trip to South Africa. Planned by my father, the trip included hunting, battlefield touring, general sightseeing and a wine tour in and around Cape Town. All along the way we were hosted by friends of my dad's. I was overwhelmed by the extent to which these people put themselves out for our group because my father was a part of it. People could not do enough for him. We were treated royally. I asked one of our hosts why he so revered my father and he said, "Because he always tells the truth and he cannot be bought." I was intrigued.

Upon returning home, a message awaited me. An old friend had called to suggest that it was about time someone wrote a biography of my dad and that I undertake the project. The coincidence of this call and the experiences I enjoyed on the Africa trip led me to this effort.

My dad is above all a connoisseur of excellence. He holds himself and all others to the highest standards. He acknowledges that only a few excel, but he encourages us all to strive for, applaud and appreciate the best in all arenas. His special gift as a teacher is to bring out the achiever in each of us. He believes that true happiness is simply the by-product of achievement. By encouraging and appreciating achievement, he leads the way to happiness. People are drawn to this.

He frames his appreciation of human achievement in a strong moral code which allows little tolerance for human weakness. His code is based on traditions of honor and integrity and acknowledges absolutes of right and wrong. This code is a beacon to those who find the world's current relativism wanting.

My dad is a voracious reader and continuous student. He is also an actor, a raconteur and a bon vivant. It's exhilarating to be with him, but demanding. He thinks and questions and requires you to do the same. This is a novelty in an age where we have become accustomed to being told what to think by television reporters and newspaper columnists.

So, what is the essence of my father's appeal and how is it communicated? What is it that the professional hunter in South Africa, the neurosurgeon in Massachusetts, the farmer in the Philippines, the cop in Phoenix and the businessman in Belgium all find in him? And whatever it is, how and why did it develop? These are the questions I hope to answer for myself in researching and writing this book. I hope I can do justice to the subject.

Prologue

May 7, 1994

This is our fifth day in South Africa. We're on the way to the hunting camp where we will stay for the next ten days. We've already had completely full days of marvelous experiences and it seems to me that I've been away from home for at least two weeks. The weather is beautiful, clear and mild. The historic election was held just before we came and they are still counting the votes to see what the majority percentage will finally be. The mood of most of the people we meet is cautious optimism. People seem surprised and very pleased that our group is here, considering the very bad press South Africa has been getting. We've been welcomed with open arms.

We've been sightseeing in and around Pretoria, visited a private game ranch where we shared our lunch with a pet klipspringer, stayed at a lovely resort, seen the beautiful Lost City, eaten crocodile kebabs, warthog stew, roast impala, mealie pap and other exotic dishes, been guests for a catered dinner and stimulating political discussion in a lovely private home in Johannesburg and been chauffeured and escorted with speed and dexterity all over by my parents' very good friend and his son.

We have climbed all over the impressive Voortrekker monument, had a private tour of Jan Smuts' house by the enthusiastic curator, had dinner with the previous commanding general of the South African Air Force and the current Deputy Attorney General for the Northern Transvaal (who is involved in writing the new constitution), seen crocodile, waterbuck, giraffe, sable, impala, warthog, dassie, zebra, red hartebeest, white rhino, black rhino, hippo, kudu, ostrich, springbok, steenbok, blesbok, baboon and a day-old roan struggling to stand.

Our group consists of me, my mother, my father, my niece, and six others. With the exception of one young woman who is accompanying her husband, these others are men who have taken at least one course of rifle instruction from my father and have been inspired to join him on a hunt in Africa. My niece has also taken rifle instruction from my dad and will also be hunting.

My mom and I are not hunters. Most of us did not know more than a few of the others before we met at the hotel in Pretoria. We are getting along well and finding we have much in common.

What has struck me forcefully is the warmth of my father's friends here in South Africa and the high regard they have for him. Everyone has been so hospitable and truly welcoming and kind. They have all gone to a great deal of trouble for our group as well, and we are all feeling very pampered and lucky to have the benefits of my dad's celebrity extended to us. The red carpet has been out since we arrived and we are making the most of it and enjoying ourselves tremendously.

Now we have arrived at Engonyameni, Danie and Karin Van Graan's hunting camp in the Eastern Transvaal. They are here to welcome us along with their two charming young daughters and the other professional hunters and members of the staff who will be helping out for the next ten days. The grounds are lovely, the theme from *Out of Africa* is playing softly as we enter the main lodge. It is a perfect setting. Stone floors, high thatched roof, spiral staircase and cat walk, stone bar, elephant stools covered in zebra hide, a full-mount leopard reclining by a small indoor fountain, a magnificent full-mount lion standing to the left, green plants and kudu and warthog and impala and wildebeest and buffalo and more and more mounted on the walls. Zulu spears and shields leaning against the wall in one corner. On the opposite side of the room, a small area is set aside for rifles and enlarged photographs of hunters and their trophies. Skins on the floor. Comfortable chairs and barstools and smiling, welcoming faces everywhere you turn. It could not be better. We immediately feel comfortable, at home and perfectly content.

There's more. We are shown our individual quarters. Danie and Karin have assigned my parents to the largest and closest of the separate cabins. They have stayed in this cabin before on a previous hunting trip almost two years ago. Something has been added. In front of the cabin overlooking a pond, Danie has built a deck and small, thatched-roof bar, fully stocked. It has comfortable seating, both stools and tables and chairs and is the perfect place to read or write, in solitude or in the company of family and friends. It's a lovely addition.

Danie invites closer inspection. There are enlarged photographs lining the interior of the structure, all of my dad on his previous hunt with other grandchildren and Danie. There is an engraved wooden sign hanging up by the entrance to the bar. It reads, "Cooper's Corner". *Danie has built this entire structure for and in honor of my dad.*

My father is surprised and very pleased and most gracious in his acceptance of this tribute. I am so touched by the magnitude of the time and effort that has gone into this that I am struck dumb. It is such a perfect gift, I am in awe of Danie's thoughtfulness. I am also perplexed and intrigued. Danie has not known my father long and the relationship has been one of professional hunter and client. Why has Danie done this extraordinary thing for my father?

For me, it is the culmination of an accumulation of remarkable efforts various people have undertaken for my father on this trip. In addition to the letters, overheard conversations, plaques, testimonial dinners and awards that I have been aware of over the years, this private bar in South Africa has finally awakened me to the fact that something unique is at hand. I am seeing my father from a new vantage point and it is startling. What is it about my father that inspires such regard?

The hunt continues, a complete success for all involved. The trip goes on and friends continue to go out of their way for us all along our route. We have a marvelous month, full of new experiences. We have made new friends, learned a great deal and enjoyed ourselves to the fullest. We will never forget this trip and we will never be the same. We are enriched, wiser and better. We owe this to my father. What kind of man is this who takes such delight in introducing others to the joys he knows? What paths has he followed to this point? What influences made him the avid student, dedicated teacher and seeker of excellence that he is? Why do his followers, who come from all walks of life and from all over the world, revere him so? Perhaps if I go back into his past, some of the answers to these questions will reveal themselves. Where to begin?

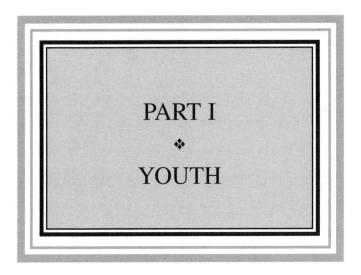

PART I

❖

YOUTH

Beginnings – Paternal

In the summer of 1939 a tall, slim, blonde young man of nineteen took part in a six-week R.O.T.C. camp in San Luis Obispo, California. He had been in R.O.T.C. since high school, so this was not new to him. One of about 250 cadets, he spent his days firing French 75's, drilling, hauling the guns around with horses, playing war games and practicing and perfecting the skills involved.

At the end of the six-week period, it came time to be graduated and the word went around that the cadets would all play a joke. On the morning of the ceremony, they would all form up in pajamas. "They can't flunk us all, so if we all do this together, we'll have a laugh." The tall blonde one refused to go along. No amount of cajoling or threats or entreaties to "be one of the boys" could move him. He felt that the point of the entire course had been to learn to be officers—to command. As officers, they would all give orders and expect their orders to be obeyed. How could they expect this of others if they were deliberately disobedient to command themselves? He would not budge.

The next morning 249 young men showed up for formation in pajamas. But the 250th, tall and straight and slim, was in full uniform. This was not a popular move with the other cadets. At the first opportunity, they threw him into the water trough. That was okay with him. He had made his point and was perfectly comfortable with the outcome. Cadet John Dean Cooper had the moral high ground and he knew it. He was absolutely sure.

> *"That sounds just like him."*
> *– LT. GENERAL VICTOR H. KRULAK*

This self-assurance and disregard of peer pressure has characterized John Dean "Jeff" Cooper all his life. He is inner-directed—a philosopher whose values formed slowly, steadily and rock-solid, like mighty stalagmites in a deep cavern. He believes in the transcendence of individual human achievement. The forces which shaped his unique set of genes were in accord—all relaying the same messages. His family, his teachers and a steady stream of books told him all he needed to know to understand the meaning of life: seek excellence in all things, seek to make truth, honor, integrity, honesty, loyalty, courage, and wisdom not simply words, but guideposts for living. His experiences in life have supported and refined his early understanding, but not changed it. Do what is right and do it to the very best of your ability. His motto is "Understand the problem. Pull your weight. Appreciate." Expect the same from others. Never give in.

* * * * * * * * * * * * * * *

Home is where character is formed. There are exceptions, but in general a young person's ideas of good and bad and right and wrong are built, bit by bit, in the daily interactions which take place in his home. It is said that a child learns the principles of life at his mother's knee. In actuality the entire family is intimately involved.

The home where Jeff grew up was a large, comfortable, two-story house at 500 North Rossmore in Los Angeles, California. That address was way out of town when the house was built and the Coopers moved into it in 1922. The house had a formal dining room which adjoined the kitchen, connected by two swinging doors. It was separated from the living room by a hall which was the entryway to the house. The Coopers ate with a considerable amount of formality in the dining room. That is not to say that they "dressed for dinner" and were served by a bevy of servants in fancy uniforms, but the table was set, the meal prepared and served by the cook and the entire family sat down to dinner together. Jeff's father believed that sitting down together at dinnertime to converse was the groundwork of civilization. Jeff accepted this belief, made it his own and later made it an integral part of his own family's life.

Conversation was the order of the day. It was not a matter of eating quickly and being excused, nor was it a matter of keeping silent while others spoke. It was a give-and-take exchange amongst those seated around the table. At the Cooper's dinner table sat Jeff, his father and mother and his older (by ten and eight years respectively) brother and sister. This is one of the reasons Jeff was more precocious as an adolescent than other little boys. All his formative years he was allowed into the adult conversations of his parents and older siblings. This is where he learned what to do and what not to do. He learned what he *ought* rather than what he *must*. What one does and does not do is a much more important lesson than what one is allowed to do or what one will be punished for doing. Morality is not formed in character by being told you must. You are led to the moral path by being told what you ought and understanding the difference.

At the head of the table sat Jeff's father, John Titus "Jack" Cooper. He was the undisputed head of the family and without a doubt the strongest and

Young Jeff with friend in the side yard of the house at 500 North Rossmore in Los Angeles, circa 1924.

Jeff's father, John Titus "Jack" Cooper.

Jeff's older brother Heinie on the front steps of the house at 500 North Rossmore in his uniform for the Harvard Military Academy, circa 1923.

most important influence on Jeff throughout his youth. Intelligent, inquisitive, circumspect, reserved, and an excellent businessman, Jack was a voracious reader who loved the romance of adventure, included as much of it as he could in his own life, and passed along this passion to his younger son.

Jack, born September 9, 1882, was a successful banker and real estate developer. He was the elder of two sons born to Harry Hershey Cooper and Euphemia Titus. Harry and Euphemia began their married life somewhere in the Pennsylvania Dutch country and moved to California before their sons were born. Two years after Jack's birth they had Thomas Percy, known as "Buzz". Euphemia died quite young and Harry then married a woman who was always known to Jeff as "Aunt Adelaide". She and Harry did not have children of their own. Harry obtained employment as a telegraph operator for Southern Pacific when it first came out west and he became head of the dispatch department. This was a significant post in those days because there was no radio or telephone and communications were all by keyboard. This made him a comfortable living.

"Grandpa", as Harry Hershey Cooper was known to Jeff, was also an inventor and adept at fixing things. He was in large part responsible for a new engine design used by the armed forces in World War I. He also worked on a method of bringing fresh water to Catalina Island, off the southern California coast.

Grandpa died when Jeff was only six years old. What stands out in Jeff's memory most is the fact that Grandpa had only one leg. The story was that he was up on Mount Lowe, not far from Mount Wilson in back of La Cañada,

From left to right, Austeene, Jack, Buzz and Grandpa, before the amputation of his leg.

which was a winter resort for southern Californians who wanted to see snow. There was no skiing in those days, but people rode sleds and sleighs and built snowmen and threw snowballs. Grandpa, who was an adult at the time, was run over by a sleigh and it crushed his right leg. In intense pain, he got off the mountain the only way possible, on horseback.

He tried to avoid amputation for many years, but the leg was increasingly the site of infection so it was sawed off, closer to the hip than the knee. All the time Jeff knew him, Grandpa got along on one crutch and his left leg.

Grandpa's courage and stoic action in the face of his injury was a story that inspired Jeff greatly. Later in life, when he read of a similar experience of Denys Reitz, Afrikaaner hero of the Boer War, he felt a special kinship because of the example in his own family.

A young Jack.

Jack was a very fine student. Of average build, he had light brown hair and was quite handsome. When he was graduated at the top of his class from Los Angeles High School he was admitted to the Leland Stanford Junior University as its first scholarship recipient. Jeff has the letter introducing Jack to the university as the "young man that Mrs. Stanford wishes to be educated at the Stanford University." Mrs. Stanford traveled down to Los Angeles to meet Jack and award him his scholarship personally.

Jack did well at Stanford both socially and academically. He was a member of the Zeta Psi Fraternity, a membership which he prized. He studied law and got a degree in law, although he did not ever pass the bar or practice law. His athletic activity was gymnastics.

Jack was graduated from Stanford in 1904 and Buzz was graduated from the University of California at Berkeley in 1906. They saved their pennies and were able to pull off a truly wonderful experience. In 1907 they packed up and moved to Paris for a full year. This was at the height of the *Belle Epoque*—probably the peak of Western Civilization—and at that time Paris was the center of everything—*La Ville Lumierre*. Jack and Buzz lived frugally on the Left Bank but frugality did not stop them from soaking up the atmosphere. Relations between the United States and France were quite cordial then and the brothers made the most of their opportunities.

Jack acquired certain attitudes that stayed with him. To the end of his days he was something of a Francophile. He picked up enough of the French language to get along and he became quite interested in gastronomy—food and drink.

In those days, Paris was about the only place where one could get a decent meal by today's standards. The West Coast of the United States was strictly, as Jack put it, "meat and potatoes, whiskey and water." The tradition of the Californios was to kill fresh beef, slice it thin and burn it black. Generally, food in the home was uninteresting and there were no restaurants of any consequence. Excellence in food and drink became a life-long interest for Jack and in his maturity he founded the Wine and Food Society of Los Angeles and served as its first president.

After the Parisian episode, Jack and Buzz settled back down in Los Angeles and set about finding suitable employment. Jack displayed and developed a knack for real estate development early on. He had enthusiasm and a keen sense of what the future would bring. He also had a rule he followed religiously. He always walked any property he was considering. (After he married, he often interrupted family outings, much to the consternation of his wife, to analyze properties in person, or to discover new properties, on the way to some other engagement.) He became successful very quickly. He and Fred Weddington laid out, developed and subdivided the town of Lankershim, which is now North Hollywood. This was so successful that Jack was able to think about supporting a wife.

He chose a petite, curvy, vivacious, dark-haired, Texas-born belle who was the ward of a very wealthy and important Glendale man. Her name was Austeene Paralee George.

A young Austeene.

8

Beginnings – Maternal

At the other end of the dinner table sat Jeff's mother, Austeene Paralee George Cooper. Quite different from her contemplative, intellectual husband, she was fun-loving, socially active, athletic and determined to be in the middle of whatever was going on.

Austeene Paralee George was born in San Antonio, Texas, on New Year's Day of 1887. The family did not reside in San Antonio for long, and Austeene lived her infancy and childhood in Galveston. Her one sibling was her older brother, Reuben George, and her father was Austin Philip George, son of Philip George and Marie DeJeutelle. Not much is known about Austin George except that he was killed in a house fire when Austeene and her brother were still children.

Austeene's mother, Daisy Dean, was one of five children of a well-to-do Galveston family. Daisy's grandparents were John Y. Lawless and Harriet Waldron. John Lawless was captain of a sea vessel and once saved the lives of his passengers at sea by his heroic action. He was awarded an engraved silver megaphone for this deed by the passengers, and it has a place of honor today in Jeff's brother's living room. Austeene always took great pride in that memento and the story captivated everyone who heard her recount it.

Harriet Waldron Lawless, Jeff's great grandmother, was born on February 14, 1819, in Bristol, Rhode Island. According to family lore, she had a hand in raising her Dean grandchildren after their mother (her daughter Harriet Lawless Dean) died. A story exists that claims she received an award from the city of Galveston for repelling an intruder in her home. She is supposed to have shot and killed him. This is another family tale that captured Jeff's attention at an early age. Harriet Waldron Lawless came to live in the Glendale mansion where Austeene spent the six years leading up to her first marriage. Harriet Lawless died at the age of 87 on September 21, 1906 in Glendale.

Austeene as a child in Galveston.

Austeene remembered her grandfather, Reuben Benjamin Dean, being a judge in Galveston. He and Harriet Lawless Dean had five children who grew to adulthood; Charles, Theresa Virginia, Mary Louise, George and Daisy. After their son-in-law Austin Philip George was killed, their daughter Daisy survived not much longer. Austeene always said her mother died of a broken heart although there is some question as to which of her parents died first. However that may be, Austeene and her brother were left orphans in about 1903. Austeene was sixteen.

Austeene's aunt, Mary Louise Dean, was born in Galveston on January 26 of 1871. She was known in the family as "Aunt Louise." She married Leslie Coombs Brand, a widower from Missouri, in Monterey, Mexico on July 18, 1891 and in 1895 the couple moved to Los Angeles. "Uncle Les" as he was known to Jeff, was twelve years older than Aunt Louise and they never had any children of their own. When Austeene and her brother were orphaned, Uncle Les and Aunt Louise arranged for Austeene to come to live with them in Glendale, along with Harriet Waldron Lawless (Aunt Louise's grandmother) and "Aunt Tess" (Aunt Louise's unmarried older sister, Theresa Virginia).

Uncle Les, born in Florissant, Missouri on May 12, 1859, started early in the title insurance and real estate business. He had a definite flair for it and ended his life as a very wealthy man. On October 28, 1895, he and Edwin W. Sargent founded the Title Guarantee and Trust Company, with Sargent acting as its first president. Both men served the company in various official capacities for the balance of their respective lifetimes and each was president at the time of his death.

Before the turn of the century, Uncle Les was attracted by the investment possibilities in the fledgling community of Glendale. He and Henry E. Huntington formed the San Fernando Valley Land and Development Company, which at one time owned a large tract of land running north from the business district on both sides of what later became Brand Boulevard. Brand

Boulevard was and still is Glendale's chief business artery.

Uncle Les also bought foothill property in North Glendale, ultimately owning a thousand acres in 1902. He built a mansion, at what is now the intersection of Mountain Street and Grandview Avenue, which was begun in 1903 and finished in 1904 at a cost of $60,000. Uncle Les named it "Miradero", but it was popularly called "Brand's Castle".

Miradero, which today belongs to the City of Glendale and is called Brand Library and Art Center, was inspired by the architecture Uncle Les saw in the East Indian pavilion at the World's Columbian Exposition at Chicago in 1893. The exterior was and is pure white with crenelated arches, bulbous domes and minars.

Leslie C. Brand in St. Louis, 1880.

It featured a large, enclosed solarium complete with fountains and tall plants in addition to several bedrooms, a parlor, drawing room, dining room, kitchen and music room. The interior was decorated in typical ornate Victorian fashion with handcarved woodwork, Tiffany zinced glass windows from Czechoslovakia, silk damask wall coverings and frescoed ceilings.

In addition to the main house there was a small clubhouse in back with a billiard room, grillroom, bath, toilet and dressing rooms leading out to the tennis courts and swimming pool. Beyond that was a covered pergola leading off up the canyon which led to the private cemetery on the hillside overlooking Glendale. There was also a nine-hole golf course.

All the grounds were elaborately landscaped and an imposing hand-hewn stone gate led up a long, palm-lined drive to the multi-level steps leading to the front porch and door.

Uncle Les was also a pioneer in aviation and included an airstrip on his property, complete with hangar. He had custom-made automobiles as well as airplanes and his staff included drivers, pilots and mechanics. He owned the first car in Glendale, a National, and could be seen touring the city streets in 1905.

Into this world of wealth and privilege came Austeene, still in high school and fresh from the loss of her parents. Uncle Les and Aunt Louise took her in and she lived with them from about 1903 until her marriage in 1909.

One of the first things they did was enroll Austeene (named after both her

Miradero in 1904.

father and Stephen F. Austin) for her senior year in the best local high school/finishing school for young ladies that Los Angeles had to offer: Marlborough School.

Founded in 1889, Marlborough School was the first school established in Southern California to produce young ladies of refinement as well as teach basic school subjects. Los Angeles was still close to its beginnings as a rough frontier town peopled by pioneers who were generally not what one might call cultivated. Pioneers seldom are. They are ordinarily the discontented, the unsatisfied and, in some cases, the rejects. They are often courageous and hard working, carving out new opportunities for themselves in unfamiliar surroundings. In such communities, cultivated society takes a long time to establish and young ladies are at a distinct disadvantage in terms of having the time or the place to learn the finer things in life which leisure produces.

Marlborough taught deportment, social dancing, dress and conduct. The first principal was Mrs. Caswell, who was extremely concerned about proper use of English and made an issue of it. Austeene also took French, rhetoric and literature classes and absorbed all the things that would fit her for a position in society to which she certainly would aspire and to which her guardians did too.

Austeene was raised to be a "lady" in the 1904 sense of the word. She had no real social pretensions beyond simply being the ward of L. C. Brand. She was always very conscious of things which meant prestige to her. Things such as the "proper" associations, clubs, dances, and parties. She developed this from being made well aware in the Brand household at Miradero of being an orphan and that it was only by the voluntary good nature of her wealthy uncle that she was enjoying a rather high life. She was never adopted by the Brands and did not take the Brand name.

Uncle Les and Aunt Louise wanted polish for their ward, not so much because she did not meet their standards, but because they also aspired to greater social heights than their beginnings had given them. There is the story of a 1928 trip to Europe taken by Jeff with his parents and siblings where Aunt Louise accompanied them. In Munich they stayed at the elegant *Vierjahrtzeiten* Hotel. At dinner one evening a dessert was brought in and when Aunt Louise tasted it she exclaimed with surprise, "Why, we have something like this at home! We call it Bavarian Cream." After a short, embarrassing pause, the waiter bowed and said politely, "Yes, madam. We are, after all, in Bavaria."

Uncle Les was very short in stature. Some sources indicate that he was as short as five feet even. He was shorter than everyone he appeared with in old photographs. He had large, strong features and evidently a very strong personality. He has been characterized as a "robber baron" and some information has it that he was particularly ruthless in his business dealings. He was also without a doubt a philanthropist, indicated at the least by the fact that he left Miradero to the City of Glendale. He also donated a city park in San Fernando and supported many causes. He also supported many relatives in various ways.

Austeene remembers him as a stern authoritarian figure. She told the story of requesting to be excused from the dinner table by asking, "Can I be excused?" Uncle Les' reply was, "Of course you can. The question is 'may' you." The proper use of English was obviously a concern of his as well. He had no education beyond high school, having had to go to work to support his widowed mother at a very young age.

In the days of Austeene's senior year at Marlborough there was no effective transportation. This was 1904. In the early mornings, she and Uncle Les would be taken by horse and buggy quite away across what is now North Hollywood to where he could pick up a train. After he caught the train to downtown Los Angeles and his office, Austeene was

Enjoying an exclusive "aeroplane party" at Miradero. From left to right, guest Ruth Roland, Uncle Les, guest Mary Miles Minter and Aunt Louise.

13

taken on to Marlborough School. She did not board, probably because she was enrolled for only one year there. She was picked back up every evening, which had to be quite an extensive effort because the horse and the buggy and the driver all had to be taken care of. In any case, she was graduated in 1904 and that stamped her as officially correct.

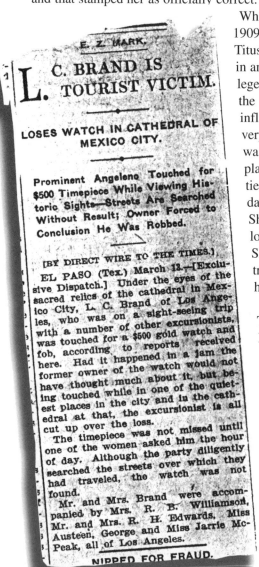

E. Z. MARK,

L. C. BRAND IS TOURIST VICTIM.

LOSES WATCH IN CATHEDRAL OF MEXICO CITY.

Prominent Angeleno Touched for $500 Timepiece While Viewing Historic Sights—Streets Are Searched Without Result; Owner Forced to Conclusion He Was Robbed.

[BY DIRECT WIRE TO THE TIMES.]

EL PASO (Tex.) March 13.—[Exclusive Dispatch.] Under the eyes of the sacred relics of the cathedral in Mexico City, L. C. Brand, of Los Angeles, who was on a sight-seeing trip with a number of other excursionists, was touched for a $500 gold watch and fob, according to reports received here. Had it happened in a jam the former owner of the watch would not have thought much about it, but being touched while in one of the quieting touched while in one of the quietest places in the city and in the cathedral at that, the excursionist is all cut up over the loss.

The timepiece was not missed until one of the women asked him the hour of day. Although the party diligently searched the streets over which they had traveled, the watch was not found.

Mr. and Mrs. Brand were accompanied by Mrs. R. B. Williamson, Mr. and Mrs. R. H. Edwards, Miss Austeen, George and Miss Jarrie McPeak, all of Los Angeles.

NIPPED FOR FRAUD.

A local news story about the Brands' travels. Notice the reference to "Miss Austeen (sic)" in the last paragraph.

What Austeene did between 1904 and 1909 (the year of her marriage to John Titus Cooper) is not recorded anywhere in any detail. She did not go on to college. She probably enjoyed her life as the ward of an extremely wealthy and influential man to the fullest. She was very striking. She had black hair and was trim and athletic. She swam and played a lot of tennis. She loved parties and people and conversation and dancing and generally the high life. She was vivacious and sexy and fun-loving and generous and spirited. She loved the theater and was attracted to it and its performers all her life.

It is not recorded how John Titus Cooper and Austeene Paralee George met. However, one can see from early photos how attractive they both were and, although they did not have similar views on most things and turned out to be particularly unsuited for each other, perhaps the physical attraction was paramount. Nonetheless, at the age of 26, Jack felt he had enough money in his pocket and that his prospects were good enough to propose. He did, Austeene accepted (with her guardians' permission, of course), and they were married on October 12, 1909. Jack had just turned 27. Austeene was 22.

Beginnings – Family

As his ward approached marriageable age, Uncle Les took precautions against fortune hunters, because fortune hunting was a highly developed occupation in those days. If a young man could manage to marry a young woman with a great deal of money he would be set for the rest of his days and could relax and enjoy the fruit of others' labors. Liaisons formed by young people are often without a more solid basis than physical attraction and relationships unsuitable for long-term satisfaction can be entered into easily and irreparably. Divorce was still very much frowned upon in polite society, so parents and guardians played a very great role in approving marital bonds.

Uncle Les made it known very clearly that Austeene would not be accompanied by one penny in the way of dowry. Any young man who wanted to marry her would have to provide for her himself, and he would have to be obviously able to do so. Jack Cooper understood this and accepted it without hesitation. He and Austeene married in 1909 and moved into a house on Hoover Street, not far from what is now MacArthur Park, which was called Westlake Park then. It was a modest house but it was not mean and they were comfortable enough. They proceeded to have two children, Jeff's older brother and sister. Harry Brand Cooper (nicknamed "Heinie" by Grandpa because of his early fondness for beer) was born on October 3, 1910 and Austeene Phyllis Cooper (known as "Phyllis") followed on November 13, 1912.

Sometime after his marriage, Jack was offered a position with the Security Trust and Savings Bank at Fifth and Spring streets in downtown Los Angeles. This position was most probably offered for two reasons. One was the innate ability he showed in real estate and the other was the influence of L. C. Brand. Uncle Les would not give the young couple anything, but he did want to insure that Austeene was properly taken care of. In the years that followed, he often gave Jack tips of various kinds which invariably led to successful

A very young, blond Jeff with nurse on the lawn at Hoover Street, circa 1921.

Young Jeff on the steps of the Hoover Street house with the family collie, Napoleon.

investments. Jack knew that his "father-in-law" was extremely shrewd and, being relatively savvy at such things himself, took the advice offered. It was a highly effective relationship.

The early years of Jack and Austeene's marriage are a mystery to Jeff. He was not born until 1920 and his parents never spoke about the past to him. They also did not celebrate their wedding anniversary. They were most likely involved in the usual early marriage activities—a young man trying to make his way in the world of business and a young woman taking care of home, husband and children.

Jack Cooper had lost a kidney sometime earlier in life, so when World War I commenced, he was 4F and could not fight. He went on with his life. This war did not dislocate society the way World War II did. It was off to one side, much the way the Viet Nam war was some fifty years later, with close to the same number of casualties as well. Jack was never a soldier and there was no personal military tradition in the Cooper household. Jeff is of the impression that members of Jack Cooper's family fought for the Union during the Civil

War and that members of Austeene's family fought for the Confederacy, but there were no stories or swords or weapons or plaques or other military memorabilia to fire the imagination of Jack's and Austeene's children. When Jeff was a little older, veterans of World War I were numbered among his parents' friends and he was suitably impressed with their ribbons and stories of flying Spads in Europe and such, but it was not highly personal.

The thing that hit the Cooper family hardest before Jeff was born was the great influenza pandemic of 1918. This world-wide epidemic of the "Spanish Influenza" killed people like rifle fire. It is hard to imagine this because nothing like it has happened since. People all over the world were sick and dying in great numbers. The virus circled the globe in nine months and left twenty-five million dead. Jack and Heinie and Phyllis were all flattened by it and Austeene had to nurse them with no help at all. These were the days before household appliances and, for the Coopers, before household servants as well. Viruses had hardly been discovered and named, much less understood. Austeene later told stories of having to bathe and feed and tend to three very sick people, and all the while friends and acquaintances were dying. Austeene never had a hint of illness, apparently being immune. In any case, the three Coopers recovered, the two children without any ill effects.

Jack, however, was debilitated. The experience of a bad case of the flu with only one kidney led the doctors to advise him to slow down and take things easy. This included watching what he ate and drank. Jack refused. He would not give up what he considered the pleasures of life in order to avoid an early death, so he went on as before.

On May 10 of 1920 John Dean Cooper was born at the Good Samaritan Hospital in Los Angeles (where his future wife would also be born, and later on his eldest and youngest children.) Because of the age spread between him and his siblings, he is practically certain that his birth was a mistake, or at least an afterthought. Austeene used to protest to him that he was always to remember that he was "wanted". This meant nothing to Jeff until she said it once too often and then it occurred to him that "the lady doth protest too much". Whatever the truth of the matter, being eight years younger than his sister and ten years younger than his brother suited him just fine. His mother called him "John Dean", but his father, despite his Yankee heritage, admired Jefferson Davis and so called his youngest child "Jeff". Jeff was handsome and bright and as blonde as his siblings were dark.

It was the beginning of a new decade, the war had just passed and there was a general boom in land development at this time that Jack caught. He was instrumental in granting loans to people in the food and beverage business, following his interest is gastronomy. He granted the loan for the establishment of Lawry's Prime Rib in Beverly Hills, which is one of the most successful restaurant stories of the time. He loaned the money to Romeo Salta to found the restaurant Chianti in Hollywood and he helped many other fledg-

Jack with two of his associates at the bank. Jack is on the right. One of the other two men is Mr. O'Melveny, a well-known name in California business circles.

ling operations with his sharp eye for what would be successful. He was involved in the development of Palm Springs. He had close relationships with the Desert Inn, which was the first luxury hotel located there, with El Mirador, which was the second, and then with the Point Happy Date Ranch which was owned by a friend of his, Mrs. Chauncey Clark, whom they visited there several times. Always he followed his instinct to view properties with his own eyes. Austeene would ask him why he did not simply look at a map or send an assistant. His insistence on setting his own foot on any land under consideration for development may have been one of the reasons he was such a success. Another reason may have been his reluctance to buy anything on credit. This caution probably saved Jack a great deal of grief when the Depression hit, and Jeff inherited this attitude.

With Jack's business success, the young family grew with the community. In 1922 they built their new home at 500 North Rossmore. Rossmore was an extension of Vine Street. If you travel south on Vine Street you will find that it changes to Rossmore at Melrose Avenue on the Hollywood border. That takes you down to Wilshire through what was then known as Hancock Park, a region of very desirable residences and good schools. Marlborough School was right down Rossmore a couple of long blocks. This was a very nice place to live and a very nice place to grow up. (The attractive house, which sat on a large lot with several levels of lush lawns and trees and roses has since been

*Jeff's older brother, Harry Brand
"Heinie" Cooper.*

Jeff's older sister, Austeene "Phyllis" Cooper.

torn down and replaced with an apartment building that covers every square inch of real estate and lends no charm whatsoever to the surrounding city.)

On one side of the dinner table sat Jeff's older brother, Heinie. Ten years older than Jeff, with hair as black as Jeff's was blonde, Heinie was charming, athletic, fun-loving like his mother, and extremely fond of his little brother. There was never anything like sibling rivalry between them and Heinie remembers spending most of his allowance buying things for little "John" as he called Jeff and teaching him how to do things.

Next to Jeff on the other side of the table sat Phyllis. Eight years older than Jeff, she also had black hair and luminous dark eyes which flashed angrily when she did not get her way. A very pretty girl and a very smart one too, Phyllis was easy to indulge and her parents did so from the beginning. She and Jeff got along fine although they were involved in totally different things and could not be considered really close. As adults, they enjoyed engaging each other in spirited intellectual discussions ranging over a broad spectrum of topics and enjoyed each other's company immensely.

All things were discussed at the dinner table, everything from current events, sports, dating and popular music, to suggestions for family outings. Plans were made for summer trips and other travels. There were few guests at dinner. Jeff remembers Phyllis bringing a girlfriend over occasionally for dinner, but never Heinie. Jefff never did because he did not care for the dinner conversation of other little boys his age. He felt they had nothing to add and did not hold up their end.

Food at the Cooper's dinner table while Jeff was growing up was normal for the time—quite uninteresting. There was no ethnic flavor at all. They did not have Mexican food, although Austeene, being a Texan, had a taste for Tabasco and always kept a bottle at the ready. They occasionally ate Cantonese food when they went out, but never tried to duplicate it at home. Much of the time their dining room was dry because of Prohibition.

Prohibition was winked at by most people but not to the extent that a respectable home would serve liquor at the table. The food for the most part was dull, which is one of the reasons Jack became an outside-the-home gourmet. The Wine and Food Society gave very fancy, lavish dinners, where they tried all sorts of exotic things, but they never allowed any dependents to attend. (Jeff was wistful after a successful elk hunting trip when he was seventeen. He brought home 270 pounds of dressed elk meat and never got to taste any of it. His father set up a Wine and Food Society dinner at which the elk was the main course, but Jeff was not invited.)

The house on Rossmore was large enough, the family was large enough and the Coopers were doing well enough financially to establish the need for personal servants. They had two or three as Jeff grew up, a cook and a maid and often a houseboy/driver/butler. Jack went to work each day on public transportation. He owned various cars, but did not enjoy driving. The chauffeur was used mostly by Austeene. Jack would walk from the house four short blocks from Rossmore to Larchmont Boulevard. There he would pick up a street car and travel down Larchmont to Third to Sixth and then all the way into town. He read the newspapers on the streetcar both to and from the office. There were no radio or television programs then and people depended upon newspapers for news. He read the Los Angeles Times and the Los Angeles Examiner in the morning and the Los Angeles Herald Express in the evening, along with any "extras" that came out.

As was the custom of the times, Jack and Austeene joined clubs. They were members of the University Club in Downtown Los Angeles and the California Club. They joined the Los Angeles Country Club, the Beach Club in Santa Monica and a little later on the Yacht Club on Catalina Island. Their membership in the Beach Club included a small cabana right on the beach in Santa Monica.

The social club is an institution brought over to America from England where clubs became extremely important as homes away from home. As London became the big city of noise, snarled traffic, dirt and crime (features that all concentrated population centers share), gentlemen of means moved their homes to the country. Their country houses are where they raised their families and entertained friends and enjoyed their leisure time. London was the place to do business. One need only read the novels of Charles Dickens to understand why no one would want to live in London. Often the country home was a long distance from London, so gentlemen with business interests to attend to in London needed places to stay when they were in town. Gentlemen could not stay in hotels, because there were none in those days. Gentlemen wanted a comfortable, quiet and secure place where they could get lodging, a good meal, a good drink, a good cigar and a cheery fire on cold nights; a place where they could read the day's newspapers in peace, discuss the day's events and socialize if they chose with other gentlemen of similar taste and position. The bases for membership are various but the principal one is simply social status. Gentlemen clumped in like groups and formed clubs.

The membership in a "gentlemen's club" (and all the clubs were exclusively male, although they sometimes had ladies' auxiliaries) was guarded rather carefully. Aside from income, standards were based on race, religion, occupation, education and social connections, among other things. Actors and entertainers were never accepted, being disreputable people by long-standing tradition. In the great days of these institutions, ladies were never accepted in the main part of any major clubhouse except possibly on special occasions such as Christmas Eve. In Los Angeles the University Club, the California Club and the Harvard Club all operated on this principle.

The justice of all this is questionable, since the merit of a human being is very difficult to assess. In the nineteenth century in America we had a rough-hewn society which became more so as the frontier moved West. As it had in England, this led to another situation where people naturally clumped in like groups. A gentleman who could read and write, knew Shakespeare and Beethoven and had cultured tastes would not be comfortable playing poker around a table in the Crystal Palace Saloon and then taking a room upstairs. At least not every night.

These clubs became an institution in the United States starting with the big cities in the East. Membership was strictly stratified. This custom came West. In Los Angeles, these clubs were all downtown. The exception was the Valley Hunt Club in Pasadena, which was founded by George Frederick Holder, who also founded the Tournament of Roses and the Tuna Club on Catalina Island for sportfishermen. Holder was an important man in early California. His book *Life in the Open* will make you long for those days.

The most pretentious club in the Los Angeles area was the California Club. This club had no athletic facilities. The University Club was at least one step down in prestige and was confined to graduates of important universities. There were also clubs with athletic facilities, such as the various country clubs. At the time these clubs were not accessible by money alone, as they so often are now. A man's occupation or the amount of money he made were not the issue. The main issue was whether or not he was a man that the other men already in the club would find compatible as to level of education, sophistication, taste and manners. Generally one had to be sponsored by a current member to be considered for membership. Of course it cost money to join and to maintain memberships, so money did enter into it at some point and depending on the specific club or clubs only reasonably wealthy people could afford the dues. Jack and Austeene were obviously successful in terms of money and social standing.

Jeff and Heinie and Phyllis enjoyed these clubs to the fullest, taking advantage of what privileges they were entitled to as the children of a member. When Jeff began to date, he would often take girls to dine at these clubs and perhaps dance. The Los Angeles Country Club was the one with which he was best acquainted. He went there often with his father and they would have breakfast in the area near the locker room. The University Club featured travelogues by members and Jack would frequently have Jeff come down and join him for slide shows about trips to darkest Africa and such things.

In the Southwest Blue Book, the social register of Southern California, along with the entry's address, phone number and family members, was a little

Heinie, Phyllis, Jeff and Aunt Tess visiting Uncle Les' Tioga Lodge above Mono Lake.

section which listed clubs. By looking at that list of clubs, one could estimate the social position of the entry, as well as something of his financial wherewithal. When it came to courtship, a parent could easily check out a prospective suitor.

Life in Los Angeles during the twenties and thirties was very nice indeed. There was no traffic. The influx of masses of people from the East had not yet occurred. The roads were two-laned but mostly paved and you could get where you wanted to go. The climate was good. There was almost no smog. Apart from the slowness of the awakening to really fine dining, it was a good life. Artistically there was the Opera House, the Philharmonic, major company productions of the latest Broadway hits, and it was the center of the cinema.

The cinema was a fascinating new business. Following the traditions of the past, the people in this new business were mostly disreputable, but the glamour and the fame generated by the new medium were most attractive. Only a very few of those associated with movies were accepted into the best social clubs of the day. These few included Leo Carillo, the heir of an old Spanish Colonial family, Joel McCrea and Robert Stack. Associating with movie people was not quite acceptable and was indulged in only by those who were inclined to be rebellious and headstrong, like Heinie and Phyllis and, to a certain extent, Austeene.

Phyllis, in an early newspaper article from her stage days.

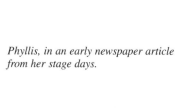

MISS PHYLLIS COOPER, socially prominent daughter of the John T. Coopers, who is receiving acclaim from Mayfairites on her first professional performance—the leading role in "Boulevard Stop," popular extravaganza, now playing at the Pasadena Community Playhouse.
—Herpel photo.

Early memories

After dinner, Jack would retire to his favorite reading chair in the living room—a chair Jeff still has and uses in his library today. Jack had a rotary book rack (which is also in Jeff's library) and he read voraciously—a reading program of his own which he did not share with anyone else. Austeene would stretch out on one of the sofas by the fireplace and go to sleep. Heinie and Phyllis would go out. When Jeff was too young to read, he would sit on the arm of his father's chair and be read to. Jack read nothing that would be called "children's books", except perhaps for the writings of A. A. Milne. The two volumes of verse, *When We Were Very Young* and *Now We Are Six* and the two volumes of prose, *Winnie the Pooh* and *The House at Pooh Corner* were favorites of Jack's and Jeff's and still are read by Jeff often. The poems and stories are endlessly entertaining, no matter your age.

What Jack read most frequently to his younger son were adventures. Jack was a romantic and adventure was his addiction. He read the works of G. A. Henty, Sir Walter Scot, Sir Arthur Conan Doyle among others. As young Jeff learned to read, he moved over to his own place on the opposite sofa and read on his own—his father handing him books. He was especially fond of Edgar Rice Burroughs and H. Rider Haggard. On Saturdays, Austeene used to give Jeff one dollar. He would walk over to Larchmont Boulevard, see a movie, buy some snacks and spend his last fifty cents on the latest hardcover Burroughs book. He read them all, from Tarzan to the Martian series and the books on the earth's core. Reading Edgar Rice Burroughs is a character-building exercise for any young person. Burroughs wrote about how people should conduct themselves and about the wonders of adventure. His villains were evil and/or weak and his heroes and heroines were faithful, strong and morally superior. Jeff was hooked from an early age and still enjoys these stories.

Austeene acquired a set of Compton's Pictured Encyclopedia, which Jeff read from cover to cover several times. What little boy could resist Volume 8 which contained sharks, snakes and swords?

> *"My friend Katie (Blackwell) said she fell in love with him in kindergarten when he arrived with a basket full of snakes."*
> *– DORIS SMITH VISSCHER*

As a small boy, Jeff's two other principal recreational activities (besides being read to by his father) consisted of shop work—building all sorts of things from scraps of lumber, metal and other miscellany—and playing violent games of tackle football on the front lawn with the other boys from the neighborhood. From a very early age, he loved the shock of tackling another little boy and going down in a tangled heap of arms and legs. He got the impression that football was an important sport—one played by gentlemen, presidents and generals and such. He never played any baseball or basketball. He never saw anyone play any basketball, although he knew that there were people who played baseball. From what he observed, football was played by important people, baseball was played by lower class people, and no one at all played basketball. In those days, baseball players were simply paid entertainers (much like all professional athletes are today), but football was a real

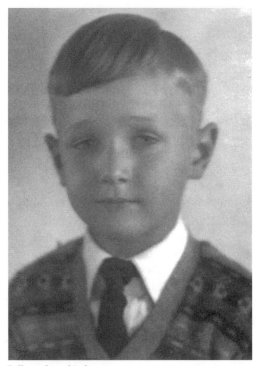

man's sport and one played it if one could. It was a much rougher sport then with not much in the way of protective gear used. It was more dangerous than it is today, player deaths occurring with much more frequency.

So football had a big influence on Jeff in his youth, although it did not continue into his later adolescence because he was not built for it, being distinctly spidery. He was 6'2" by the time he was fifteen years old, with not much weight to spread around.

Still he loved football and played sandlot after school in both junior high and high school whenever a game offered itself. It is the only

Jeff, at about kindergarten age.

25

team sport that ever attracted him. He was not and has never been a joiner, although his father joined many organizations. When school let out, if there was no football game, he rushed to build things in the garage shop, or read.

> *"Upstairs in the back there was a double sleeping porch where Jeff and I slept. He used to spend a hell of a lot of time reading up there. He was a walking encyclopedia.*
> *Virginia was the housekeeper and she was crazy about Jeff. I don't remember who did this (Jeff did) but a buzzer was rigged up by his bed so he could buzz into the kitchen. There was a code for various snacks. Virginia would bring things up to him and he would lecture her about the things he had just read."*
> *– HEINIE COOPER*

Austeene was an avid tennis player and tried to interest her children. Heinie became quite good, but Jeff never developed any passion for the game. He felt it was a great deal too much trouble to get players and equipment together and get to a court. They did get groups together on an occasional Sunday morning to go to the country club and play, but beyond that he never stayed with it. The Los Angeles Tennis Club, where the Pacific Southwest Tournament was held annually, was within walking distance from the house at 500 and they used to walk over there on weekends during the school year. Austeene maintained a box there and it was a very pleasant social occasion to watch the play and visit back and forth between boxes.

It does seem odd that Jeff did not take to tennis more than he did. He was certainly built for it, being tall and slim and long-legged and blessed with very fast reactions. It was also a gentlemanly sport and one well-suited to individual achievement. However, although he did enjoy it, he never really loved it and never competed.

He learned to ride a horse, although he remembers no lessons. He simply got on a horse whenever one was around and did what came naturally, getting better as he gained experience. It seemed to him that everyone rode horses because people were engaged in all sorts of activities which involved riding. Equitation was a necessary skill much like swimming. One would think it would have been common to send all children to riding school, but Jeff never went. He remembers a time over in Arizona when he was in the White Mountains chasing cougars and they came to a spot where the path was blocked by a large fallen tree, three feet in diameter. The guide said they would have to jump it. Jeff replied that he did not know how to jump a horse. The guide said, "You don't have to know anything. The horse will do the jumping."

Heinie remembers being entranced by his little brother. He would spend at least a part of his allowance buying toys with which the two of them would play. Electric trains were a favorite, as was a mechanical pylon with a big arm and a plastic airplane on the end. It had two controls and a motor and they could make the plane take off and fly and land. They set this up in the middle of the living room, much to the irritation of their mother. Heinie put up a swing set for Jeff, bought him an archery set, and has fond memories of "pampering him".

> *"My father was crazy about him. He and Jeff were even closer than he and I were.*
> *I remember one thing that frightened me so badly I never have forgotten it. Jeff was with me one day and I had a big axe and there was a tree out in the front yard that was dying. I told my dad I would cut it down. Jeff was about six or seven and he came out with me. I whacked this big tree and the axe went through the trunk and out the other side and just passed by Jeff's neck. I could have cut his head right off."*
>
> *– HEINIE COOPER*

When Jeff was growing up, automobiles were still fairly new inventions and not everyone owned or drove one. Motoring was adventurous then because most cars were not particularly reliable, roads were not awfully good and service stations were a hit or miss proposition as far as both availability and

Jack (center) and Heinie (left) on a visit to Uncle Les' Tioga Lodge. (The man on the right is unidentified.)

ability to service cars. One of Jeff's earliest fascinations was the huge, custom-made Locomobile owned by Uncle Les. This was called the "Tioga Wolf".

Uncle Les had a large summer vacation compound at the top of the Sierras on Tioga Pass called the Tioga Lodge. Getting there was an operation because there was no practical way. There was a railroad that ran up the Owens Valley and stopped in places like Independence and Lone Pine and would make whistle stops. Uncle Les' place was at the top of the Tioga Pass which was reached by a road which went right up the east side of the Sierras and was comprised of a series of switchbacks. This was too much for any normal car. Uncle Les specified to the Locomobile people what he had to have. It was a big, elaborate open touring car into which he could put a whole family of guests and their luggage and chug up the side of the mountain to the top of the Sierras. This was the "Tioga Wolf".

Locomobile was one of many automobile manufacturers in operation in those days. Oldsmobile was another as was Hupmobile, Marmon, Pierce Arrow and Stanley Steamer. Oldsmobile has been absorbed by General Motors for a great many years, but Ransom E. Olds was the inventor, designer and proprietor of Oldsmobile first, and that kind of individual effort and creativity is how many of the first automobile companies came into being.

One of the challenges involved in getting to the lodge on Tioga Pass was simply getting the Tioga Wolf to Leevining, which is the location of the railroad station from which it picked up its load and departed at the bottom of the hill for the lodge at the top. In the springtime it would be a big operation. Uncle Les would obtain the services of two drivers and two mechanics and their equipment and they would take off for Leevining. They couldn't get any tires to make the trip so they would fill tires with twigs and straw because the pneumatics of the day would not hold. They would chug off from Glendale, make it up through Palmdale and the passes, across the desert and up to the bottom of the hill. The car broke down every hundred miles or so and they would fix it and continue. Automobiles were much simpler machines at this time.

When the Tioga Wolf reached Leevining, Uncle Les and his guests would pick up the train at the Union Station in downtown Los Angeles at Olvera Street, and take it to Leevining where they would stand down. When they arrived, they would see this huge gray machine waiting there, all polished up, and they would all pile in and chug up to the lodge.

The Tioga Wolf was only used in the summer time. The rest of the year it resided in a garage on the grounds of Miradero, and Jeff used to peer in at it in silent awe whenever he visited there. It was maintained for many years after Uncle Les' death, but it was lost in the confusion of World War II and Jeff does not know what became of it. Hand-crafted and one of a kind, it was quite something!

In 1925, L.C. Brand (Uncle Les) died of cancer at Miradero after a long ill-

The Tioga Wolf at Mono Lake.

ness. When he became too sick to climb the stairs to the front tower bedroom he shared with Aunt Louise, they moved him down to a middle bedroom on the ground floor, just beyond the front parlor, and he died there on April 10. He evidently died slowly and in great pain. This left an impression on Jeff that he has never shaken—that all cancer deaths are lingering and extremely painful.

Uncle Les left the bulk of his considerable estate to his widow and she lived at Miradero with her unmarried sister, Aunt Tess, for the next twenty years. With Uncle Les' passing went the elaborate parties and fly-ins and columns in the society pages of the newspapers. Aunt Louise and Aunt Tess lived quietly. Jeff remembers visiting often and playing alone on the grand, terraced steps leading up to the front door. He does not remember ever seeing anyone else on those steps as a youngster, since family and informal guests always came in the back door. The grand, imposing path to the front door was reserved for formal occasions.

> *"My feeling was that these ladies........... had this huge estate to man-age, and it was not in a particularly good state of repair. They had been hit with a New Year's Day flood in 1934. The canyon behind them had a summer house and a tennis court and a swimming pool. The pool was full of mud, and rocks as big as automobiles had come down the canyon and lit in various places. I assumed that they were not in a financial position to restore what had been lost."*
>
> *– CHARLES BRAGG*

APRIL 11, 1925.—

CAPITALIST TO REST 'MID VERDUGO HILLS

BRIEF RITES FOR BRAND TOMORROW

Capitalist Will be Laid at Rest in Verdugo Hills After Private Service

With a brief and simple service, the body of Leslie C. Brand, one of the empire builders of the Southland, who died early yesterday morning after a long illness, will be laid at rest tomorrow in the Verdugo Hills.

The funeral will be conducted privately at Miradero, the capitalist's residence estate north of Glendale, and interment will take place in the family burial plot on the estate. The service will begin at 10 o'clock.

Leslie C. Brand

VERDUGO HILLS TO CLAIM BRAND

Uncle Les' obituary.

The Cooper household at 500 North Rossmore did not entertain often but they became famous for their annual Christmas party. This party became a tradition very early and, for Jeff, it was the biggest event of the year. Austeene spent a good deal of time sending out personalized invitations which she sealed with sealing wax and a stamp. They always had the same verse written upon them, composed by Austeene:

> *"The same old Christmas in the same old way*
> *From ten to two on Christmas day."*

The time was only an affectation because people generally stayed up late on Christmas Eve and no one was up early enough to be at the Cooper's by 10 a.m. Still, the house had to be ready. A pattern developed. They always had live music. Jack hired a seven-piece band and everything would be taken out of the living room for the band and the dancing. Jack would set up the bar in the sun room. He featured the same punch every year. It was most effective. He felt ordinary party punch was too weak and too sweet. Jack never let that happen to his punch. His was potent and widely imbibed. In addition to making the Christmas punch, the only other things that Jeff remembers his father doing around the house were mixing the cheeses on the service cart and picking up blown newspapers. Jack did not believe in gentlemen doing any other chores.

In addition to the punch, Jack had up in his dressing room on the second floor a bottle or two of very choice whiskey. This was not for everybody. When anyone showed up whom Jack knew to be a connoisseur of Bourbon-type whiskey, they would retire upstairs for a shot or two. These parties got to be very exciting.

They had to have everything ready by 10. This meant that Christmas mornings in the Cooper household were early ones. Jeff was a nuisance to everyone because he would insist that all presents be distributed by sunrise. He generally would waken the household by 5 a.m., and with many moans and groans from his siblings, they would all go down to the living room where the Christmas tree was up in the corner and they would open their presents. So all the presents would be opened and admired and commented upon and put away by fairly early in the morning. Jeff upheld this tradition with his own family as well.

The musicians would arrive at about 9:45 and set up. Then there was a definite blank spot until about noon. During this time Austeene would fret that no one was going to come. But come they did. The main entertainment was dancing, mainly Charleston-type steps and lots of jazz. After Jeff turned 16 and had his driver's license he took over from his brother the task of getting the ice for the party in the morning. Some of his most pleasant memories have to do with getting the car out about 9 a.m. on Christmas day when not another soul was out. All he would encounter at that time of day in the Hollywood region was a stray cat or two. This was delightful. He would go to the ice machines and return with enough ice for the rest of the day.

So the party got going about noon and since the times indicated on the invitation meant nothing, the band did not pack up until about 5 p.m. By this time everyone was pretty well inebriated. It seems likely that there would have been accidents driving home, but Jeff remembers none. He did lose a couple of acquaintances during this period to auto crashes, but these had nothing to do with drinking and nothing to do with Christmas.

Food at the party was Austeene's responsibility. She always had a large ham, served with small buns and mustard and she served Christmas cookies called *Pfeffernussen*—small and hard and hot with pepper.

Each family member invited guests to the Christmas party. Heinie and

Phyllis were fond of inviting important and famous people to the party whenever the opportunity arose. This included people in the entertainment business, since Phyllis was an aspiring actress, Heinie was an aspiring singer, and Austeene dabbled in acting and dancing on stage whenever she could, mostly related to her charity functions. Jeff remembers that it was considered quite sensational to have both Lana Turner and Rita Hayworth at the party at the same time. He also remembers Joel McCrea and Randolph Scott in attendance as well. Jeff tried setting up a few post-party dates, but he soon abandoned this practice. He was not at his best after an entire afternoon of his father's punch. He had some difficulty getting up off the sofa. Heinie remembers twenty-six Christmas parties.

"I did not meet Jeff until I was in my late teens, but everybody knew of Jeff Cooper. My mother knew his mother, they were very close, and I knew him when I saw him because he was so handsome. He had piercing blue eyes. Everybody was always talking about Jeff Cooper. They traveled with a lot of the movie set which nobody else did. Everybody else was in awe of the movie people. They had a Christmas party at that house on Rossmore every year and mother and Austeene were such good friends that mother was invited to bring us children. I always looked forward to going to that party. Jeff did not know who I was and I never would have had the nerve to even open my mouth and say hello, but I was watching him for years before I finally met him."

– DORIS SMITH VISSCHER

Travel begins

In 1926, Jack Cooper did a truly extraordinary thing. He decided to pack up his family for a nine-month trip to Europe. He wanted to travel, knew that travel was an enriching and rewarding experience, and wanted to enjoy a lengthy adventure with his family. He was a successful businessman/banker, but he was employed by the bank and allowed no more than the normal amount of vacation time.

Jack informed his superiors at the bank that he wished to take his family to Europe for an extended vacation—nine months. They told him that this was impossible, he had only two weeks allotted and besides, they needed him. He then politely told them that he was going to take the vacation anyway. They then told him that he would have to give up his position at the bank. He said that was fine. He did not care greatly for the job—it was too confining. He wanted to be out and about and visit exotic places and see what was over the next horizon. He resigned his position and set about making preparations.

Thus he introduced Jeff, an inquisitive and precocious six-year-old, to the sophisticating effects of travel. This was enormously exciting for the whole family, but was most effective on Jeff. Travel became an almost yearly ritual for the family and travel has been a love of Jeff's since this first trip to Europe in 1926.

They started across the continent by train, with the first stop in Chicago. There they took a day room for the ladies to primp. Riding across the plains and the desert in the days before air conditioning was a dirty affair, with sparks and soot to contend with. While the ladies primped, Jack and his sons went to the Field Museum. In Chicago they received the telegram informing them of Grandpa's death. This dampened their spirits but the trip was underway and they did not change their plans.

The Chicago Field Museum was where the Man Eaters of Tsavo were on display. These two lions, killed by Patterson in 1902, were very badly mounted, but there they were. These were the lions that stopped construction of the railroad from Mombasa to Nairobi by eating so many of the workers. Jeff was enthralled

They took the 20th Century Limited from Chicago to New York, which was an overnight. It was called a luxury train, but it still had no air conditioning. Then they booked into a nice hotel and spent two weeks in New York, shopping and seeing shows. Live entertainment was popular and you could walk down the streets of the city at night safely in those days.

Austeene and Phyllis shopped for all they would need for Europe. Then they got on the steamer and took one of those marvelous trans-Atlantic crossings. This was one place where food and drink were decidedly gourmet, a great pleasure for Jack especially. Usually the passengers were taken to Southampton on the English side but occasionally to Le Havre or Cherbourg on the French side. Then the continental travel began.

On these crossings, Jeff decided to take up fencing in the gym on the ocean liners. They always had fencing masters and Jeff would include working out with the "pro" in his shipboard activities. He quickly showed a talent for it, being slim and very fast. Jack, being interested in history and entranced with the romance of the past, always made a point of visiting all the museums in the places they visited. He and Jeff would be sure to look up any arms collections with a great deal of enthusiasm.

The logistics of these adventures necessitated a fantastic effort on Jack's part because one really needed a great deal of luggage to travel in those days and all the luggage for five people for nine months took up a large amount of space. All of that luggage had to be assembled, labeled, organized, found and transported from place A to place B mainly by muscle. Simply getting aboard the ship in New York was a big operation. It is amazing to think of the skill and determination and general competence and extreme patience displayed by Jack in getting this mob all the way over there and all the way back again without serious mishap when nothing was convenient. The secret was tips. Jack went everywhere with a sheaf of dollar bills in his hand, tipping everyone. It all worked out. Jack also devised a plan for decorating the luggage with matching insignia to make it easier to identify and assemble. Jeff uses this method and finds it surprising that not everyone does. When a black bag comes down the ramp to the carousel displaying a colorful logo of your own design, you can spot it blocks away and no one mistakes it for any other. All it takes is a little paint and imagination.

(See "The Crossing" from *Another Country* and *To Ride, Shoot Straight, and Speak the Truth* by Jeff Cooper.)

Other than the lions in Chicago, the thing that struck Jeff most about his first trip was the fact that people spoke different languages. This fascinated him. He immediately liked the sound of French and began to attempt to speak it right away, picking up quite a bit the way children will do.

The family had a fine time. When they returned, the bank called Jack and offered him his old job back. He accepted, returning with some reluctance. His office (from 1926 to 1930) was at Fifth and Spring streets in downtown Los Angeles. It later moved to Sixth and Spring. He traveled there by walking and taking the street car. There was no parking problem, traffic problem or smog problem. But the office was four walls and a ceiling and he found this not very exciting. He took more and more to getting out whenever he could, insisting on visiting sites in person. He traveled all over Southern California, Arizona and Nevada by car and began to travel whenever he felt the pull of adventure and thought he could arrange it.

The 1926 trip was the first of the family trips. Jack decided to do it again in 1928 and again in 1930. Each time he went through the same routine at the bank. They told him he could not leave and he would tell them he was going to do it anyway. He would resign. Then he would return and they would offer him his position once again. He apparently had enough of a reputation as a wizard with land deals that they took him back happily each time.

Also in 1926, the family acquired a house on Catalina Island and, when not traveling, spent summers there. Jeff remembers this as a very comfortable place, although he also recalls that they had no water supply, relying on a cistern to catch rainwater for washing. For drinking and cooking water, Austeene used to haul up a five-gallon glass jug of Arrowhead from down on the main street all the way up to the house, which was a good ways up the mountainside.

Austeene was a magnificent swimmer, swimming across Avalon Bay from Sugarloaf to the other rock and back two or three times a week. The family warned her of the danger of doing this since boats were continuously going in and out of the bay, but she persisted, being a woman of decided spirit. She must have been the one to teach Jeff how to swim, although he does not remember a time when he could not swim and remembers no lessons. He would fall off boats and docks for fun and simply wend his way to shore from wherever he was. His usual attire was a bathing suit which had a top. Jack had a banking associate Jeff knew as Mr. Stringfellow. He owned a 37-foot fishing cruiser. Jeff would purposely fall over the side, go under the boat and come up on the other side to alarm the guests and get attention. He swam fully as much under water as he did on the surface and never gave a thought to danger. He was always within sight of land and could swim to shore, crawl out and make his way home. Summers on Catalina were 60% boating and swimming and 40% hiking. Later on, hunting and shooting would be included.

"One time we went to Catalina on the steamer 'Catalina' which was built for the island. We sat on the upper deck one day and Jeff was sitting next to me and some other people were around. Jeff started to

35

Jack would commute to Catalina on weekends. He took the "big red car" from Pacific Electric in downtown Los Angeles, within walking distance from his office, right down to the pier at San Pedro where he picked up the steamer which would take him across the Catalina Channel in about an hour and a half to Catalina Island, where he would walk from the pier up to the house.

On the second family trip to Europe in 1928 (this time with Aunt Louise along) they had an audience with the Pope. Jack and Austeene were not Catholic and were not religiously connected at all, but Jack had enough contacts to be able to be granted a group audience with His Holiness. This was very exciting to them all. They went to the Vatican in their Sunday best and lined the room in a circle. The Pope appeared and made his way slowly around the circle, holding out his ring to be kissed and saying a word here and there. Jeff was eight years old, standing in front of his mother with his bright, golden hair setting him apart from the crowd. The Pope stopped and looked at him and asked Austeene, "American?" She said yes. He then asked, "North American?" and she again replied yes. He reached out and put his hand on Jeff's head and made the sign of the cross and gave him the blessing, "*In nomine Patris, et Filii, et Spiritus sancti.*" Jeff comments to this day that that blessing is the reason he has been lucky in so many ways for so long.

In 1929 the Great Depression happened. Luck held for the Cooper family largely because Jack did not believe in consumer credit. He was of the philosophy that if one could not afford a thing with cash up front, one should not buy. This philosophy was as uncommon then as it is now. So when the stock market crashed in 1929, this was a great disaster for many, but not for the Coopers. Anyone reading about it today would be appalled at the horrors of the Great Depression, which were not minor. To Jeff, a nine-year old, they did not exist at all. It may be that his mother had to get by with fewer new clothes and that his brother and sister were short-rationed on a couple of items. He does not remember. He does know that it did not bother him at all. He had the same clothes and the same schools and the same friends and the same food. He knows that his father lost a lot of money, but it was not enough to influence significantly the family's lifestyle. They did not have to sell any cars or give up the house on Catalina or give up clubs or travel. The servants kept right on working for them and life continued. Jeff remembers no one at school (and this was public school) reporting having to do without or make any changes. It seemed to Jeff to have no effect at all. He remembers his father later making the remark, "In the days when we thought we had money......", but he never felt the effect of whatever it was to which Jack was referring.

Jeff in Munich during his second trip to Europe in 1928.

Watching history programs on public television would lead you to believe that every American was standing in a bread line in 1929. Jeff's grandson was given a school assignment to write a paper on the horrors of the Great Depression and he was directed to interview his grandparents to obtain first-hand accounts. Jeff was of no help to him at all.

By the time of the 1930 European trip, Jack and Austeene had grown excessively apart. Heinie was 20 and Phyllis was 18 and they were entering upon their own lives. They were through with high school and becoming independent. Jeff was only 10, but a very self-contained little boy who entertained himself quite well. Austeene had taken up the high life with clubs and dances and parties and charity work. Jack did not follow. He was evidently well-liked and enjoyed socializing, but never to the extent that Austeene did. He was a reader and a thinker and he enjoyed solitude and the great outdoors and exploring new frontiers. Austeene liked none of that. Jeff was only 10 but he remembers a significant incident.

They had taken a northern route from Germany to Norway to Sweden to Finland to Russia and back. In Oslo, Jack and Austeene had a major battle. Jeff was in the next room and heard much screaming and yelling. He believes this was the end of the line as far as his parents' relationship. Austeene moved out of the room she shared with Jack and took Jeff with her to other quarters in the hotel. Although they went on with the trip, Jack and Austeene were only polite to each other after that. They agreed to go their separate ways. They did not divorce and they did not maintain separate living arrangements, but they were seriously estranged and would remain so until Jack's death in 1942.

The other great impact of the 1930 trip was Russia. Jack wanted to see how or if Communism was working. It was drab and dull and uninteresting and the impression Jeff received from the people everywhere was fear—real physical fear. It impressed Jeff very much because it seemed to him that everybody in Russia at the time was terrified of not seeing the light of day the next morning. At 10 he did not understand the politics but he caught the mood.

He and his father were visiting one of the big art galleries in Leningrad. They were part of a group, because it was forbidden to move around in Russia without being part of an organized group. They did not want anyone to see anything that was not specifically on the tour. So, they were in a gallery and the girl guide, who was 18 or 19, was holding forth in English at the other end of the group. Jeff and Jack saw something interesting down a side corridor and down it they went. The guide went along to the next stop and counted the group. When she found that two were missing, she almost had hysterics. She was the first person Jeff ever saw who was abjectly terrified. They were left with the impression that she thought she was going to be killed for her mistake. This left a strong impression on Jeff. He had never been anywhere where he had seen fear like that. That was Russia in 1930.

They all came back to the hotel one afternoon to find that all of their belongings had been gathered together in a sheet and moved to other rooms and dumped on the floor because some party of important government officials had arrived and needed their rooms. This was unpleasant, but to Phyllis, who was 18 years old and used to getting her own way, this was absolutely unacceptable. She took one look at her lingerie and cosmetics lying there on the floor and she turned and looked at the hotel man and she charged. She screamed and ran right at him like something out of a horror movie. Perhaps her intention was to scratch his eyes right out of his head. He turned and ran in terror down the corridor and Phyllis chased him all the way down to the stairwell.

Another lasting memory of Russia for Jeff was the food. It was mostly foul. The only notable exception was the Russian rye bread. It has the reputation for being very nourishing because it contains a lot of foreign matter, the origin of which is better left undiscovered. It is solid and dark and moist and kind of sour. Jeff liked it very much and lived on very little else while in Russia. The rest of the family suffered somewhat, especially Heinie, who was 20 and had a big appetite. He tried something that they served in the hotel dining room and came down with violent dysentery. He was quite ill for several days. They despaired of getting out of the country, because if you could not make your schedules in Russia, you were stuck.

They did make it out and Heinie recovered. They proceeded to Warsaw, which had nothing to offer, and then to Prague. Prague was not much of a place then but it was a great improvement over anything to the East. The family wanted a good meal because they had been on rather Spartan rations for 14 days. Jack checked with the hotel management and organized a special dinner. This took a long time because the hotel was not normally set up to serve such an elaborate meal. It had to be a special occasion for them to prepare such a dinner, the kind they would be called upon to serve to visitors of importance, royalty or other dignitaries. Heinie thought he would starve to death waiting. It took about four hours from the time they got the order to the time the meal was served. Jeff remembers a great big table and a feast. He remembers no details other than some wonderful beef, which was worth its weight in gold. He thinks he ate about three pounds. Heinie ate until he was tired and then ate some more while his little brother watched in admiration.

That look into the Russia of 1930 left Jeff with very strong impressions. He had a first-hand glimpse of Communism at work, something few Americans have seen, and it helped shape his political views strongly at an early age.

The Cooper household was not free of prejudice, anti-semitism being the norm in their household. Jeff was conscious from an early age of being a member of the most privileged class. The Cooper's servants were both black and white and this was not an issue that was ever discussed, nor was there any labor trouble that Jeff can recall. He mixed with black and white and his-panic and oriental in school and never thought anything about it. However, the Coopers were definitely anti-semitic and did not think that one associated with Jews. This prejudice stayed with Jeff until the Six Day War.

Even as a very small boy, Jeff began to believe that the measure of a man is how well he can fight. He accepted the fact that fighting is what men do, have always done and will always do. He calls this his "warrior mentality". He makes judgements about people based on their individual achievements and a man who does well in whatever fighting comes his way has Jeff's respect and admiration no matter who or what he is. Thus the brilliance, ability and courage shown by the Israelis in the Six Day War changed Jeff's opinion of an entire group of people forever. After that war there was a series of small engagements in which the Jews distinguished themselves as probably the most serious soldiers of the post-World War II era. Jeff has always been most influenced by personal experience and observation, so an inherited prejudice fell easily by the wayside in the light of what he saw and understood for him-self. Today more than half of his closest friends are Jews, although he often has to guess at who is and who is not because this is not of any real impor-tance to him and he never asks. In many cases he simply does not know the ethnic or religious background of a friend. He simply accepts them on the basis of their accomplishments.

After 1930, most of the traveling was done by Jack and Jeff during the sum-mer months so as not to interfere with school. They went to Ireland, Spain, Mexico and they kept on traveling at regular intervals. This was marvelous for them both. Jack was able to indulge his adventurous spirit with an equally adventurous companion—one who soaked up the impressions and atmos-pheres of the various places they visited with enthusiasm and a wide-eyed curiosity and appreciation.

In 1933 they took the train down to Mazatlan from Los Angeles. The wild parrots flying free captivated Jeff—it was his introduction to the semi-trop-ics. They stayed first at the plantation of a good friend of Jack's, Don Luis Bradbury. (To this day one of the buildings between Fifth and Sixth streets in downtown Los Angeles is called "the Bradbury building".) He had a plantation outside of Mazatlan. At night there were sentries pacing outside the bedroom windows, walking about with big sombreros and bandoliers and lever-action rifles. Jeff was fascinated.

Back in the hotel in Mazatlan where they stopped on their way to the plantation there was kept a pet boa constrictor for rat control. At 13 Jeff was tall and skinny, so he had some trouble getting this big snake up around his shoulders for a photograph. But he succeeded and this was a high point for him.

They traveled down from Mazatlan to Mexico City where they visited some ruins which did not impress Jeff very much. From there they flew to Cuba. Commercial aviation was in its infancy at that time. They flew in a Ford Trimotor—the old corrugated iron plane with three engines—noisy as could be. From Mexico City they flew to Vera Cruz—Vera Cruz to Campeche—Campeche to Mérida where they went to Chichen Itza and Uxmal. It was pretty wild in those days and they had to fight through the underbrush to get there. There Jeff concurred in the widely-held theory that there are no more Maya because they fell off their own temples.

From Mérida they flew to Havana with two stops at Cozumel and Santiago de Cuba for fuel. This flight was made in a Sikorsky amphibian which had the main hull at the bottom and two engines mounted above, with both a lower and an upper wing. They took off from Mérida on land and landed in a lagoon at Cozumel where there was nothing at all. They nosed up on the sand and jumped from the hull onto the barren beach. This was very exciting for a youngster who had been absorbing adventure stories at great length.

From Cozumel they flew to Santiago de Cuba and then to Havana. In Havana, Jack was particularly impressed with the quality of the local beer. They then flew to Miami and took the train back to Los Angeles. Jeff had picked up a few Spanish phrases and a lifelong taste for *refritos*, and

Jeff in Mazatlan at age 13.

40

the impression he gained of Mexico was very different from what a typical border American might have.

At the time, the stereotype of a Mexican was of a lazy bum sitting in the shade with a sombrero over his eyes and wearing dirty white pajamas. Young Jeff picked up an impression of Mexico which was much more aristocratic—blooded horses and braid-trimmed trousers and silver-mounted machetes and things like that. He has not lost that impression. No amount of drug-dealing gang members can alter his opinion of the "real" Mexican who has an image of which to be proud. The conduct of various Mexicans on various occasions in various international incidents has been exemplary. Years later when Jeff went down the Rio Balsas with two Mexican soldiers he drew the conclusion that if the Mexican army were made up of men like his companions, they have a good army. He has a much more positive feeling about Mexico than many other southwesterners.

The attitude that Mexicans were to be looked down upon derives largely from the Mexican War of 1847 when it became customary in the American Southwest to decry anything Mexican. When Jeff was a boy in Los Angeles there were no restaurants which laid claim to serving "Mexican food". They would claim to serve "Spanish food" which was entirely in error. The food was, in fact, Mexican, but it was not popular to say so.

Nevertheless, Jeff's impression of Mexico was definitely good and years later when we took a family car trip down to Mexico City and back, that attitude came through clearly and we took our cues from him.

In 1934, Jack and Jeff went to England and Ireland. They took a ship to Southampton and then went on up to London. They happened to hit a very hot day in London and saw a chalkboard sign outside a pub advertising "iced hock and seltzer." They thought that sounded good. Hock is a general English term for any German wine. Nobody ever iced anything in England, but they did that day. They mixed a light, fresh, fruity and dry German wine with seltzer and served it over ice. The two of them had big tumblers of Rhine wine and soda over ice. Jeff still remembers how good that tasted.

They continued over through Wales and took a ferry across the Irish Sea to Dublin. They traveled across the island by hired car and train to Aran on the west coast. They admired the surf and the green and the horses and the large, friendly shaggy dogs—and the fuchsias by the mile. There were beautiful purple and lavender colors in all the hedges around all the buildings. They got quite cold while walking across a causeway in the sea spray and then came back to a feast of pink salmon—served cold! Everything is served cold there in the summer, whether the guests are cold or not. They also visited the Guinness brewery in Dublin and that tour was a high point for the two Cooper men.

Jeff learned that when the British first invaded Ireland, they landed in the Dublin area and settled there. They felt the Irish were not people with whom one would want to associate. After all, they lived in holes in the ground and wore skins. So the British set up their beach-head around Dublin and built a fence all the way around it. This fence was built of palings. In Ireland, you were okay if you were on the inside, but if you lived "beyond the pale" you were not acceptable. That's what the British thought. Of course the Irish have a different point of view.

In 1936, when Jeff was sixteen years old, he and his father took a summer trip to Spain. This impressed them both greatly. They took one of the Italian liners from New York to Gibraltar. Gibraltar was interesting—the big rock and the Barbary apes. They went on up inside to other interesting places. First was Ronda. Ronda is now the headquarters of the Spanish Legion. It's more notable for people who read Ernest Hemingway. If you have read *For Whom the Bell Tolls* you know of the occasion where, in the first part of the movement, the communists murdered all the aristocrats in a village and threw their bodies off the cliff. That's Ronda, and it is very spectacular. It sits on the edge of the cliff and the gorge between the two parts of the town is separated by a bridge and everything is vertical.

They went on to Granada. Jack, always the voracious reader, would hand his son books on the countries they would be seeing and say, "Before we go, read this!" So he gave Jeff *Tales of the Alhambra* by Washington Irving so he would know all about the Alhambra and its romantic Moorish past. That was very wise and Jeff got the most out of their travels in that way.

They saw Granada and Sevilla and went up the Giralda Tower and saw various other sights. Then they went on up to Madrid. The other book that Jack had given Jeff to read on the boat on the way over was *Death in the Afternoon* by Ernest Hemingway. Jeff really absorbed this book, as had Jack. When they got to Madrid they could actually talk to the Spaniards about the bulls. The Spaniards were so used to foreigners who could not stand the thought of bull-fighting that Jack and Jeff, who were enthusiastic about the activity, immediately became bosom buddies with everyone. They were treated to tours of several *ganaderias* where they raise the bulls and *tientas* where they separate out the cows for breeding. They traveled by hired car with Ernesto, a local driver who knew the country well.

They saw a number of bull fights, perhaps twenty. They had Jeff's copy of *Death in the Afternoon* autographed by several matadors and obtained auto-graphed pictures and souvenirs. Jack was very much interested in the production of sherries so they went to various vineyards to see how that was done. They drank *manzanilla*. It was traditional to bring a bottle of *manzanilla* to the bullfight and keep it between your ankles and finish it by the time the fights were through—that way you would have something to throw at a matador if he displeased you.

They saw a *corrida* in almost every town they visited—Granada, Sevilla, Córdoba, Aranjuez, Toledo and a few in Madrid. In Córdoba they had front row seats. Jeff was still very blond in those days. The matador was Armillita Chico. He fought his bull just right and got both ears and the tail. He did not get the kill *recibiendo* but that is very rarely seen. He was smiling and parading and when he saw Jeff, standing out in the crowd as a blond young foreigner of sixteen, he tossed him the tail. Jeff still has it. Thus he developed an appreciation for bullfighting which lasts to this day.

This trip to Spain was just before their civil war, so well written about by Hemingway in *For Whom the Bell Tolls*. This was a grim war which Jeff has studied deeply. Like most civil wars it was very savage with much killing of innocents, torture and excesses. Jeff's visit there just prior to that war gave him a special feel for the actions and the consequences of that conflict.

The bond which developed between Jack and Jeff was deep and profound. It has always been a regret of mine and my sisters that we never knew our grandfather. He died just after our parents were married. Our memories of Austeene, however, are vivid. She lived to be ninety-eight and died in 1985 in Los Angeles at the house on Rossmore. We saw her often as we grew and came to know her well.

Austeene was bossy, opinionated, warm, generous, spunky, earthy, sentimental, critical, stubborn, theatrical and generally fun to be around. She was only a few inches over five feet tall and always fairly plump that I recall. Pictures she kept on the wall from some of her stage performances showed a curvaceous, dark-haired beauty with flashing eyes.

Austeene felt it was definitely a woman's prerogative to lie about her age and she did so all the time I knew her. I think I have pieced together her motivation. She could not have hid her true age from Uncle Les and Aunt Louise, nor from Jack. However, after Jack's death in 1942, she was courted by Warren Watkins, who became her second husband in 1945. She was a widow of 55 with three grown children. He was 44. She carefully reconstructed her history by shaving off about six years, thus being a widow of not quite fifty and, in her opinion, a much more acceptable wife for a man of 44.

Thus we all grew up with the story of her having been orphaned and coming to live with Uncle Les and Aunt Louise when she was a poor little girl of nine (she was 16). She told us all she was married at 18 (she was 22). She blamed the relative failure of her first marriage on the excessive age difference between herself and Jack of 10 years (it was 4 years and 4 months). Warren died in 1976, but by this time, the stories had been told too often to be refuted. When she was well into her nineties, I think she struggled—to be openly proud of her longevity she would have to admit to having deceived us. When she died, we had some trouble finding out the true year of her birth. The page in the family bible which recorded her arrival had been torn out.

I think she was somewhat incredulous when she looked at her younger son, wondering what kind of prodigy she had produced. She was very proud of his accomplishments, but they had almost nothing in common. Conversations between them never lasted more than a very few minutes. Jeff had learned this axiom at an early age and took it to heart: *Small minds discuss people, average minds discuss events and superior minds discuss ideas.* Consequently, Jeff has always steered conversations to the highest plane, while Austeene wanted to talk about the latest party at the country club and the activities of her society friends. She was somewhat in awe of him while he tolerated her.

> *"I knew both Jeff's father and mother. I knew Austeene better. She was a real tiger in almost any situation. She was very prominent and busy socially. She was a very active person and certainly the opposite of her son with respect to small talk."*
> *– CHARLES BRAGG*

After I married, my grandmother and I often talked on the phone. She would always ask me how my sex life was. She felt this was a very important part of life and wanted to assure herself that everyone she cared about was doing well in that department.

> *"I went to see Austeene when she was dying and she always used to say, 'Have love in your life—like Jane Ellen and Jeff. That's the most beautiful love story.'*
> *– DORIS SMITH VISSCHER*

Austeene was unique and larger than life—a force of nature. In our own ways, we all miss her. I certainly do.

Austeene Paralee George Cooper Watkins, Jeff's mother.

CHAPTER

Early school – travel continues

At about the time of his marital estrangement, Jack Cooper made what seems to have been deliberate alterations in his child-rearing practices. Up to this point he had left the bulk of those duties to his wife, being busy making a living. Austeene had been an indulgent mother and Jack was not particularly happy with what he saw as the result. Heinie, handsome and charming, was rather a playboy, interested in driving the latest car, dating Hollywood starlets and minor European royalty, playing sports and partying. He was not ambitious nor did he have any goals beyond continuing the good life. He was nothing like his father, having no serious intellectual or philosophical bent. Jack once referred to him as *"el estúpido"* in front of others and he was not kidding. Heinie was given a short trial term at Stanford, due to the influence of his father's association with that school, but he could not do the work required. He transferred to the University of Oregon, but he never was graduated. He married a young woman named Roberta Mullineaux, but the marriage did not last more than a couple of years. He had a good voice and tried to establish himself in a singing career, but it never took off. He was an excellent ballroom dancer and a fine personal athlete, but he was not an achiever.

> *"I was close to my mom. She was an exuberant person who loved*
> *life and was full of personality. I was a hell of a lot like her."*
> *– HEINIE COOPER*

Phyllis was of a more intellectual makeup, but she was rebellious and spoiled. She liked to smoke and drink and acting like a lady was not her cup of tea. Beautiful and adept at attracting men and then dropping them for the next conquest, she was graduated from Marlborough and then went off to Sarah Lawrence and returned after one year—too confining. She then entered

45

into a very short marriage with Onslow Stevens, the director of the Pasadena Playhouse, where she was an aspiring actress. Phyllis was more like her father than her older brother was, but her lack of direction and discipline was disappointing to her father.

"Phyllis was intellectual in every way. She was also very sexy. She really had an aura. My mother was very sexy too. Phyllis was like both mom and dad. She was not exuberant and joyous like her mother. She was more serious.

Her first husband was Onslow Stevens, an actor. He had another girl who threatened to jump off a building if he did not come back to her. So he did and the marriage ended abruptly. Then she married Niven Busch because he was such a good writer. That was the only reason she married him."

– HEINIE COOPER

Heinie in his Coast Guard uniform, World War II.

Jeff's birth, being an afterthought as it was, cramped Austeene's style somewhat, and when he turned out to be so very independent from an early age, she was happy to leave him to his books while she got more and more wrapped up in the social whirl which was Los Angeles in the "roaring twenties".

Jack stepped in. From handing Jeff books to taking him to his clubs for meals to taking him on automobile excursions all over the Southwest, Jack recognized a soulmate in his younger son and he delighted in encouraging their similarities. He probably felt that giving his older children everything they wanted whenever they asked had fostered in them a lack of discipline and ambition. He sought to make a difference in his younger son's development.

Jack and Austeene were both generous people and Heinie had

been handed almost everything he wanted from the beginning. This included boats, cars and money. Heinie did not do well in school and this annoyed Jack, who felt it was a young man's primary job. While a gifted athlete in individual sports, Heinie never wished to put himself on the line. He never went out for big-time tennis, although he could have, and while he was very fond of cars, he never considered putting himself to a test on a race track. Jack provided him with a series of very impressive automobiles and boats. This included a Bugatti Type 35 —a sensational automobile —in which Heinie succeeded in constantly evading traffic police in the days before radar. Heinie developed great skill with small boats which served

The earliest photo of Jeff Cooper with a gun. Here he is about six years old on the front porch of the house at 500 North Rossmore.

him well in World War II because that's what he did in the Coast Guard. Every time he wanted anything, Jack gave it to him.

Jack decided that his youngest child should not be handed things simply because he expressed an interest. He developed a system of requiring Jeff to earn what he yearned for which was a different tactic. He tried to make sure that what his youngest got was what he *really* wanted.

Jeff had been introduced to shooting at an early age by his brother. Heinie remembers having a BB gun and a pump pistol with which both he and Jeff played. Jeff remembers being hooked at the age of eleven, when Heinie let him shoot his Colt Woodsman down at Hamilton Cotton's place in San Clemente. (This became the "Western White House" under Nixon.) Heinie did not teach Jeff to any great extent, but little brothers learn by watching. Jack was not a shooter and never gave his sons any instruction of any sort about marksmanship. Jeff's extensive reading of adventure stories gave him some knowledge as well and practice is a great teacher. He also subscribed to and read the current sporting magazines and gun editors. He paid attention and he remembered.

At the age of thirteen, Jeff decided he had to have his own 22 rifle. The object of his desire was a Remington Model 34, introduced in the early months of 1934 and retailing for the princely sum of thirty-four dollars. That was a lot of money. Jeff approached his father, praising the excellence of the weapon.

Jack asked the price and then offered to give Jeff half that if he could come up with the other half. This was asking a great deal, since Jeff got no allowance and he was off to Catalina for the summer. He came up with a plan.

Jeff often worked as boat boy on Mr. Stringfellow's boat, but this was not for money. He worked for the privilege of being on the boat. There were a lot of fishermen at Avalon. Some were guests of the Coopers, some guests of Mr. Stringfellow, some they met on the beach and some they met at the Yacht Club. These fishermen tended to exaggerate. Jeff, being blessed with an extremely good memory (photographic I am convinced), acquired the Pflueger catalogue and memorized all the listed current world's records for all the game fish in the world. (Pflueger made fishing tackle and accessories.) He hustled those fishermen and involved them in small wagers regarding the size of fish. Most bets were for fifty cents. An occasional high-roller would wager one dollar. Bing Crosby made the mistake of betting Jeff that there was no difference between "light tackle" and 3/6 tackle, and so he added one dollar towards the price of Jeff's first rifle.

During that summer, Jeff accumulated the necessary seventeen dollars. When he returned to town he received his 22. Jack was impressed with Jeff's ingenuity and the fact that he really wanted that rifle. That's how Jeff got his first gun which he still owns and shoots regularly off the front porch of his home.

Jeff went to public schools. The education he received there was exemplary and he has no complaints about its quality. He was a good student. He was not at the top of his class, but he was right up there with mostly all 1's and 2's in grade school and then A's and B's when he was in junior high and high school. He got more A's as he got older and realized the importance of good grades.

"I first met Jeff Cooper in the 8th grade at John Burroughs Junior High School in Los Angeles. ...we seemed to get along. He's by far my oldest acquaintance. Jeff has always been different. As I recall, Jeff's bedroom was on the second floor of the house at 500 North Rossmore, and it verged on being a sleeping porch, sort of exposed. He had, even at that time, a loaded gun under his pillow. The thing that he did that bugged his mother—he got a fencing foil and stuck it in the ceiling just inside the door, so that anyone who came into his room in the dark would run into the silly thing and it would fall out and make a hell of a racket."

– CHARLES BRAGG

Jeff (standing second from left in last row) in elementary school at The School of the Little Green Trees. Even at that age, he hated those flowers!

He remembers distinctly that many of his teachers emphasized messages of importance which corroborated ideas he heard at the dinner table at home and which he read on the sofa in the evenings. For example, Miss Champion, Los Angeles High School civics teacher, told her class that there was no such thing as a free lunch. She said the government has no power that is not yours, no money that is not yours and whenever the government is going to do anything, you are going to be doing it. She told her class to keep that in mind.

She then hit them with the doctrine that rights and privileges are contingent upon duties and responsibilities—that nothing is free and that anything you get in life you are going to earn, and that includes liberty. This was good, rousing stuff. It still is, although finding it in any school today would be difficult. She told her eleventh graders that they would learn these principles or they would not pass her class, and that her class was required for a diploma. If one did not pass it in the eleventh grade, one would be required to take it and pass it in the twelfth grade. Miss Champion let her students know that she would still be there, expecting them not only to know and understand what she was teaching, but to be able to explain it to her in whatever foreign language they were studying as well. She was totally devoted to the importance of civic duty and Jeff learned her lessons well.

Jeff was always weak in mathematics because he never came across a teacher who could tell him why he would need any of it. The exception was Mr. Brubaker in geometry. The traditional way of teaching arithmetic is to give the students a book and tell them to do the problems on a certain page and then grade them. Jeff could do the work, at least most of the time, but he couldn't see what it was good for. In algebra he reached quadratic equations and could not see to what use one would ever put a quadratic equation. Mr. Brubaker was unusual, first of all because he was a man and most public school teachers in those days were women. He also was a humorist and joked with the students in class even though getting chuckles out of high schoolers is a chore. He showed them how geometry is philosophy and shows one how to think. He showed them the beautiful logic of A squared plus B squared equals C squared and the attraction of the fact that this has always been so and will always be so after man has vanished from the face of the earth. Jeff loved the certainty of it.

The students got a heavy dose of good old-fashioned indoctrination from the music department. The music teacher at Los Angeles High School was Mrs. Morgan. As Jeff puts it, "I feel sure that she sits high amongst the angels at the right hand of God—because she was marvelous." She taught band and chorus. She had her students memorize the words to songs of heroism and valor and dignity and excitement and Jeff still remembers them all.

> *"You, who have dreams, if you act, they will come true.*
> *To turn your dreams to a fact, it's up to you.*
> *If you have the soul and the spirit, never fear it,*
> *   you'll see it through.*
> *Hearts can inspire other hearts with their fire,*
> *   for the strong obey when a strong man shows them the way."*

The chorus sang those lyrics (from *Stout-Hearted Men*; music by Sigmund Romberg, lyrics by Oscar Hammerstein II) and they are just some of many like that. This was indoctrination into the morals and ethics of the culture which has vanished today. Mrs. Morgan was determined to get these messages across to her students and she succeeded. This was public education in the 1930's. Jeff was receptive—perhaps more than most—and there were no contrary ideals being espoused at home or in the literature he read with such passion.

In high school, he discovered the R.O.T.C. and started using the 22 Springfield training rifle at the range they had set up under the concrete bleachers on the football field. He and his friends played around and taught each other how to shoot, using the regular 50-foot course. When they felt they were good enough, they could try out for the high school rifle team. If you made the team, then the practice ammunition was free! There was a limited free supply for the ROTC battalion, but the rifle team got unlimited ammo. Jeff thought this was very desirable, so he decided to try out.

At this same time he discovered the center-fire 22's and the lead one at the time was the 22 Hornet. This struck him as a massive and important cartridge

50

Jeff in his R.O.T.C. uniform, Los Angeles High School.

and he determined to have one. He settled upon the Savage Model 23D and again approached his father. The price was about fifty dollars. His father, mindful of his experiment, told Jeff that if he made the team, he would buy him the gun. So Jeff tried out, made the team, and got the Hornet.

"The major thing that initially developed out of all this was a mutual interest in guns. We used to go down to the hardware store in central Los Angeles called Hoegee's, (the William H. Hoegee Company), *a fascinating place. It had a shooting gallery in the basement. They had a wonderful inventory of handguns and rifles.*

There was a public shooting range that we used to go to occasionally and then we would also go to the Brand house in Glendale and go up in the hills behind it and shoot. There were these two lovely old ladies (at least they looked awfully old to me) living in this huge house. (This was Aunt Louise and Aunt Tess.) *The house had a whole bunch of light fixtures—sconces here, there and everywhere. About half the bulbs in those sconces were out. It was Jeff's idea to take out those burned-out bulbs and use them for targets. The ladies had fits over that."*

– CHARLES BRAGG

Jack Cooper was interested in land—that being his business. He was mostly interested in land development in and around Southern California, but that did not limit him. He would travel northward to Oxnard and Santa Barbara and to the foothills of the Sierras and the Sequoia area. After Uncle Les' death and the abandonment of the Tioga Pass lodge, Jack and his sons went up several times into the Owens Valley and took pack trips up into the Sierras. Often the motor trips would include pack trips on horseback. They would drive to a ranch location and take horses from there. In Arizona, Jack was fond of the White Mountains and he liked the country around Prescott (one reason Jeff lives there today) and Flagstaff. In Southern California he traveled southward to San Clemente, which grew due largely to the influence of his friend, Hamilton Cotton.

For Jeff, motor trips are separated in his mind between the times when his brother drove and the later trips when Jeff did the driving and went alone with his father. Heinie was a good driver and loved cars, but he was reluctant to go along on these excursions as chauffeur. He had his own private life and interests. When Jack told him they were going to such and such a place for the weekend, Heinie would complain and try to get out of going as best he could. Jack would insist and off the three of them would go. Jeff believes Heinie really liked these trips after they got out of Los Angeles and he realized that he was stuck. He would then relax and enjoy himself. They went on pack trips in the White Mountains and in the Rockies in both Wyoming and Colorado. The Jackson Hole country was a favorite. Austeene and Phyllis never went along on these outings. They did not like "roughing it", so they stayed in the city and were chauffeured by the family's driver.

As soon as Jeff got his license, Heinie abdicated all driving to him. Heinie went along on only one trip after Jeff could drive and they shared the driving. After that, it was just Jack and his youngest. They got along better with each other than with anyone else. They were kindred spirits. They spoke of history, geography and adventure. They did not speak of intimate or personal things. This was not their style.

Automobiles were still rather primitive and service for them was not easy to find. Thus they were accustomed to carrying what they needed for repairs with them in the car. If a fuel pump broke down, they would simply rebuild it there in the road. Heinie taught Jeff the basics of car mechanics. Jeff remembers being alone in the car and far from anywhere when he had his first flat tire. He had never seen one before, much less changed one. He sat down and gave it some thought and figured it out for himself. He remains fond of that technique in teaching situations, believing that one does not need to be taught or shown how to do everything. Learning how to think and reason are better tools for survival.

The roads were somewhat difficult and often the heat was great and there was no air conditioning and keeping the engine from boiling when you went through the lowlands was always a geographical problem. Jack liked to leave Los Angeles at the close of business Friday and drive down in the heat to Parker or Needles. They would go to bed early and get up at about 3 a.m. to be able to catch the coolest time of day to get out across the desert before they hit the escarpment at what is now Kingman or Wickenburg, in Arizona. If they did not do this, their chances of getting up the grade there (which still exists today) without boiling over were not good. They always carried plenty of water in addition to light bulbs and fan belts and distributor heads. Much of the country was not paved and they did more than half of their exploring on dirt roads. These varied from quite good to unidentifiable. The road from Kayenta to Montrose, Colorado, degenerated into a gully and they had to find their way around between rocks and other obstacles. Their trips got pretty adventurous. They always packed along personal weapons and whenever there was an opportunity, Jeff would get out and do some shooting. Then he would religiously clean the weapon because he adhered to the traditions of Stewart White and Theodore Roosevelt—you don't let the sun set on a dirty gun.

Shooting, hunting and girls

I t's probable that Jack Cooper was highly satisfied with the way his younger son was developing and took great pleasure in helping to mold him. He likely regretted not having taken the same strong role in the development of his two older children. He arranged for several independent experiences for Jeff, with an eye toward helping him mature into a well-rounded individual.

The first of these was a summer stint in the National Guard when Jeff was sixteen. Sixteen was too young, but Jack pulled some strings and Jeff found himself in a summer camp in San Luis Obispo. This was very educational. Jeff was a buck private and spent his time picking up cigarette butts, tightening tent legs and scrubbing out garbage cans. He did not care too much for this and decided that menial labor did not hold any attraction for him as a career choice. They had an Armenian mess sergeant who was really good. He was justifiably proud of the fact that his floors were so clean one could eat off of them. He kept them that way by keeping the privates on their knees with scrub brushes a good deal of the time.

Communication duty was also not pleasant. Whenever the wires would go out, three privates would have to go out and find where the wire was broken and repair it. This was twenty-four hours a day. Jeff did not relish being pulled out of bed at three in the morning to go wandering out in the bush looking for a break.

This was a taste of the dogface life at the bottom and it encouraged Jeff to be an officer, which is of course what the ROTC was for—the Reserve Officer Training Corps. So he stuck with it all through high school and signed up immediately for the ROTC at Stanford.

Jack also arranged for Jeff to go on a commercial tuna cruise. Jeff is not sure how his father arranged this. He only knows that Jack told him to go down and see the ship's captain in San Diego and that he would be taken aboard as a crewman. Jeff did not want to do this much, but he did not question his father. What his father said went.

This was a brutal experience and Jeff did not enjoy it at all. It was cold and wet and exhausting, hauling tuna over the side amidst blood and fish guts. He worked for wages and his desire not to be stuck doing something like that for a living was further strengthened.

A much more enjoyable summer job which Jack arranged for Jeff was as a dude wrangler in Arizona. Jeff was already a pretty fair horseman. Wrangling dudes was much more to his taste. He was responsible mainly for the horses and their equipment, but he also served as guide and instructor, baited fishing hooks and cleaned fish—whatever was needed by visitors except food and food preparation. Dudes had to go everywhere on horseback in those days because hiking was not popular and there were no recreational vehicles. They would most often go out on day or two-day trips into the mountains. This was great fun because it was social and the dudes were generally well-to-do families who were enthusiastic about the whole experience. Many were Easterners who were seeing the "wild west" for the first time. They would build campfires and sit around and sing. Jeff would flirt with the dude girls.

These were not exactly typical summer jobs since Jeff did not get them for himself, but he worked for wages and absorbed all that the experiences could teach him, which was what Jack had in mind.

About this time, Jeff decided he had to have a 30-06. From all that he read and heard, this was the ultimate cartridge and something he clearly must possess. He approached his father who asked the cost. Jeff told him, "Seventy-nine fifty." Jack thought a minute and then inquired if the L.A. High School ROTC rifle team was going to compete city-wide against all the other ROTC battalions and if they expected to win. Jeff said, "We're going to try." Jack said, "If your rifle team wins, you get the 30-06." The team won and Jeff got his new rifle. It's in his armory today.

To his way of thinking, a 30-06 is the perfect cartridge and has been since 1906. Current literature will tell you that it is hopelessly outdated. In Jeff's opinion this is balderdash. If you cannot do it with a 30-06, you cannot do it—with a few exceptions such as elephant and buffalo. In any case, he has used and loved that gun all his life. He has done the best shooting of his life with that gun. He got into top form when he was a senior in high school and has never shot better—as well, but not better.

Jeff started hunting at an early age. He was not tutored by anyone but learned by reading and listening and paying attention—committing to memory those things that made sense to him. It never occurred to Jeff that not everyone hunted. With the singular exception of his own father, everyone he knew hunted. One of the first things that one did when visiting the homes of friends in those days was to break out the guns and examine them and admire them and discuss them.

Jeff and his first trophy, the 1937 elk.

His first hunting was on Catalina Island, scrub goats being the quarry. When he was about sixteen, some friends of Jack's arranged a deer hunting trip and Jack asked that Jeff be taken along. Jeff was unimpressed with his father's friends when, on the first night of the trip, they stayed up late drinking bourbon and playing poker. He was even less impressed when they encountered some distant deer on the following day and immediately started blasting away, hitting nothing and scaring away all the game. When the smoke cleared, one of the men asked Jeff, "Did you get a shot?" Jeff looked disdainfully at him and replied, "If I had taken a shot, we would now have a deer." That must not have endeared him to the group—he was not asked to go along again.

His first big game hunt was for elk in 1937, just after his graduation from high school. It was his idea. He asked his father and Jack, not being a hunter, agreed to the trip but did not choose to go along. Jeff packed up his 1936 Ford station wagon with sleeping bags and rifles and, with Art Rasmussen, a distant cousin, drove up to Jackson Hole, Wyoming. Their outfitter was Bill Scott, from the southern part of the Hole up above the Hoback. They had a fine time, packing in for about ten days. Jeff secured a massive bull which for many years graced the wall of Kerr's Sport Shop in Beverly Hills because there was no place to put it at 500 North Rossmore. (I suspect there was room but Austeene nixed the idea of a great big elk looking down on her Christmas party guests.) Art got a nice bull too. Jeff was using his brand new 375 and Art borrowed the 30-06. Art took his elk with one shot, while Jeff took four shots to get his down. Jeff had to wait several years before getting to eat elk he shot himself since this was the meat that Jack donated to the Wine and Food Society dinner.

In high school, Jeff was a fairly big frog in a fairly big puddle. He was commander of the ROTC battalion, the only major in the line-up, and he was a member of the honor society and the senior board, which was what passed for student government. Los Angeles High School was extremely stratified in those days—there were castes. These were in no way based on race or religion, but rather on seniority and achievement. Seniors were very conscious of the fact that they were vastly superior to the underclassmen. Only seniors were allowed to wear corduroy trousers, and there were other privileges regarding lunches and breaks and things of that sort. There were over four thousand students. It was in no sense egalitarian, but extremely socially stratified. There were important people, less important people, the common people and the under-class and everyone knew where everyone else stood.

There was a racial mix in Los Angeles High School in 1937, but it did not figure into anything to Jeff's knowledge. He sat on the senior board next to a brilliant young black man who was an honor student and a track star. Everybody admired him and nobody brought up the subject of his race. Whether he was bothered by this he never said, at least not to Jeff. In the ROTC battalion there was a Chinese lieutenant and a Japanese sergeant and nobody gave a thought to their race. They were simply cadets. Jeff looks back on this with a sense of bemusement and wonders why everyone is mad at everyone else today when they weren't back in 1937.

In his senior year, when he was battalion commander, a major, in the ROTC, Jeff was invited out to the Los Angeles Country Club by a group of gentlemen which called itself The Golf and Poker Club. They golfed by day and played poker by night and they were influential and affluent people. They asked him out to talk about hunting rifles, about which he knew a few things, having done some hunting and read extensively. He got through the presentation and got a nice round of applause. One member of the club, Charlie Cotton, a very important oil man in Southern California, took Jeff aside and said, "I don't know if you are very sharp, young man, but you have a lively curiosity and an excellent memory and that will take care of most of it."

That comment proved to be right on the mark. Jeff does not have a record-breaking I.Q., but he appears to. This is due in large part to his intense curiosity about just about everything and his astonishing memory, as well as a love of reading, an ability to read vast amounts quickly and a dedication to the

Jeff as a senior in high school.

idea that "superior minds discuss ideas." His curiosity is relentless and very motivating to others. His memory is phenomenal and, because his desire to learn leads him to read constantly, he has a warehouse of knowledge on almost every subject at the ready, in his head! This, which was apparent to Charlie Cotton in 1937, has only become more pronounced as the years go by.

Jeff discovered girls in high school and became a life-long, enthusiastic appreciator of "the fair sex". He quickly discovered that dating was not feasible without a car and a driver's license. As soon as he turned sixteen, he talked his father out of an automobile. Unlike his older bother, he used some logic by convincing his father that a station wagon was just what the family needed for trips since they could pack all their gear in the back. So his first car was a 1936 Ford station wagon. This was the car he later took to college.

Jeff soon became aware of another distinct social stratification in existence which dictated boy-girl relationships. There were girls who did and girls who did not and it was quite clear to Jeff upon very short acquaintance which category they were in. Jeff thought all girls were great, but he knew early on that it would be ungentlemanly of him to try to convince a girl who did not otherwise. If he could find a girl who did, all the better.

He developed a three-phase approach which worked well for him and must appear to be quaint ancient history to today's youth. The first date was dinner and a movie. (Jack approved of dating and kicked in all related expenses.) The second date was dinner and dancing, dancing being more intimate. There were many places to go. There were many very good nightclubs and it was not forbidden for adolescents to enjoy them. The third date was the beach—specifically Santa Monica Ocean Park, which was full of concessions such as the Ferris wheel and the roller coaster. Jeff discovered that this was a great softener-upper. When he took a girl on the roller coaster, it gave her the chance to indicate quite clearly how interested she was in him. He always made his passes after leaving the amusement park. This was his one, two, three punch and it usually worked well.

He discovered, being a smart young man, an excellent student with a good memory and having a keen interest in the subject, that females were more subtle and complex in the erotic sense than males and he always kept that in mind. He also adhered to the principle of keeping his mouth shut about his romantic encounters. Both these precepts added to his desirability as an escort, as he was well aware. He was horrified to find that at fraternity gatherings in college it was quite common for the young men to discuss their conquests openly. This was foreign to Jeff and he never played that game. No one ever taught him this. He was simply more mature than his peers, due to his extensive reading, travel and the society of adults.

When Jeff was a senior in high school his good friend, Charles Bragg (known forever as Briggles), set him up on a date with a pretty, bright junior girl named Jane Ellen Marks. They took the station wagon and, true to Jeff's formula, they went to a movie. It was a double date with Briggles and their good friend Betsy Fricke. Although they did not date exclusively from that date forward, the die was cast.

Jane Ellen, about the time she met Jeff at
Los Angeles High School, 1936.

Beginnings – Janelle

"I think one reason I admire Jeff so much is that he is married to Janelle."

— CLIFFORD DOUGLAS

"For many of us, part of our respect for Jeff stems from the fact that he is married to Janelle."

— PAUL KIRCHNER

"I seriously doubt that Jeff would have succeeded so grandly without a woman so supportive and devoted to his life's work. I've often said that it is neither fair nor accurate merely to speak of Jeff Cooper. It's Jeff and Janelle, like Lewis and Clark or Currier and Ives."

— BARRETT TILLMAN

"(Jeff is) husband to one of the most gracious, charming and delightful of ladies (doubt not her core of steel, though—else how could she have managed Jeff for more than 50 Years?)"

— FINN AAGAARD

"I think I introduced Jeff and Janelle. That was almost an instant match. I don't think either one of them ever looked askance after that."

— CHARLES BRAGG

"The luckiest thing in my life was latching on to Janelle who is the only person I have ever known who has no flaws."

— JEFF COOPER

On May 31, 1920, just twenty-one days after the birth of John Dean Cooper in the same hospital in Los Angeles, Eleanor Jane Marks was born. This was the name entered on her birth certificate, although she was called Jane by her father, Jane Ellen by the rest of her family and later Janelle by everyone. She was the second child, first girl born to Jasper Glenn Marks and Florence (Floy) Pixley Marks. There is no doubt that the single most influential person in her development was her mother.

The Pixley family can trace its ancestry back to the tenth century. Turgar, the first Earl of Picheslei, was a contemporary of Ethelred II, Canute and Edward the Confessor (965-1016). Later relations came from England to the United States as early as 1662 and the family was always proud of its pioneer heritage. Floy Pixley spoke often of one of our antecedents who was a titled English lady, Lady Frances Wood. She seemed to think this would inspire us to adopt more ladylike manners than we might otherwise be inclined to display.

Janelle's grandfather on her mother's side, DeWitt Clinton Pixley (known as D.C.), was a very important man in Orange, California. He came from Illinois in the middle of the nineteenth century with his wife, Florence Boring Pixley, and one young son, Walter. They settled in Orange and had four more children, Frances, Florence (Floy), Alma and Osman. He was a director of the first flour mill in the county and then went into banking, establishing the first bank in Orange and then the first building and loan association. He was a pillar of the community church and there is a Pixley Street named after him in Orange.

The Pixleys were very productive, solid citizens who can be credited with helping to get Orange started. D.C. Pixley was also one of the first pioneers to visit Big Bear Lake and buy land and build. He used to pack his family in horse-drawn buggies with donkeys carrying supplies for the trip from Orange to Big Bear, which took three days. It became their favorite vacation spot and the compound with several cabins on three acres of land is still in the family and is still used today.

Janelle's grandmother, Florence Boring, was a descendent of the Buchanan family which produced the fifteenth President of the United States, James Buchanan. He was a Democrat, whose lackluster administration immediately preceded the Civil War. For these reasons, the Marks family, staunch Republicans, always played down this connection.

On her father's side, Janelle's grandmother was Eva Esther Stonebraker. She was born in Wisconsin in 1862 and came to live in Hampton, Iowa in 1871. Her ancestors had names of Stonebraker, Day, Holmes and Enoch, with birthplaces ranging from Virginia to Illinois to Tennessee to Missouri. (We have traced some of this lineage as far back as 1796.) Janelle has no memory of her grandmother Eva, who died of "heart trouble" in the year following Janelle's birth.

Janelle does have one photograph which shows her with her Grandfather

A romanticized portrait of Turgar, First Earl of Picheslei.

The earliest photo we have of a Pixley. This is Janelle's great grandfather, Osman Pixley, 1828-1903. He was married to Lady Frances Wood.

Janelle's grandfather, DeWitt Clinton Pixley, center. His brothers are Arthur Homer on the left and Harvey on the right.

D.C. Pixley's house in Orange, California.

An early Big Bear photo shows a very young Jane Ellen with her grandfather on the left and her father on the right.

Janelle's grandfather on her father's side, William Frederick Marks, taken in 1924, the year before his death, when he had just turned 70 years old.

Marks when she was about two, but she has no memory of him either. He died when she was five years old (the same year Jeff's great uncle L.C. Brand died). His name was William Frederick Marks and he was the co-owner of the largest wholesale hardware outlet in all of Southern California.

William Frederick Marks was born in 1859, probably in Wisconsin, to Philip Marx and Marie Schaefer. Although little is know of them, they appear to have been of German extraction. Their son William married Eva Stonebraker in Hampton, Iowa in 1882. In 1883 their only child was born there. He was Jasper Glenn Marks, Janelle's father.

Early in the 1890's William Marks joined with his father-in-law, W. J. Stonebraker, to form "Stonebraker and Marks, Dealers in General Merchandise." About 1900, William and Eva moved to Los Angeles where William joined with H.P. Hoffman to form "Hoffman-Marks Co., Dealers in General Hardware" at 226 South Main Street.

Their son, Janelle's father Jasper Glenn Marks, stayed behind in Iowa in order to complete high school in Hampton where he was the "graduation speaker". Janelle's brother has a copy of the speech he delivered on that occasion. He joined his parents in Los Angeles in 1902 and immediately enrolled at Stanford University, joining a student body which included Janelle's future father-in-law, Jack Cooper.

William and Eva made their home in Los Angeles at 1318 West Third Street. It was a solid structure with pillars of stone and twenty-one cement steps leading up from Third Street. A huge pepper tree graced the back yard.

Janelle's father, Jasper Glenn Marks.

The hardware business prospered, and William and Eva were able to purchase an orchard in the San Fernando Valley, several farms in the San Joaquin Valley, and some acreage in western Arizona.

Jasper Glenn Marks, Janelle's father, was always known as Glenn. He studied accounting at Stanford, where he was graduated in 1906 during the turmoil that followed the great San Francisco earthquake of that year. He recounted that he was asleep in his dormitory bed when that quake struck, was bounced around considerably, and acquired a lifelong terror of sudden earth movements. After graduation he worked for his father's hardware firm and became an officer thereof. Glenn was a charmer, good-looking, fun-loving and well-liked.

Floy was more serious. She was raised very strictly, taught to be a lady and was very much dedicated to being correct, to doing the right thing and to observing very strict moral standards. She went to Sunday school at the First Christian Church of Orange and attended elementary, junior high and high school in Orange and Los Angeles. She attended Cumnock School for Girls in Los Angeles as a finishing school.

Janelle's mother, Florence "Floy" Pixley.

Her father offered her the choice of a college education (her sister Alma went to Stanford) or a trip to Europe. She, being seriously interested in music, chose Europe and studied piano for two years in Germany. When she returned, she gave piano lessons to private students until she married.

Floy and Glenn were acquainted before Floy went to Germany. There was some business connection between the Marks' hardware business and the Pixley's banking business. In any case, they married in 1910, a year after the marriage of Jeff's parents. Floy was 25 years old and Glenn was 27. The ceremony took place in Orange in a wedding described by the Orange newspaper as a "brilliant affair" and written up in much detail. The newlyweds took up residence at 252 South Benton Way in Los Angeles, then moved to a new home, built by Glenn, at 153 South Gramercy Place, Los Angeles, in 1914. Here Janelle's brother, Jasper Glenn Marks, Jr., was born in 1916, and Janelle in 1920. Here they grew up and this is the home where they brought their children for visits until Floy left for a convalescent hospital in 1975.

When the house was first built, Gramercy Place was still a dirt road. The house was white with large stone pillars at the front porch. It was one story with a basement, attic, two bedrooms, one bathroom and maid's quarters. A third bedroom with bathroom was added later on as was a separate garage. It was not as grand as the Cooper's residence at 500 North Rossmore, just a few miles away, but it was well-built and comfortable, just right for a family of four and a maid.

Above: Baby Jane Ellen.
Right: Jane Ellen enjoying a pony ride.

153 South Gramercy Place, Los Angeles, 1920.

Glenn and Floy were very different. Glenn was an avid Shriner who attended all the conventions, a popular and very social young man. He was described as "a delightful person". Floy was less out-going and has been described as "Victorian". As they had children, Floy became dedicated to bringing them up correctly and Glenn reacted with a decided lack of responsibility. He took to philandering. Janelle remembers that it "got pretty bad" and she recalls the tension created by the situation. She remembers being awakened once by the arguing of her parents when her dad came home late and her mother confronted him.

Floy once told Janelle that she never really had a chance to get to know Glenn very well before they were married because of the conventions of courtship at the time. They were seldom alone and never for any length of time. Each was considered a "good catch", both being from successful family backgrounds.

Things came to a head in about 1929 and Glenn moved out. Floy felt that there was a terrible stigma attached to being a divorced woman and she did not want to grant Glenn a divorce. He was finally able to obtain one in about 1939 because of the time elapsed since the date of their separation. He married again in 1940 to Margaret Melinda Butler who remained his wife until his death in 1970. She had a daughter named Mary Margaret who in turn had a daughter of her own named Melinda. We used to stop by and visit them on our way to see Floy each time we came to Los Angeles. "Grandpop", as we called Glenn, was a charming man and we liked Margaret, Mary Margaret and Melinda very much.

The Marks family fortune was mostly lost in the stock market crash of 1929, unlike that of the Cooper's. This was bad timing as it came along with the break-up of Floy's and Glenn's marriage. The seven ranches in the San Joaquin Valley that Glenn had inherited from his father were not good things to own during the thirties. The farmers had a rough time. Glenn evidently did not spend what little income he got from the farms wisely and he was forced to sell them, one after the other. One of the last things he had to sell was the Arizona acreage that his father had picked up so optimistically years before.

Glenn eventually landed a job with the California State Board of Equalization as an accountant. He was able to acquire two apartment buildings, one of which he lived in until his death in 1970.

Things were rather tight for newly-separated Floy and her two children. Glenn provided what he could and Floy was able to keep the house, but thrift became a way of life that passed down from her to Janelle very strongly. Floy finally borrowed a considerable sum from her father and invested it. She taught herself the art of investing and became so good at it that her stockbroker, a fellow by the name of Adams who worked for Merrill Lynch in Los Angeles, used to call her up and ask her advice. In this way she was able to

Jane Ellen's brother Jay.

provide for herself and her children quite adequately, as long as they were careful. They were able to afford a maid. She was a German woman named Anna and she did all the cooking. Janelle, who has become a most accomplished gourmet cook, did no cooking at home and had her first instruction in a cooking course offered at Stanford University!

After the breakup of the marriage, Floy asked her son, Jasper Glenn Marks, Jr., to change his name to Jay Pixley. He accepted the change of his first name but not his second and so became Jay Marks. He was thirteen and remembers being very fond of his father and very much saddened when his parents parted company and were divorced. He also remembers a concurrent newspaper article in the Los Angeles Times which described how it was possible to eat on a total expenditure of ten cents a day. This must have been a very traumatic period for thirteen-year-old Jay and nine-year-old Jane Ellen.

Jay and Jane Ellen attended Cahuenga Grammar School, John Burroughs Junior High School and Los Angeles High School. By virtue of their address on Gramercy Place, they were scheduled to attend Virgil Junior High School on Vermont Avenue but Floy felt that the district was shoddy and did not want her children to go there. It was too far east and west was nicer. West was Hancock Park and the Wilshire District (where John Dean Cooper was growing up). So Floy somehow got special consideration and her children attended John Burroughs. (Jeff was also a student there, although Jeff and Jane Ellen did not happen to meet there.)

Jay and Jane Ellen also were supposed to attend a high school other than

Los Angeles High School, but again Floy obtained special permission because she was determined that her children should obtain the very best in education.

Both Jay and Janelle concede that they were basically raised by their mother. Their father was "in the wings", but his personality was such that his philosophies gave way to the stronger influence of his wife. She was determined and dedicated and very sure of what needed to be done. She was also able to a remarkable degree to keep to herself what must have been her intense bitterness with regard to Glenn's affairs and desertion. Although Janelle refers to her father as being irresponsible, it was always apparent that she felt affection for him and Floy did not attempt to interfere with her children's natural warm feelings toward their charming, if wayward father. When we, her grandchildren, came on the scene, she knew of our visits to her former spouse. Although she never talked about this, she never attempted to influence us negatively.

Floy was a strict disciplinarian who nevertheless provided her children with all the love and support they could ask for. There was never any doubt in their minds that their mother loved them fiercely and had only their best interests in mind in all that she did. She carefully taught them the difference between right and wrong as she saw it. She instilled in them a need to be thrifty, not wasteful, lead a good moral life and to expect good things to happen to those who worked hard and did right. She believed, as she had been taught by her parents, in the worth of individual initiative and achievement. Thus Janelle's moral code, developing simultaneously with Jeff's, was identical in all important ways and again the schools reinforced what each learned in the home.

When Austeene's and Jack's relationship came to a virtual end, Jeff was ten years old. When Glenn's and Floy's marriage ended, Jane Ellen was nine years old. Each bonded most strongly with the more solid parent, Jeff with his father and Jane Ellen with her mother.

Floy emphasized education and encouraged and rewarded her children's obvious intelligence and aptitude for academic study.

Both children were excellent students. Jay was a great reader. He remembers being particularly fond of Zane Grey and another series of books about a boy named Max Tidd. Max was a fat child who wore glasses and was so bright that he was always getting his comrades out of trouble. This impressed Jay very much—the idea that not only do the good guys win, but intelligence can work as well as physical prowess.

The Marks children studied and got good grades and took their education seriously. When it came time for Jay to enter college, there wasn't enough money to send him to Stanford, as Floy desired, so he attended the University of California at Los Angeles for his first two years. Floy also wanted Jane Ellen to attend Marlborough, but again money was just too tight.

In 1938, D.C. Pixley died, and the money Floy inherited allowed her to send

Jay to Stanford for his final two years of undergraduate work. (Later, Standard Oil of New Jersey provided scholarships for Jay's graduate schooling and he obtained his doctorate in Geology in 1951.) She also was able to send Jane Ellen to Marlborough for her senior year of high school. Marlborough School did not like to accept girls for only one year, but Floy got special consideration again. She managed to obtain dispensations for her children whenever she put her mind to it. She was smart and determined and very much a lady and her approach with these various school officials was obviously effective.

Floy proved herself to be quite adept at financial management. In the years following her father's death, she did very well for herself and all her heirs in playing the stock market. Janelle's skill in money matters and hard-earned lessons in thrift were to prove invaluable to Jeff, whose own attitude toward money is much less careful.

My memories of "Grandpop" as we called Glenn, are not strong, although they are most pleasant. We never were able to spend a great deal of time with him. He had a new family and we lived in another town, at least for most of my life. On the other hand, my memories of "Bama", as we called Floy, are quite clear. She was soft-spoken and affectionate. She was always immaculate, both in her person and her home. She was obviously well-educated, well-spoken and intelligent. That she loved us was clear. She, like most grandmothers, wanted to have her grandchildren with her whenever possible and spoiled us just a little. She did not have any domestic help when I knew her and did all her own cooking. She was interested in the benefits of exercise and healthful nutrition before anyone else and was a perfect model of good habits. She was a true lady.

Floy as her grandchildren knew her.

School, travel, Janelle

John Dean Cooper and Jane Ellen Marks had much in common. Similar in background and education, their differences are more quickly delineated. Jeff was the more sophisticated because of his extensive travel. Jane Ellen was less worldly and a little shy. Jane Ellen had learned the virtue of frugality out of necessity, while Jeff had a cavalier attitude about money. Jeff was also cavalier about academics, although both were excellent students. Jane Ellen applied herself with much more industry. Jeff was intensely inner-directed and very much at home with his own company. Jane Ellen was more other-directed, developing a social sensitivity and diplomacy which turned out to be a perfect foil for Jeff's lack in that area.

One activity they shared which they both loved was dancing. Jeff obviously took Jane Ellen on his famous second date and they stayed in that mode for several years. Jane Ellen was a conspicuously good dancer from a very early age, graceful and possessed of a perfect sense of rhythm. Jeff applied himself to this new skill with the intensity he always displayed when he was interested in something. They eventually won several dance contests. They made a striking couple. He was tall and slim and straight and blonde. She was brunette, slim and graceful. As was common for the time, dancing played a very large part in their courtship.

Jane Ellen thought Jeff was very exciting from the beginning. She found his company stimulating. He was not "one of the boys" and she always felt that when they talked about things, he would not run off and tell his friends. He was not that kind. He thoroughly enjoyed engaging in deep conversations and would often ask her questions such as, "What do you think is really important?". That sort of thing was not common and Jane Ellen was entranced. Other young men made small talk, but not Jeff.

Another thing that impressed her was that he was willing and able to take her to very nice places. The first opera she ever saw was Faust at the Philharmonic with Jeff. They went first to the ladies' annex of the California Club for dinner. That was something the Marks did not do, particularly after Glenn left. Jane Ellen was absolutely petrified. She was wearing a long, formal dress, and felt comfortable about how she looked, but she was nervous about how and what to order for dinner. She left it up to Jeff and he was fully up to the task. It was very quiet in the dining room, with thick carpet and hovering waiters—very elegant. Jane Ellen was quite awed by the whole thing. She considers this the start of her cultural education.

Although Jeff and Janelle are the same age, somewhere along the line, Jeff got one entire year ahead of Jane Ellen in school. She then skipped a half year in elementary school and they went all the rest of the way through school with Jeff one half year ahead of Jane Ellen.

So in 1937, John Dean Cooper was graduated from Los Angeles High School, booked in at Stanford University and became forever after known as "Jeff" to everyone. He did not have any trouble getting in because he had aced out the aptitude test, had an A- average in high school and his father was a wealthy alumnus. Jeff had no particular desire to attend Stanford but it was a good school and his father expected him to attend. He always tried, to the best of his ability, to do what his father expected of him. So he did not argue the point. He simply packed up the station wagon and went.

Jane Ellen on graduation day at Marlborough, June of 1938.

Meanwhile, Jane Ellen was facing her senior year in high school at a new school — Marlborough. This was intimidating for her since she had the disadvantage of joining a new class and the additional problem of trying to hold her own with young ladies of more means than she. She felt herself to be a little bit of an outsider. There were a number of young women with very impressive old family names. Betty Helms, for instance, came from the family who founded the Helms Bakery. Jane Ellen was socially acceptable but she felt uncomfortable much of the time. She got befriended by Doris Smith and that helped. They are still friends today.

"I knew (of) Jane Ellen long before I ever met her because she was a legend in John Burroughs Junior High School. She was so smart and she was so pretty and all the boys had a crush on her. I still run into people who say, 'Oh, Jane Ellen! Do you remember her?' I did not really get to know her until we were both dating the same boy, Dwight Hart, in high school. She came to Marlborough in her senior year. I thought she was so gorgeous. In those days, no makeup or anything, she just still was a knockout. Also, I knew what kind of grades she came in with. She did not get any academic honors because they did not honor those grades from L.A. High School, but she did graduate California Scholarship Federation because of her points that she earned at L.A. High School. It was not until she graduated from Stanford (that her record was rewarded)—cum laude or something. I never had any doubts about how smart she was. But she was so beautiful and so sweet. I mean I have never met anybody who was genuinely sweet clear through like Jane Ellen. And it was good for me because I had a bad temper. I don't think I ever showed it to Jane Ellen. I wouldn't have wanted her to know."
– DORIS SMITH VISSCHER

For Jeff, Stanford proved to be a widely different atmosphere from that prevalent at Los Angeles High School. High school had been stratified, but Stanford made an issue of being egalitarian, which surprised him. He found, for instance, that the president of the student body was a hasher in a sorority house. While he knew there was nothing exactly wrong with that, it did not fit his sense of decorum. He got used to it. He also found that most people went to Stanford because they thought it would enhance their prestige. This did not occur to him at all. He just did not consider what others might think important, except for a very few people.

Jeff got into Stanford as a prospective transfer to the United States Naval Academy, so he was in pre-engineering, as was necessary. He was intended for Annapolis. Engineering did not excite him very much because it emphasized mathematics which was not his forte. On the other hand, the ROTC program was field artillery and he found this to be pretty fascinating. Field artillery involved field guns and the field guns were seventy-five millimeter guns—the renowned *soissant quinze* (75) of World War I. They were drawn by horses, not by trucks, so that meant that they had to have both the horses and the ability to manage them. This was complex and Jeff liked it a great deal.

Jeff also knew that he had to be an athlete of some kind at school because that was the custom, so he signed up for collegiate competition fencing, remembering his instruction on board ship during the ocean crossings to Europe when he was a boy.

The ROTC battalion was not much on close order drill, which Jeff knew well, but it was very high on equitation, of which he knew something. The P.M.S.&T. (Professor of Military Science and Tactics) was Colonel Allen, a grand old gentleman from the Virginia Tuckahoe country who was more interested in horsemanship than grade point averages. Jeff had enough skill with horses that he was noticed by Colonel Allen and was selected as "battery guideon." This was the cadet who rides by himself, not on the gun carriage, but out on the right front of the battery—and when they change direction he takes position at the right front in the new direction and the people "guide" on him. The man chosen to do that has to be able to manage a horse and a banner at the same time. This was fun.

Jeff was not very interested in the scholastics at this point. It seemed to him, being a practical sort, that he had only to put in one year before he transferred to the Naval Academy so it did not really matter much what he did in class.

There were social fraternities and sororities at Stanford at that time and they set the social scene. If you were a person of a certain type you were in a fraternity, and the fraternities were stratified according to their prestige. There were Class A, B and C fraternities. Jack was an old grad and a member of the fraternity known as Zeta Psi, and the "Zete's" were one of the three Class A fraternities on campus. (The others were the Deke's (Delta Kappa Epsilon) and the Phi Delt's (Phi Delta Theta).)

Jeff was rushed Zete. He was not a great mixer or partier, but his father's membership counted a lot and he pledged Zete that winter. That meant that after living in the main hall, Encina, during his freshman year, he could move into the Zete house the following fall of 1938, should he choose to stay.

At the end of his freshman year at Stanford, Jeff decided he did not want to go to the Naval Academy. He had the appointment and knew that he would be considered ungrateful, but he did not look forward to living a cloistered life for four years—and it was cloistered in those days. He felt that he was too mature to submit to being a "plebe" and he did not see that it would get him anywhere. Besides that, he would lose an entire year. He understood that if he went to Annapolis he would be starting as a plebe and his freshman year at Stanford would count for nothing. He would be better off to stay at Stanford for the next three years and obtain his commission upon graduation. Although Stanford could not graduate him as a regular, they could graduate him as a Second Lieutenant, Field Artillery Reserve—with a year's seniority.

Jeff and his Zete pledge class at Stanford. He is in the front row, on the right.

At this time, the United States was not yet at war, but the rest of the world was and it seemed quite obvious to Jeff that the situation was going to become a world catastrophe and that the best thing to do was to get ready. That attitude shook up a lot of people. Jeff heard later at reunions that he was the only man in the Zete house who took it for granted that in a couple of years the United States would be in a full-sized war. So, he stayed at Stanford and changed his major from engineering to "Political Science".

The reason for this switch, like so many decisions in college, was due to one particularly good class given by one particularly good professor.

There is nothing less scientific than politics, but Jeff was inveigled into taking a course called "Political Panaceas" which people said was good. This was essentially an overview of political philosophies. They defined and compared democracy, theocracy, aristocracy, etc. from Plato to Jeremy Bentham and Burke. Jeff found this theorizing about politics very attractive and this led to his change in majors. He still felt that his choice of academic major made no difference. The war was coming and he would soon be in it so he took what he enjoyed.

In the summer of 1938, Jack and Jeff took another luxury liner across the ocean—this time to Germany. Germany was at that time at the absolute peak of the Nazi triumph and the place was very impressive to an outsider. Jeff still had not personalized any political theory and he did not know much about Germany, but he did notice that it was very spick and span. Germany tends to be that way, but the Nazis emphasized it.

The mood in Germany seemed to be very upbeat. The Germans had their pride back after having lost it in World War I. There was a feeling of cozy snugness that Jeff has never felt as strongly anywhere else in the world in all his travels—a feeling of warmth in every pub and cafe.

Jack arranged for a visit to Dachau and on the way they made a memorable visit to an SS barracks. Jeff had been working for three years in close order drill and spit and polish in ROTC and the Germans did that very well. Jeff particularly liked the singing. One group broke into song while they marched and they sang in parts. They must have spent at least a few hours a day doing nothing but singing. The aesthetic effect was very good. The SS people were the cream. They got paid more and there were higher recruiting standards. They were very handsome—tall and straight and generally blond and blue-eyed. They marched well and they sang well and they looked good. Jack and Jeff were very impressed.

At one demonstration they saw in Berlin in a gymnasium where they were doing exercises, three soldiers came out in full black field uniform, with black jack boots and long overcoats and packs on their backs. They had steel helmets with chin straps and Mauser rifles slung over their shoulders. They approached a horizontal bar and did full swings up to handstands in full field equipment. This was obviously done to impress people, and it did.

At Dachau, there was no special sense of doom or foreboding—it appeared like any other prison. Jack and Jeff were unaware of what was going on behind the scenes and they were not about to be enlightened by anyone.

What was striking to Jeff was the difference in his impressions of the two major tyrannies of the time, the Bolsheviks and the Nazis. He saw the best side of the Nazis—they gleamed and glistened. And he saw nothing but scruffiness and squalor with the Communists. Everything about Russia was crummy whereas everything about Germany was sharp as a tack. In Russia, one encountered fear in everyone. They saw none of that in Germany. How could they? Everyone who had need to fear was in hiding. One possible clue they had was from a guide they had in Munich who said, "Well, you understand we don't get where we are for nothing—there is a price to pay."

When Jeff returned to Stanford as a sophomore in the Fall of 1938, Jane Ellen came up as a freshman. With her outstanding grades from a top-notch school, a score in the highest category on the aptitude test, an alumnus for a father and her brother a current honor student, she had no trouble getting in. Floy had to scrape together every extra penny she could to send both her children to Stanford at the same time, but she managed it and was justifiably proud and happy to be able to do so.

Jeff moved into the Zete house, and Jane Ellen pledged Pi Phi, one of the three best sororities on campus (the others were Kappa Gamma, "Kappa's" and Kappa Alpha Theta, "Theta's"). Jane Ellen lived in Roble Hall as a freshman (where her oldest daughter would later live as well.)

*Jeff and Jane Ellen,
trying a little archery
in Big Bear, 1938.*

When Jeff first arrived at Stanford, the ratio of men to women was about three to one. There was a great deal of competition and freshmen were at the bottom of the totem pole. He did not date anyone exclusively, and he also had Jane Ellen on his mind. When she arrived, he wanted to pin her down to a steady relationship right away, but she would have none of it. She wanted to enjoy the college social scene to the fullest. She told Jeff that she did not want to be tied down just yet. As she later said, "It was the very best idea because after I 'played the field' I decided that he was definitely the best and I had a basis for comparison." Jane Ellen, who had been a little plump in high school, lost her baby fat and had an absolutely stunning figure to go with her good looks, charm, sweetness and intelligence. She was very popular and in demand and she enjoyed her college years immensely.

One of the activities that Jeff and Jane Ellen enjoyed together while at Stanford was "tea dancing" in San Francisco. In those days it was dangerous to go to or come from San Francisco after dark, not because of any criminal element, but because it was a long way home and the old Bayshore Highway had an evil reputation. It was narrow, dark and winding and had no center-line. After an evening of dining and drinking and dancing, it was simply a risk to take that road all the way back to Palo Alto. People were killed on it all the time. It was mostly a problem of falling asleep and driving off the road. So tea dancing was the answer Jeff came up with. True to his form, it was not common or popular, but still great fun. They went to the St. Francis Hotel at tea time. About the only other people at tea were members of ladies' clubs and retired couples, and few of them. They generally had the entire dance floor to themselves. Soon they would form a rapport with the band leader and he would play to their tastes. They did the most common step, the fox trot, but mostly they excelled at waltzes, rhumba and tango. They both have delicious memories of those afternoons, and they could come home while it was still light and avoid the Bayshore Highway problem.

In Los Angeles during breaks from school, they used to go down to a place on Sunset Boulevard called the Club Zarape. It was a Latin place up over a market on the edge of the Mexican section of the city and it was a bit of a dive. Today going to a place like that might be risky at best, but then it was quite safe. They had a nifty band there for some years led by Nilo Menendez, who was a musician of some reputation. Jeff and Jane Ellen would get there as soon as it opened and stay there until they started putting the chairs on top of the tables. Anthony Quinn was a regular patron during this time. They danced the nights away—wonderful exercise. They drank endless "Cuba Libres" (rum and cokes), but never got tipsy because they danced off the effects of the alcohol. They did the rhumba, variations of the rhumba like the danson, the samba when it was introduced and the tango.

They got so good that they took the grand prize one night at the Club Zarape in one of their impromptu dance contests. Jeff regards this as a highlight of their dancing days because they were competing against Latinos in Latin dances! The judges were Latin as well. There was no formality or preparation involved. The contest was a process of elimination with continuous dancing. They did the rhumba, danson, samba, tango and cha-cha. They won a little tin cup which they still have and cherish.

At the old Hotel Del Monte, one of the prime resorts of the California coast, they would go down on football weekends and dance. One evening, when they were in full formal dress, Jane Ellen in a long gown and Jeff in white tie and tails, they won the waltz contest. The prize that night was a great big bottle of champagne.

Jeff describes dancing as "a man and a woman blending their physical activities into a pattern of grace in response to beautiful music." It was wonderful, erotic, fun and essentially courtship. The more Jeff and Jane Ellen came to enjoy each other and each other's dancing, the better they got as a couple. As much as they enjoyed themselves, so did the spectators. What a pair they must have been! Today, the films of Fred Astaire and his various lovely partners can give you a glimpse of the part such wonderful pair dancing played in courtship during the 1930's and 1940's.

At this point, Jeff took part in a psychological assessment program to earn some extra credits which led to a rather startling discovery for him. A chosen group spent hours answering questions about themselves and taking tests. The results categorized people into various personality types. Jeff's test scores showed him to be an *aesthete*, along with only about 6% of the population of the world. This came as a shock to Jeff, who expected to be pegged a warrior or philosopher or romantic, anything but an aesthete, which brought to his mind images of Oscar Wilde. As he thought about it, it began to explain things which he had observed but not given much thought to before, and it made sense.

He found that he really does look at the world through lenses which accentuate beauty and reject ugliness and that this is unusual and rather perplexing. He feels there is an abstraction of beauty which is not exactly a matter of training or custom, but objective observation. Beauty can never be totally objective, but Jeff believes that there are standards which last over time and which can be regarded as factual. That 94% of the population does not share his point of view he finds disappointing and often irritating.

To an aesthete, things which are beautiful are pleasing and things which are ugly are displeasing and that adds an interesting dimension to everyday interactions. When Jeff sees a young person with baggy clothes, slumped posture, hat on backwards and open mouth, he is repelled. Conversely, when he sees someone he considers good-looking, he is predisposed to be pleased with the inner person as well. This may seem normal to some of us, but it is greatly exaggerated in an aesthete such as Jeff.

The same is true for his appreciation of everything from machines to graphic arts to music to animals to dancing. He takes aesthetic pleasure in a great many things: classical ballet, leopards, modern cruiseships, World War II battleships (but not those of World War I), Minoan dress, Nefertiti and Catherine Deneuve.

Aesthetics affects him as a hunter in various ways. While sheep hunting is certainly the most challenging physically, it also takes the hunter into the grandest landscapes of the world, and the great joy of a sheep hunt for Jeff is primarily the wonderful country in which mountain sheep are found. Many people consider leopard to be a princely trophy. Jeff does not. He has no illusions about the leopard—it is a ferocious beast that eats all kinds of things including house pets and small children when it gets the chance. He has no objection to other people killing leopards, but he will not. He will not because he considers the leopard too beautiful to shoot. He does not feel that way about kudu or impala or numerous other beasts which might be seen as equally beautiful. But an aesthete *knows*.

The last application of the question of aesthetics is to the complexity of social interrelations. Jeff really enjoys looking at beautiful women in person, on the screen and in print. He knows that he does not escape the occasional connotation of lechery, because most men look at a beautiful woman and think of sex. Jeff does not necessarily, and can admire the view in itself, appreciating line and form and visual pleasure. It's a good thing too, because one is never too old to look.

As a sophomore, Jeff became a part of the varsity fencing team. He had

Jeff and the Stanford varsity fencing team. He is in the middle of the back row.

developed an interest in history as well as his warrior mentality at an early age. Naturally he gravitated toward the implements of fighting and became interested in firearms. However, men had been fighting without firearms for far longer than with them, and he was fascinated with ancient warfare as well. Bladed weapons of all kinds were of interest to him, but especially the various swords used by heroes down through the ages.

The fencing foil and the sport involved had evolved into things which bore little resemblance to actual fighting, much like target pistols and target shooting. Still, it was a semblance of combat which appealed to him. It also was an individual sport and it rewarded speed and dexterity, two of his greatest strengths.

Elwyn Bugge was the fencing coach at Stanford and he recognized Jeff's greatest weakness as a fencer right away. Jeff always wanted to go *in*, far beyond the point where scoring counted. Mr. Bugge told Jeff often that he did not have to try to come out the opponent's back, just a touch on the chest would win the point. Going in too far exposes a fencer to his opponent and can lose the match. Jeff tried to conform, but not too hard. He felt that the object of the sport was to simulate combat and the object of combat was to kill. Therefore what kills should be what wins. Jeff's greatest strength in fencing was his speed and he often made points on pure speed, scoring a hit before his opponent realized the match had started.

At the same time, Jeff came to realize that in a real fight, the fencing foil was not a good weapon anyway, and going clear through your opponent would only slow him down and then only if he realized that he was skewered, which might not be for some time. He once saw another Stanford man hit about six inches down from the right armpit by a broken blade which went in about four inches. The man did not know he was hit. Only when others brought attention to the blood sheeting down his side did he realize that skin had been broken.

In later study, Jeff realized, much to his regret, that nothing has ever been written down about how to use any sword well in an actual fight by anyone who ever did it, and that studying the modern fencing foil would not do the trick. Probably the greatest practitioners of the sword were the Spaniards in the 800 Year War—they mostly won. El Cid and the Conquistadors could have told us much. Sir Richard Burton, one of the great 19th century adventurers and discover of the source of the Nile with Speke, is the only great practical swordsman who made an attempt to write down the technique. He finished Volume I, which was the history of the sword, but died before he got to Volume II. As Jeff says, "This is a lesson to us all."

Jeff felt that it was practically his duty to do well for his parents, particularly for his father, and it never occurred to him that he should resist. One occasion he remembers with particular pride. He was a sophomore, first year on the Stanford Varsity Fencing Team. When they went up against Cal (the University of California at Berkeley), their traditional rival, the match was held on the Berkeley campus and Jack came up to see it. There are five bouts in a fencing match and five members of a team and each member met each member of the opposing team. Jeff was in top form that day and went through all five members of Cal's team one at a time. He beat all five of Cal's best (including Stone, their top man who usually beat Jeff) while his father watched.

While his own children were growing up, Jeff came to realize that one of the greatest joys in life is seeing your own child perform well in a competition or recital or other forum for performance and achievement. He looks back with tremendous gratification on that fencing match, knowing how much pleasure he gave his father that day.

Hunting, travel, Janelle – war!

In the summer of 1939, Jeff spent six weeks in ROTC camp, spent two weeks hunting in Canada, spent some time in Catalina and pursued Jane Ellen.

At San Luis Obispo, Jeff learned a few new things at ROTC camp. In addition to the incident of the final day's formation where he solidified his position as a dedicated individualist, he discovered the five-minute reveille. This was an exercise which took place between the first note of reveille and the marching off to breakfast. Five minutes. From dead sleep to fully dressed and ready for inspection with your tent made up, your bed made and everything ready for the officer of the day to inspect. Jeff, had he considered it beforehand, would not have thought it possible. They did it in the field artillery to impress upon the cadets that it *could* be done. If they were suddenly alerted to move out, the entire battalion could be in operation in five minutes. They did this regularly, every day.

Jeff also learned that he was invulnerable to poison oak. The area around San Luis Obispo was covered with poison oak. One evening, Jeff had control of a section, consisting of a gun (French 75) and a caisson, two horse-drawn vehicles which carry the gun and the ammunition. They had to put them totally under cover so that they could not be seen from the air by the next morning. They hacked and hewed and hauled and by sunrise the next day they had it totally covered in poison oak. Jeff had no reaction at all but a couple of the cadets had to be hospitalized.

Next came his second hunt for big game. He went alone with his 30-06 and 50 rounds of ammunition, which was all the Canadians would allow. Jack did a certain amount of research for this, taking pleasure in the planning and the result, if not the trip itself.

Jeff went to the east slope of the Canadian Rockies in the province of Alberta, across the ridge from British Columbia. He went up the coast by train and then picked up the Canadian railroad and took that train eastward just across the ridge. He jumped off at a whistle stop with his gear and was met by Miles Moberley, a Creek Indian who was on his first trip as head guide. The outfitter did not go along. One junior-grade hunter on a fourteen-day outing was not worth excessive overhead. They also had a cook. They got on their horses and headed north to Jasper National Park.

Miles and the cook wrangled the horses, the cook wrangled the food and Miles and Jeff hunted. They rode for a day and camped, then another day and camped, and the third day they made it to the edge of the park and went out to the north—spectacular country.

They had third-string equipment and Jeff's tent leaked and the cook was only mildly interested in cooking, but they had plenty to eat. The first few nights they ate grayling, a type of trout. On the third day Jeff killed a caribou, one shot, fairly long range, and they ate that. (It's mounted on the wall of D.C. Pixley's cabin in Big Bear Lake, California.) They also had bacon and flour and mostly tea to drink.

Although Jeff had several licenses, the purpose of this hunt was the mountain sheep, *Ovis canadensis*, the bighorn of the Rockies—one of the grandest trophies in the world by anyone's standards. They concentrated on that. This was very hard work. They hunted the main valley and up on the spurs and the main ridges, which were above the timberline. They would take the horses to the edge of the trees and then hike up to the ridge tops and glass the coun-

Jeff and his Canadian caribou, 1939.

83

Above: Jeff and his prize-winning Bighorn sheep, 1939.
Left: The ram holds a place of honor on Jeff's wall today.

tryside. It rained for days and when it was not raining, it was foggy and misty. They would break camp, move several miles and set up another camp. They saw a lot of moose and goats, but no sheep and also no grizzly bear, for which Jeff also was looking. They had caribou steaks for breakfast, a slab of caribou between two biscuits for lunch and caribou stew for dinner. And it rained.

After five or six days, the sun came out. Jeff was awed by the grandeur of the vistas. Watching the sun come up and move over the eastern walls of the Canadian Rockies held him entranced. It boded well for the hunt and that day they scored. They spotted a huge ram and Jeff shot him at a steep downward angle from about 90 yards. (This ram was a national first prize and has a place of honor in Jeff's house today.) The mountain sheep was even better to eat than the caribou, which was delicious. Later Jeff told Jack that he thought the mountain sheep was the best eating meat in the world. Jack said, "You mean the best eating game, don't you?" Jeff said, "No. I mean the best eating meat—the best I ever tasted."

Now they looked for goats, Jeff having decided to leave the moose for last, having seen several on the bottoms of the canyons. They moved on up to the other side where the cliffs were even steeper to look for goats. Here they ran

The Canadian goat.

into another hunting camp, a very luxurious hunting camp peopled by two wealthy Chicago businessmen. They visited for awhile and Jeff discovered that they knew nothing at all about what they were doing. They had purchased the very best of equipment from Marshall Field's in Chicago and had beautiful custom Springfields built for them by Griffin and Howe in New York. But they didn't know how to shoot. They didn't even know how to focus their telescopes. They had telescope sights which were not common in those days. They were nice guys and very much in awe of Jeff's ram. They told Jeff and Miles how they had fired 55 times at a goat the day before and as far as they knew they had not touched him even once. Jeff showed great restraint and did not offer comment or advice.

They found a goat and that was memorable, not so much the finding or the shooting, but the climb. They managed to maneuver themselves above three animals and Jeff took what looked to be the biggest with one shot, perfectly placed, at about 200 paces. The terrain was too steep to allow them to get anything other than the head and the hide out. It is mounted in a gun store back east.

So Jeff had his goat and now they started moving back toward the park, looking for moose. One afternoon, they spotted what looked to be a big one in some jack pines which had burned and fallen. Jeff took aim at about 100 yards. The animal was so big that Jeff had some trouble deciding where to place the shot. He did the best he could and squeezed off. Nothing happened. He worked the bolt, got back on and took up the slack. The moose did not move. He thought what a shame it would be to have taken three animals

85

The Canadian moose.

with one shot each and to spoil the record with this one. Then the moose top-
pled gently to the ground. The moose turned out to be another national first
prize. It is mounted in Packmayr's in Los Angeles. It was butchered and
brought in, but Jeff did not get to eat any of it. It was too near the end of the
hunt and they still had plenty of caribou.

So he had four animals with four shots and two national first prize trophies.
Jeff got the feeling that the outfitter was a little annoyed at the size of the trophies. After all, this was just a junior-grade hunt, one gun for only two weeks,
and not a money-maker for him. Jack must have been pleased with his son's
performance. He could not have done better.*

Jeff and Jane Ellen got closer and closer. Janelle remembers it this way:

"He was the best because he was the most interesting. He coped. He was
sophisticated. He had a car. He was well-traveled. We had a lot in common
in terms of our ethics and standards. We had been raised similarly. He was
definitely a learning experience. He was tall and slim and blonde and handsome and dashing. He did everything well. We liked everything we found out
about each other as we got to know each other better. We used to drive back
and forth to Stanford together, and that meant seven hours at a time together.
It was a gradual growth of friendship and love."

*NOTE: This hunting trip is written up in *Another Country* by Jeff Cooper.

"I knew him mostly because Janelle, my cousin, was going with him. I was always kind of in awe of him, especially in the beginning, because he was a class ahead of us in school and he was so regal looking. Janelle just thought he was so wonderful and I took my cues from her."

– VIRGINIA DEAN ARTHUR

"Jeff in college was such a presence! He commanded attention wherever he went. He had an aura about him that made people sit up and take notice. He's always been that way."

– DORIS SMITH VISSCHER

The Marks family would spend as much of the summers as they could in their cabins in Big Bear Lake with the extended family. Jane Ellen would invite friends to visit and Jeff came often.

"Then I really got to know him when Janelle had me up to Big Bear and he would come up to see her. One time we really actually had a conversation. ...when he was appointed to drive me back to Balboa....we had that whole drive to talk. He told me then that Jane Ellen was the girl he was going to marry. When I asked why he said, 'Because she has everything and besides that a wonderful disposition and probably the only girl I have ever met that I thought I could get along with for life.' He knew what he wanted......"

– DORIS SMITH VISSCHER

Dating, circa 1939.

Stanford R.O.T.C., 1940.

Back at Stanford in the field artillery ROTC, Jeff took up the study of the service pistol. Prior to that time, he had shot a few 22's, but nothing serious. The field artillery battery featured no riflecraft, only the cannon themselves and the sidearm of the officer, which was the straight service pistol, a .45 1911 semi-automatic. The pistol shooting at Stanford was strictly routine, conventional military target shooting, shooting at bullseyes from the offhand position, slow fire and timed fire.

In addition to that, however, they did fire the mounted course which required them to shoot from the back of a horse, describing a figure 8 and shooting at silhouette targets at very close range. Jeff earned his expert badge with mounted pistol at that time and may be one of the few left who can boast that he is qualified officially as a mounted pistol expert.

It so happened at Stanford at that time that an alumnus had set up an annual award for a field artillery cadet who had a B average or better academically, who was a commissioned officer equivalent and who shot the highest score with pistol on the Army course. Jeff won that award and the pistol that was presented to him. That is the pistol he took with him to World War II and he still has it today.

So college life continued. Jeff and Jane Ellen both did well academically. Socially, Jane Ellen continued to meet and enjoy dating other young men, while feeling more and more that she had already met the most special of them all. Jeff fenced and shot and rode horses and continued to try to convince Jane Ellen that there was no other for her than he. Both were all the while aware, especially Jeff, that the world situation was looming darkly.

In the summer of 1940, Jack planned another trip with Jeff, this one a month-long hunting and camping trip to the Yukon. Again, Jack did not participate in the hunting, but this was the first trip where Jeff hunted and Jack went along.

They took the train up the west coast to Vancouver and then flew by stops up the inside—Edmonton, Prince George, Watson Lake and up to Whitehorse on the Yukon River by stages in a series of airplanes. The last one was a Bellanca floatplane—a very big, strong, heavy airplane with a reputation for durability and reliability, but in no sense luxurious. Jack had made arrangements by mail with Gene Jacquot who already had a reputation up on Burwash Landing which is some hundred miles north of Whitehorse. They spent the night in Whitehorse and flew the next day by charter Fairchild floatplane to Burwash Landing, on Kluane Lake. For Jack and Jeff, this was paradise.

Burwash Landing was a compound where Gene Jacquot and his Indian wife and all sorts of children and in-laws and relatives hung out. The buildings were sunk down into the permafrost so that you had windows at ground level. No sheets, but skins. Jeff and Jack found that sleeping between nothing but furs is very luxurious.

Off to one side there was a kennel full of sled dogs who were ecstatic at the attention Jeff gave them. He opened the gate, went in and made their acquaintance amid much jumping, tail-wagging and sloshing of tongues. When he went back in the lodge, the locals all looked very alarmed. They told him that if he had fallen, he might never have got out of the kennel alive. That never occurred to Jeff and perhaps the locals were exaggerating.

The next day they got into the floatplane and followed the track of the outfit which had been sent on four or five days before to go westward into the foothills of the St. Elias—a magnificent range of mountains. Look at the map of where Alaska joins Canada, come down almost to the ocean and that mass of ice is the St. Elias range. They were on the inland side, where there is not so much rain and mist. They flew to Teepee Lake, where the outfit had not yet arrived. They got out and all the stuff was handed ashore and the plane took off, leaving just Jack and Jeff and Gene alone on the beach. The three of them made camp as best they could right there.

The first thing that impressed Jack and Jeff was the wolves. Jeff had never heard wolves before. To this day, he has never heard wolves as impressive. Coyotes yip, but these wolves sounded like pipe organs in a much lower register. The next day Jeff found tracks out on the beach and cut a piece of paper to fit. They measured 6 and ½ by 5 and ¼. That is a big paw. Jack and Jeff were in their element again.

They had told the pilot to pick them up at that very spot in 28 days. That was the time contracted for. When he disappeared, that was a thrill. That was what Jack really liked. He was always being hassled by business and he loved being somewhere where there was no communication with anyone.

The next day the outfit showed up and that included the main hunter, Carl Chambers, who was half-Indian, and George the Indian horse boy. They got the camp set up properly. Gene had left Alsace when he was a young man to avoid conscription—he did not want to fight any wars. In his adolescence he had been apprenticed to a pastry cook. He served as camp cook (chef is a more proper term for him) and his food was just superb. Jack and Jeff were properly enthusiastic and appreciative.

The weather was cold at night and crisp in the daytime and clear most of the time. Jack puttered around camp, building a refrigerator by digging out the side of the permafrost. He fished for grayling and scouted around.

Jeff and Carl and George went looking for a prime sheep—not the *Ovis canadensis* but the *Ovis dali*, the Dall Sheep—pure white. There are a good number of them but they are not easy to get. They are the best eating meat around, but the locals only go out for them on special occasions, caribou being much easier to get, bigger and also good to eat. There were no goats in this area. There were sheep and moose and grizzly bear and caribou, but the caribou were all still in velvet and Jeff considered himself strictly a trophy hunter at this time and he wanted a sheep.

They looked all over but saw no big sheep. After three days they got hungry and had George shoot a smallish sheep because in those days Indians had no limits on their hunting. Jeff was anxious for Jack to have a taste since he thought so highly of the meat. When Jack tasted it he agreed with Jeff's assessment.

Gene liked to make soups and he also made good use of what was at hand. That included masses of blueberries and a kind of wild salad green. He made cole slaw out of that and a blueberry meringue pie which struck Jack and Jeff as out of this world. They had sheep and grayling and also fresh fruit and fresh vegetables. They had the entire four weeks and they enjoyed every single day. They were rained out on a couple of occasions and even that was just fine. Jeff welcomed a respite from the hard hunting. They could sit in a camp chair with the rain beating down on the canvas overhead and read a good book. They had good company and excellent food.

The shooting did not present a problem to Jeff so much as the getting to and from. He got the scope on a nice ram at one point but had just run across a slope and was too winded to take the shot. He had learned from Townsend Whelen not to risk wounding an animal and he took these lessons seriously. They went down the mountain and got caught on a spit by the water, which had been melting all day and building. In that country, all night long the water freezes and the water levels drop lower and lower in the streams. In early morning, the streams are at their lowest and are often just a few feet across and can be jumped. All day long the sun beats on the glacier and the ice melts and when you return to the same stream in the afternoon, it may have become a raging torrent that cannot be crossed. This happened to Jeff and Carl and George.

A bear had spooked their horses which had broken their halters and gone back to camp riderless. The delay gave the water a chance to rise and they were caught on a sand bar, where they had to spend the night. There was no way to get warm. They built a small fire and would rotate themselves, trying to keep from scorching on the fire side while they got frostbitten on the out side. There was no way to sleep. It was perfectly still and calm with a full moon and it was cold. They waited it out. The water went down and the next morning they crossed the stream and headed back to camp. Gene and Jack were not overly worried, but it was a trying experience—probably the most trying Jeff had ever had up to that point.

They went out to a fly camp, looking for more sheep. This was a bare min-

Jeff and his Yukon Dall sheep, 1940.   *One of the Yukon bears.*

imum set-up—just blankets and enough food for one meal. They went for one day and ended up spending four days there, subsisting mainly on chocolate bars. Every time they got into position it was late in the day and they did not want to go back. Still, they never really got a good chance at a really good ram. When they returned to camp, Jeff ate two bowls of soup, two bowls of cole slaw, five grayling, two sheep steaks with all the trimmings and a big wedge of blueberry pie for dessert. He was not starving, but he was hungry.

Jeff finally got a nice ram. It was a very long shot but there was no way to get closer. Jeff only dared take the shot because he was not winded, was able to get into a solid prone position, was not in a hurry, knew exactly where his rifle was shooting and was in good practice. When he took the shot, rocks flew behind the ram and Carl called the shot high. Jeff was sure his hold had been right and did not change it for the second shot. Carl again called it high, but Jeff held in the same place again and squeezed off the third shot. When they got to the ram, Jeff could put his hand across the three hits. He feels that his shooting on that day was as good as he has ever done.

In the next days, Jeff took a moose with one shot and three grizzly bears. The bears were offered for nothing in those days and were considered to be almost like varmints. The first bear he hit ran, and he shot again and missed. He wrote in his journal that it was the first time he had ever shot at a game animal and missed. A black mark for the day. He hit him with the third shot and he went down. This was a very unusual bear. He had a white collar which made quite a sensation with the locals. They thought he was magic.

The second bear he hit right through the heart with the first shot, but the

Jeff's Stanford senior picture, 1941.

bear was not going to pay heed. They had to chase him some distance before the second shot stopped him. The third happened when the trip was winding down. George disturbed a female grizzly who followed him back to camp. Jeff was sleeping in. At the shouting, he rolled out of his sleeping bag, grabbed his rifle and want after her. He did not get back into camp until about 3 in the afternoon, still in his pajamas. He kept that particular pair for a long time. As the Groucho Marx story goes, "Remember the time I killed that elephant in my pajamas? How he got into those pajamas I'll never know." (Jeff had these bears made into rugs. I remember lying on them as a child in front of the fireplace, and playing with their teeth.)

Jack was fascinated by the processing of the moose. He observed that the only thing left was the lungs—everything else was taken. Moose fat is prized in the Yukon. They make shoes out of the hide and cook all the bones. They make glue out of the hooves and use all of the viscera except the lungs.

Jeff and Jack were reluctant to go back. When they reached a ridge where they could see Teepee Lake, Jeff told the others that he wanted to make it the rest of the way alone. He took his horse and rode for one half day through virtually untrod wilderness. For him, this was a great feeling. He saw several moose and a bunch of wolves. Glorious!*

About two days later, the floatplane showed up. They kept hoping it would get snowed out and not be able to pick them up, but no such luck. Then and there Jack decided to come back up to Burwash Landing for a full eighteen months, two full summers and one winter. He was captivated with life in the Yukon. That seems an odd decision for a Los Angeles banker, but that was his plan. He would have done it had not his untimely death interfered.*

Back at Stanford for his senior year in the Fall of 1940, Jeff continued in his study of political science and with his ROTC and fencing activities. He per-

*NOTE: This hunting trip is written up in *Another Country* by Jeff Cooper.

suaded Jane Ellen to accept his fraternity charm, and that meant that they were serious.

He never again matched the glory of his sophomore match against Cal, but he had another memorable fencing triumph. Al Snyder was a Stanford man who had lost his right arm at the shoulder as a child. From the age of five or six he managed with one arm. He was a great swordsman and once achieved a ranking of second in the United States. While Jeff was on the Stanford team, Al Snyder was in amateur athletics for the Olympic Club in San Francisco and the two teams occasionally met for informal sessions. The first time Jeff met Al, he resorted to his great speed and got him down four to nothing—there being five points in a match. During a break, Al looked over at Jeff closely and Jeff could see the wheels turning in his head. Al made his mental shift, put his mask back on and went to work, winning the next five points in a row and taking the match five to four. Still, a masterful showing for the younger man.

During his senior year the Marine Corps came around with their recruiting officer and offered the first, second or third cadets in the ROTC battalion a regular commission in the Marine Corps. This gave Jeff the chance to have both a regular commission and keep his year's seniority—the best of both worlds. Jeff was ranked second in the battalion. When the number one cadet declined, Jeff accepted right away. He had no tradition with the Marine Corps and he had more friends in the Army, but, being an aesthete, he really liked the look of those sky-blue pants with the red stripe down the side.

The Marine Corps, having no academy, was authorized by Congress to come around to the major universities that had ROTC programs and offer the top men in each cadet battalion regular commissions in the Corps. The Army must have howled when this plan was first approved because it meant that their best men were likely to be scraped right off the top to join the Marine Corps.

So now Jeff's near future plans changed. He would graduate from Stanford in the Spring of 1941, spend the summer as usual with Jane Ellen, family and friends, and in the Fall, report to San Diego for his physical and then go directly to Basic School for a one-year course of instruction in military subjects. If all went well, he would be commissioned in September, complete the year's course and have his seniority dated back to the date of his commission. This struck him as a good plan.

After Jeff's graduation in the Spring, Jack again had a trip planned for the two of them. Jeff, more serious than ever about Jane Ellen but mindful that they were both only 21 and she had another year at Stanford to complete, invited her along. This trip was a swing out through the great West, to include camping, fishing, hunting and general exploring.

The three of them packed up and took off in the station wagon, going first across the desert up the hill at Wickenburg to Prescott. Then up across the

Navajo country through Kayenta. This was not particularly attractive. As they went on the road got worse and worse, sometimes deteriorating into a couple of tracks. They got to Mexican Hat and then to Monticello, not far from Four Corners. That country was wild then. They got up to Ouray and then on up the west side of the Rockies. They found themselves up in the country near Rifle and Meeker and they packed in there on a fishing expedition. They went in on horses and did some fly fishing—good fun.

Then they traveled on up to Wyoming and at this point, Jeff was dropped off at Lander with a guide to go antelope hunting and Jack and Jane Ellen went on up to Jackson Hole. Jeff and his guide went out in a pickup truck and hunted pronghorn for about five days.

In the middle of this hunt, they came over a ridge and found a big festivity going on, sort of like the party in *Oklahoma* with trucks all around. This event was held by the "Sweetwater Homemakers' Club". The Sweetwater was the local river and the Homemakers were the local ranch wives for miles around. They had a shindig and it was a great one. It was very "Old America" despite being in the summer of 1941. It included all ages. The old codgers sat and rocked and yarned, the men milled about, the ladies served food and the young people chased each other about among the willows. They all manifested a strong feeling toward Jeff as a sort of sacrificial lamb. Jeff considered himself a professional soldier who liked fighting and looked forward to more of it, whatever came his way, and it never occurred to him that he might be a victim. They gave him advice to not take chances and not try to be too much of a hero. The cultural memory at that time was of Marine second lieutenants in World War I. Jeff was touched by all of this, but at the same time felt very confident because he was such a good shot. That, of course, makes little difference but he had the arrogance of youth.

The 1941 Wyoming Pronghorn.

Jeff got a record pronghorn out of this hunt. Within minutes of leaving the highway at the beginning of the hunt, they came across a very big buck. Jeff passed him up because it was too early in the hunt. On the third day, he killed a record antelope, but will always think that the first one was bigger. Again it was a one-shot kill. He was getting used to that.

Jeff got ferried up to Twogotee Pass going into Jackson Hole where Jack and Jane Ellen had set up the main camp. They packed in there, going up on horses for several days. There were great, enormous electrical storms in the Rockies. It was spectacular.

Jane Ellen later told Jeff that she thought she was being tested by the two of them as to her ability to cook and build fires and swim and ride horses and such. This never occurred to Jeff. He never thought for a moment that she could *not* do these things, and more. They all had a fine time. They went back to Jackson Hole, packed up the car and drove home. This was pretty much a full month.

At this point, it was obvious that the war was coming. It was already in full cry in Europe and North Africa and there was no question in Jeff's mind that the United States was going to be in it soon, and that the world would never be the same.

Janelle on her first hunting/camping trip with Jeff (and his father), 1941.

He and Jane Ellen said their goodbyes at the end of the summer and she returned for her senior year at Stanford. Jeff reported to the base in San Diego where he passed his physical and received his commission. Date of rank: 6 September 1941. In his class there were 96 officers and he was 93rd on the list because they were ranked in seniority entirely by age and he was a little young for his graduation from college. He was never an enlisted Marine and he never went to boot camp. He went directly to Basic School.

Marine Basic School in those days was an improvement over the Military Academy because they took young men who were fully civilized by four years in college and had received their academic degrees and gave them one full year of military subjects. Unlike West Point where you had to take history and English and other basic courses, Marine Corps Basic School was a nine-month academic year of nothing but military.

Basic School was arduous and demanding, but the level of the student body was very high. It had been carefully selected. The majority were honor graduates from major universities, but there also were selected enlisted Marines (about 10 in the class) who had been commissioned, and then there were some dozen Naval Academy graduates who had opted for a Marine Corps rather than a Naval commission. All were "high achievers" and this was a problem for the staff because they were hard put to come up with challenges that the class could not meet. The students had all executed similar exercises with their own subordinates in other services.

The duty was interesting and difficult, but not as trying as it might have been because as commissioned officers they could not be pushed around physically, nor was it considered appropriate to confine them to quarters on weekends. The school was held at the Navy Yard in Philadelphia which was a rather primitive establishment even at the time. It was down the road from the center of town and on weekends the men sought the bright lights to see what was going on in Philadelphia.

The answer for Jeff was—nothing. Any town is a good one if you know the right people, but this did not happen for Jeff. One friend named Stanley Graf (known as Bosco) who had been a classmate of Jeff's at Stanford got into the Navy about that time and he was an ensign in Philadelphia. He got hooked up with the Mainline social group and as far as he was concerned he had died and gone to heaven. Every spare hour he had he was out at various estates outside of town swimming and riding horses and generally having himself a fine time. As a Stanford graduate and Naval officer, he was a distinct prospect for families who had marriageable daughters.

For Jeff, diversion came in New York City. The train service was pretty good and it only took a couple of hours to reach the city. Jeff spent most of his weekends in New York. It wasn't nearly as expensive then as it is now and even on a second lieutenant's pay he could afford the good life. He stayed in fine hotels and ate in the best restaurants and saw the best shows and took in the latest Hollywood films.

On Sunday, December 7, 1941, Jane Ellen was studying for the next week's classes in her room in the Pi Phi house on the Stanford campus. Jeff was in New York, returning to the St. Regis Hotel from seeing a movie at Rockefeller Center. Japanese bombers, flying low to avoid radar detection through the Kolekole Pass on the island of Oahu, came over the sleeping United States fleet at anchor in Pearl Harbor and dropped their deadly cargo. The world slipped sideways and changed forever.

Basic School, 1941.

96

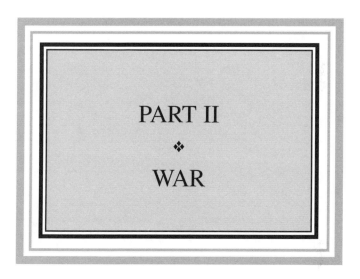

PART II

❖

WAR

Marriage

I t is perhaps not possible for anyone under the age of sixty-five today to understand the changes wrought by the Japanese attack on Pearl Harbor. Everything changed and it changed radically. The entire focus of everyone's lives shifted. Not only were military and political policies suddenly shifted, but social interactions were all immediately altered. A common rage united everyone behind the war effort and focused everyone's activities on providing what support they could to that effort. It also focused men and women on the distinct possibility of sudden loss of life, limb, support and happiness. They looked for ways to forget for a few moments and reached for what happiness was available while they still could.

Jane Ellen's first reaction to the news from Pearl Harbor was to call Jack and see what he might know, although he knew no more than anyone else. Jeff's first reaction was to write to Jane Ellen and ask her to marry him. She wrote right back and said yes.

Jeff was fully aware that marrying a Marine second lieutenant who expected to be leading infantry at the beginning of a major war was not a good prospect for any woman. The chances of being a widow quite soon were very high, as were the chances of being left a young widow with a child to support during wartime. He explained this to Jane Ellen and did not pressure her in any way. He told her he would like them to be married, but left the decision up to her. She never hesitated.

At Stanford, rumors of a Japanese attack on the west coast of the United States persisted and they went through a period of blackouts and other preparations which faded as time went by. At Marine Corps Basic School, they did not immediately pull Jeff's class out of the classroom and send them off to war. Decisions needed to be made as to how best to use junior grade inexperienced Marine lieutenants. That took awhile.

SOCIETY

Los Angeles Times

WEDNESDAY, FEBRUARY 4, 1942

Jane Ellen Marks Engaged to Lieut. John Dean Cooper

Stanford Co-ed Passes Candy to Pi Phis Tonight

BY CHRISTY FOX

Coming as a complete surprise to their friends here and in Northern California is the announcement being made of the engagement of Jane Ellen Marks, daughter of Mrs. Pixley Marks of 153 S. Gramercy Place and J. Glenn Marks, to Lieut. John Dean Cooper, son of Mr. and Mrs. John T. Cooper of 500 N. Rossmore Ave.

The young bride-elect will pass candy at the Pi Beta Phi house at Stanford tonight to tell the news to her sorority sisters. No date has been set for the wedding.

Lieut. Cooper and his mother are motoring north today to join Miss Marks for a few days.

Jane Ellen was graduated from Marlborough before continuing her education at Stanford where she is now a s e n i o r. Lieut. Cooper, Jeff to his friends, is a Zeta Psi from Stanford and a lieutenant in the Marine Corps.

JOINS BRIDES-ELECT — Announcement is being made today of the betrothal of Jane Ellen Marks to Lieut. John Dean Cooper. The bride-to-be will pass candy tonight at the Stanford Pi Phi house in Palo Alto. Lansdowne photo

Newspaper engagement announcement, 1942.

100

In the meantime, they were all concerned about their upcoming ten days of scheduled Christmas leave. They wanted to go home, show off their beautiful uniforms, and have their own private send-offs with their loved ones. They all were sure that Christmas was off.

When the class assembled on the afternoon of the day prior to their scheduled leave the commanding officer, Colonel Clifton B. Cates, came into the classroom and said, "Gentlemen, I don't know whether your leave is on or off, but I have not been told that it's off, so the sooner you get out of this room the luckier you will be." Then he stepped aside to avoid the stampede for the door and the Christmas leave of 1941 was on.

Jeff got back to California as soon as he could, traveling by air. Jane Ellen was down from Stanford on her Christmas break. Jeff gave Jane Ellen his fraternity pin and they discussed plans to marry. Their parents were against their getting married, for all the right reasons. This included the fact that Jeff, as a newly commissioned officer, was forbidden by regulation from getting married for at least two years. Also, married women were forbidden to live in sorority houses, so Jane Ellen would have to hide her marriage or find other housing. Marriage would necessitate secrecy and deception which went against the grain of everyone involved. They told no one except their parents of their intentions. Jeff remembers that when he told his father, Jack said, "How can you? You are forbidden." Jeff replied, "I'm not sure how I can but I'm going to do it anyway, because the way the situation is, it really doesn't matter."

During the Christmas holidays, they had a memorable time. Jeff wore his gorgeous "undress blues" and everywhere they went, Jeff was wished all the best things in life by everyone from taxi drivers to waiters to people on the street. The general feeling was that the young men in uniform were all going off to die for the country and people everywhere wanted to show their gratitude while they could.

Jeff and Jane Ellen decided to get married in secret as soon as they could. They could not pull this off during the short Christmas break, but they resolved to accomplish the deed at the next possible chance. They knew they had to wait for Jeff's orders before they could make any additional plans. He returned to Philadelphia and she to Stanford to wait.

At Basic School, the decision was announced that the class would be considered graduated at the end of January, 1942, and would receive their orders then. As the war machine picked up speed, they needed to get this class out and the next one in. The men were given their choice of assignments. (This memory always makes Jeff smile wryly since no one got anything he chose.) There were five choices: Fleet Marine Force Atlantic, Fleet Marine Force Pacific, Seagoing Atlantic, Seagoing Pacific and Base Defense Weapons (manning the 5-inch guns which are mounted around Naval bases to repel surface ships). Jeff put in for FMF Pacific first, FMF Atlantic second and Base Defense

The soon-to-be-married Jeff.   *The soon-to-be-married Janelle.*

Weapons School third. What he got was Seagoing, but he did not know that at first because his first orders were to report to the Naval prison at the Navy yard in Vallejo, California. This was close to Palo Alto and Stanford, and he had six days of leave before he was to report.

Jeff and Jane Ellen saw their chance. They figured this might be the last leave Jeff would get, perhaps for the rest of his life, so he wended his way from Philadelphia to Palo Alto. In the Pi Phi house at Stanford, it was the tradition to gather all the members in a circle and pass a box of candy to announce one's engagement. They did this and then took off in Jeff's latest car (a 1941 Ford station wagon) ostensibly to go back down to Los Angeles for a visit. Instead they headed for Nevada.

> *"He cut a really glamorous figure when he came back to campus after he had graduated. He...(came)...to take Janelle someplace in his Marine uniform with the cape. He...(made)...an appearance and had everybody gasping. He was gorgeous!"*
> *— DORIS SMITH VISSCHER*

> *"The thing I remember most was, in 1942, Janelle and I were living in the Pi Phi house because we were in the same pledge class and lived there the last three years of our college. I knew things were quite serious between Jeff and Janelle.....Janelle confided in me that she and Jeff were going to go off to Reno to be married. She really just alluded to it so that I would not be burdened with the secret.....We*

had a wonderful housemother named Mrs. Gardner and I was pres-
ident of the sorority. I sort of confided in Mrs. Gardner about this,
but there was no way I was going to spill the beans. After all, blood
was thicker than water and it was not like Jeff and Janelle could live
together. I just thought this was so exciting to think my cousin was a
married woman! It was so romantic. Janelle seemed so sure from the
very first that this was who she would marry."

– VIRGINIA DEAN ARTHUR

Jane Ellen had called her mother and Jeff had called his father to tell them of their elopement. Jack, accepting his son's decision with good grace, called ahead and contacted an attorney friend of his in Reno and asked him to assist Jeff and Jane Ellen in the arrangements. He also reserved the honeymoon suite for them at the Riverside Hotel in Reno.

So the young couple headed toward Reno. Jeff was in his Marine "service greens" and Jane Ellen was in a silk dress, stockings, high heels and a fur coat. The rain was coming down heavily in Palo Alto when they left and it got no better as they approached the foothills of the Sierras. It was February 5, 1942.

Halfway up toward the Donner Pass Summit, the rain turned to snow. Jeff got out to put chains on the tires. A little further up there was a salesman stuck in the snow. Jeff pushed him out and he went on, but the chains on the station wagon slipped and became wrapped around the axle. Now they were in deep snow with more coming down and they could go no further. They were near the summit in the quiet early dusk of a winter evening, with the beautiful, heavy white flakes drifting down and no traffic whatsoever—stuck. They had heat in the car as long as they kept the engine running, but they knew they would eventually run out of gas. They huddled together and discussed what to do.

By merest chance, the last vehicle to go through the pass before they closed the road came by. Jeff flagged down the driver and he took them down to the maintenance station on the Truckee, Nevada side of the mountains. Several days later, after a call to the auto club, a tow truck had to probe to find the station wagon.

It was now night and there was no transportation available in the heavy snow. Jeff found someone who agreed to drive them down to Reno for ten dollars. In Reno, they were not sure what to do. It was very late, but they were not married and spending the night together was not an option. They knew they had reservations at the Riverside Hotel and they had the address of Jack's attorney friend, but it was now about 10 p.m.

By making a few calls, they discovered that the attorney was attending a play that night and they made their way down to the theater. The attorney made his own car and driver available to Jeff and Janelle and they were driven to Minden, where they obtained the marriage license, and then to another lit-

On the Stanford campus, preparing to elope.

tle town called Gardnerville where they found a pastor whose name they will never forget—Grimshaw. They were married at fifteen minutes past midnight on February 6th, 1942. Then they were driven back to the Riverside Hotel where they had an abbreviated but wonderful honeymoon for the next four days. They were both 21.

They had to keep the fact of their marriage secret. The rule was that a regular military officer of Army, Navy or Marines was required to refrain from marriage for two years after being commissioned. There was some sense to this rule because junior officers are more or less like rounds of ammunition—they are expendable and certainly should not have families. They should also be extremely mobile and go where they are told immediately, without distractions. It was a sound rule, but it did not work for war time. Jeff's and Jane Ellen's situation was not unique.

Jeff was, however, jeopardizing his commission. As Janelle recalls, "Looking back, it was a severe step to take. I think Jeff understood the significance of the coming war more than anyone else and he wanted to grasp whatever happiness he could while there was still time, before he got in the middle of the conflict. I was certainly guided by him. It meant kicking over the traces. Jeff does not have that much respect for rules and regulations made by mere mortals for....reasons that (no longer) make sense."

With their car recovered, they drove back to Stanford where Jeff dropped Jane Ellen off at the Pi Phi house and he reported for duty at the Navy yard. Jane Ellen immediately went to see Mary Yost, the Dean of Women at Stanford. She told Dean Yost that she and Jeff wanted to get married, not that they just had, and asked her what current policies applied. The Dean was a reasonable woman and she said that she realized that the war changed things considerably. She told Jane Ellen that although the rules stated that no married woman could live in a sorority house, she understood that Jane Ellen would be separated from Jeff. She also knew that Jane Ellen had excellent grades and had earned unlimited "late leaves". She therefore granted Jane Ellen permission to continue to live in the Pi Phi house after her marriage, knowing it would only be until Jane Ellen's graduation in June, just four months away.

They were "in the closet" for not quite two months. The rule regarding marriage for junior officers was rescinded on April 1, 1942. Jeff and Jane Ellen took that opportunity to go away for the weekend and then tell everyone when they got back that they had just got married. (A newspaper announcement of their engagement followed the passing of the candy at the Pi Phi house. It stated, "No definite date has been set for the wedding." After the April rule change, they immediately arranged for an announcement of their marriage. It states that they were married on April 4, 1942.)

On March 2, 1942, less than one month after the marriage, Jack Cooper died. He had entered Scripps Institute in La Jolla, California, for a complete physical. While there he suffered a fatal stroke. He was 59. Jeff obtained emer-

Jack Cooper – Jeff's favorite photo of his father.

gency leave for the funeral. Mourners gathered at the house on Rossmore for the eulogy. The burial took place at Miradero, in the private cemetery in the canyon behind the house.

The impact of Jack's death on Jeff was shattering. Jack was the deity of Jeff's youth. He knew everything and did everything and provided for everything and he was the center. He was suddenly gone. But Jeff was on full duty as a second lieutenant of Marines and he had a war to fight. The impact of Jack's passing was very much mitigated by that fact—like having a close comrade fall beside you in a fire fight. Jeff simply carried on.

Jeff's first assignment at the Naval prison in Vallejo lasted only a few days and that was all to the good. He learned immediately that prisons are an abomination and that he wanted nothing at all to do with them for the rest of his life. As an intense individualist who valued human achievement and dignity, the idea of crowding wrong-doers in a pen with other humans to guard their every movement was repellent to him. He has always felt that escape or attempted escape from prison should not be punished—it is what any and every human being *should* do when faced with incarceration and what should be expected. The situation changed for the better in a short time and Jeff was reassigned to the Naval Ammunition Depot.

The prison and the depot were only a few yards apart, but duty at the Ammunition Depot, while not what Jeff expected as an infantry officer, was a great deal more agreeable than duty at the prison. Since none knew of their marriage, Jeff lived in barracks-style quarters at the depot and he and Jane Ellen surreptitiously stole a few hours at a time whenever they could until his regular orders came through.

Jeff's regular orders, as he by now knew they would be, were seagoing. So he checked out of the Ammunition Depot and went down to the docks in San Francisco Bay and took his first look at the U.S.S. Pennsylvania, BB 38, mounting twelve 14-inch guns and eighteen lesser guns. A creature of the old

Navy, where they wore whites for meals, she was a 35,000-ton battleship just back from Pearl Harbor. She had been in drydock in Pearl Harbor, probably the only reason she had not been sunk there. She had been damaged somewhat and had been sent to San Francisco to get her out of the way while being repaired. At the same time, they needed some replacements in personnel and Jeff's assignment was as the new junior officer of the Marine detachment on the "Pennsy." Although he had no way of knowing it at the time, this was to be his home, with few interludes, for the next 30 months.

The Pennsy went out rather quickly in May of 1942 for the Battle of the Coral Sea, but did not see any action. That exchange ended in a stand-off. The decision was made to bring her back to San Francisco to rebuild the topside and enhance her gun capabilities.

Jane Ellen waited until her graduation from Stanford in June of 1942 to find an apartment for the two of them. It was on Bay Street in San Francisco. Jeff was able to leave the bachelor quarters and Jane Ellen settled in to being a homemaker. The young couple soon found that they were going to be parents, the baby being due around mid-February of 1943. Jane Ellen's obstetrician was in Los Angeles, but he gave her a referral to a San Francisco doctor for her monthly check-ups. Her cooking class at Stanford now came in handy as she tried out recipes on a husband who, despite his youth, had very sophisticated tastes. She decorated their apartment, kept in close touch with her mother, prepared for the baby and began the educational process all military

The Marine officers of the U.S.S. Pennsylvania, 1943. Left to right, Jock Elliot, Harvard, Jeff Cooper, Stanford, McLennan, University of Texas.

Jeff, on the left, had not yet learned to keep his finger off the trigger until his sights were on the target.

spouses must go through to understand the rather labyrinthine world of military protocol.

They socialized with the Naval officers from the Pennsy and with Jeff's sister Phyllis and her current husband, Art Balinger, who was a new Army lieutenant. Art was awaiting his orders and since war plans were very secret, Art and Phyllis said their goodbyes every weekend. Fortunately, the Pennsy was visibly being repaired, so Jeff and Jane Ellen did not have to go through the same emotional rollercoaster as the Balingers. They enjoyed themselves in San Francisco as much as possible, while the war loomed ever closer.

When Jeff went aboard the Pennsy, there were 100 enlisted Marines including a top sergeant and a gunnery sergeant, and three officers—a captain, a first lieutenant and a second lieutenant. Jeff went aboard at the bottom, as the second lieutenant. As he did, the captain went out, and that captain was Bob Cushman. Cushman later became a very distinguished marine in World War II, with several medals, for whom Jeff later worked on a couple of occasions, and who finally wound up as Commandant of the Marine Corps. While they did not form a really close friendship because Bob was much senior, Jeff and Jane Ellen became friends with both Bob (whom they always called "sir") and his wife Audrey and touched base with them several more times as their careers progressed. As Bob Cushman went out as captain aboard the Pennsy, Bob Ridell came in.

Early war

T he duties of a Marine officer aboard ship are not demanding in an infantry sense. They are demanding in a naval sense, and Jeff did not know anything about being a Naval officer, so he had to learn how to be a Navy ensign by osmosis. He pretty much left the handling of the Marine detachment to his two senior NCO's. Senior NCO's in 1942 were, for the most part, very good men, so Jeff had excellent support. The detachment was run from an administrative standpoint mostly by the Top and the Gunny and about the only time Jeff was called upon to do anything "Marine-wise" was to stand formations when they put out honor guards and to administer punishment when necessary.

Punishment seldom needed to be administered. Jeff recalls his detachment as honorable men going about their duties and getting on with the war and about the only thing that would come up once in a while was a fistfight. There would be some broken teeth and smashed noses and the officers would have to decide what to do about it. Jeff never assigned a man to a court martial the entire time he was on board the Pennsy. The sergeants handled all the more minor infractions, not by brutality, but by making sure that the men knew the rules, knew when they had transgressed and knew that there was a price to be paid.

Marines on a battleship serve a number of functions. One is ceremonial— they perform guard duties for command and flag officers who come aboard and they stand guard over the ship when it's in port. In action, the Marines in those days manned the anti-aircraft guns. The Pennsy had a number of different kinds of anti-aircraft guns and the Marines were distributed amongst them, always in units together.*

The curious relationship of the sailors to the Marines is the subject of many

*NOTE: See: "The Guns" in *Another Country* by Jeff Cooper.

amusing stories. It was a function of oneupmanship all the time. The Marines would insist that the sailors couldn't be trusted with firearms and the sailors would insist that the Marines did not know port from starboard. They went on and on like that. It was all in the spirit of friendly competition, although the Marines and the sailors did not associate with each other socially in the enlisted ranks.

As to the officers, this was not true. There were only three Marine officers aboard and they associated freely with their contemporaries amongst the Naval officers. The main source of officers for the Navy, Army, and Marine Corps, was from the graduates of the major universities of the country. It was considered in those days that if you had a bachelor's degree from a serious university you were almost automatically commission material unless there was something wrong with you. Therefore, if you were a graduate of Harvard or Northwestern or Berkeley, you signed on as an ensign in the Navy—the equivalent of a second lieutenant in the Army or the Marine Corps.

The Naval Academy graduates and the university graduates would rib each other unceasingly. The Academy boys would make the point that the trouble with the "civilians" was that they had never had a "plebe year" in an academy. The suffering and harassment of the plebe year at any of the academies was considered to be a rite of passage without which a man did not know how much he could stand. That was important then. So the academy graduates teased the others, saying they had never really been put to the test. The "civilians" retaliated by saying that the academy boys never really had a college education, insisting that the academies were really only glorified trade schools where they taught people how to be technicians rather than cultivated men. This good-humored ribbing kept up their spirits and helped ease the monotony of drill.

One might well wonder what a battleship's personnel do during a war when they are not in a battle. The answer is drill. Constantly. They had abandon ship drill and gun drill and collision drill and fire drill and pay drill. The men tried to get as much sleep as they could, but when they were not asleep or on watch, they drilled. Half the watch time was spent drilling too because men would get called away. This was onerous and tedious, but necessary. In recent times, one can recall incidents where ships have gotten into serious trouble when an emergency arose and the crew did not react correctly or quickly enough. In 1942 the brass made sure no American ship would be caught unprepared in terms of what to do. The men on board the Pennsy knew every inch of the ship and how everything worked and they worked it all 25 hours a day.

The Pennsylvania's second round of repairs complete, she again went to sea. The U.S. Navy did not know quite how to face up to the superior power of the Japanese Navy in the Pacific, so they did a bit of patrolling and a bit of churning around, drilling all the while. On some occasions they had a chance to use their heavy guns in practice before their actual war began. They moved on down the Hawaiian chain to Kahoolawe and later to the big island of Hawaii. They worked with both the main battery and the secondary battery. For Jeff, this was interesting because all guns are of interest to him, and having been a shooter all his young life it was a pleasure to use the guns and see how they worked. They had various gun drills, including anti-aircraft drills where they would shoot at various types of targets in the air. The best of these were "drones"—unmanned aircraft which were launched in various ways and flown by radio direction into simulated attack. They were costly and the men were cautioned not to "kill" them if they could help it.

The Pennsy was part of the fleet formation at the battle of Midway in June of 1942, but she never got to fire a shot. She was on the north flank, assigned to prevent the Japanese from trying to break away to the north. She had the massive gun power to stop them, but they did not come that way. So Jeff lived through the most decisive battle of the Pacific war without firing at all. They were in solid fog all the time. The only casualties suffered in that part of the fleet, apart from the industrial accidents which are a fact of life aboard a battleship, were on the California. Their spotting aircraft came back and crashed into the ship. They were trying to put down and instead hit the ship. That's how thick the fog was.

The Battle of Midway, although nobody realized it at the time, was one of the turning points of civilization. Up until that time the Japanese Navy owned the Pacific. At Midway, in a matter of only a few minutes, Japan lost control of the Pacific and the world. Admiral Spruance's dive bomber swarm that hit the four Japanese carriers was composed of not fewer than nine and not more than twelve naval combat pilots. Between 10:00 and 10:25 in the morning the Japanese lost the war. This was a moment of extreme drama, and like many such moments, nobody knew. The Japanese had their major carriers sunk or disabled. They lost something like 220 of the finest naval aviators in the world, and they could not replace them. When the carriers went down, these highly trained naval pilots were left up in the air with nowhere to go. They simply plunked into the water. Very few of them survived. The surviving Japanese ships, destroyers and such, were hightailing it back to Japan and the Americans were not interested in saving Japanese lives. This was a savage war and that savagery has been lost today. Perhaps that is all to the good— many people would be uncomfortable to know how ruthless their grandfathers could be. All they wanted from the Japanese was their death.

When Midway was over, American PBY's (patrol flying boats) flew back and forth across the ocean looking for survivors. When they saw an orange life raft, they would land and pick up the men. When they saw a black life raft, they would cruise in low and slow, turn the 50 calibers loose and kill everyone aboard. This was brutal. This was the way it was.

When American pilots had to bail out of their aircraft, they usually could make it into a life raft. If they were lucky, they would be picked up by their own men. If unlucky, they would wash up on the beach of a Japanese island, whereupon the Japanese would proceed to revile them, abuse them and behead them. After the war, Jeff formed a close friendship with C.F. "Bud" Reynolds, a colonel of Marines who sat on some of the war crimes trials in Japan. Bud had kept a picture of a Japanese naval officer, a lieutenant commander, in the act of beheading an American flyer, who was bound and kneeling, while the sword was in the air. The important thing is not that the Japanese officer killed the pilot, but that he had his picture taken while in the act and saved it as an important souvenir of his war service. "Here I am, killing a helpless man." Very different.

Midway was the end, or the beginning of the end. The Americans did not realize this at the time. Perhaps the only person who had an inkling was Admiral Nagumo, who had led the attack on Pearl Harbor. He must have looked at the reports and contemplated long and hard on what to do next.

Of course, propagandists always lie, or at least obfuscate the truth. There was propaganda on both sides, but in the United States, which was and is a more open society than any other, lies were and are harder to make believable.

The Pennsy saw a lot of ocean but was supposed to keep out of sight until required. Exploiting the temporary advantage of Midway, the U.S. moved into the offensive stage at Guadalcanal in the Solomon Islands. Fighting there took place in September and October of 1942, but the Pennsy was not involved.

Guadalcanal was a dreadful experience. When Jeff heard that the Marines had landed he thought that was it and that the island was surely taken. What he did not know was that it was not a sure thing at all and the outcome hung in the balance for months. Major General Alexander A. Vandegrift was in command and his plans officer (G3) was Merrill Twining, a man Jeff would later serve under on a couple of occasions. He was a very distinguished officer—brother of Nathan Twining who later was chief of the Air Force. Merrill Twining was given the job of designing the plans for withdrawal from Guadalcanal. Nobody was aware of that at the time. Not only were the American people not told but even the troops were not told that the situation was as desperate as it was on Guadalcanal for a short period. Part of the ground attack was led by Colonel Clifton B. Cates, the same man who had sent Jeff's Basic School class on their Christmas holiday less than one year before.

Guadalcanal was more dreadful for the Japanese than for the Americans because they were overconfident. They had gone to war with the notion that the Americans were pushovers; that they were soft, pleasure-loving, easy; that they didn't know what it was to work hard and they had no tradition of valor; that the tradition of *bushido*, the gallantry of the Japanese soldier, would simply wipe them out.

The Japanese were also told by their officers that if they just got to their feet, screamed, drew their swords and ran at the Americans they would win the action. All they got was shot.

On Guadalcanal, the Japanese did not get shot so much as they died of disease and starvation. Only one out of four of the Japanese who died on Guadalcanal died as a result of American gunfire. The rest succumbed to malnutrition, malaria, dysentery, dengue and exhaustion. The stories which came out later about what it was like on the Japanese part of the island were horrifying. One Japanese staff officer was sent ashore and arrived in the dark. All he could hear were whispers from barely seen figures begging him for anything at all to eat. He went inland for a mile or so, walking through a corridor of dead and dying. Another officer later said that at one point when trying to get back up the island all he could think about was food. He simply could not force his mind away from that one subject. The only way he could keep his feet was to think about food with every step. Once they had lost control of the air, they could not resupply. Out of about 42,000 Japanese on Guadalcanal, less than 10,000 survived. The Americans did not feel sorry at all.

The Pennsy then put in to the harbor at Long Beach on February 5, 1943, just in time for Jeff and Jane Ellen's first child to be born.

The baby was due on February 14, 1943. Jane Ellen decided to give up the apartment on Bay Street in San Francisco and move down to Los Angeles to stay with her mother while Jeff was gone. At this point, no one could guess how long that would be. She left San Francisco in late January, having been advised to make the trip by overnight train because she was near to term. There was heavy rain around Santa Barbara and the railroad tracks washed out. They put all the passengers on buses and Jane Ellen bounced all the way down to Los Angeles. The baby was still two weeks late, arriving on March 1, 1943.

It was strictly luck that put Jeff in Los Angeles at the exact time of his first child's arrival. Whether it was good luck is debatable. Jeff acknowledges that he was no help at all and Janelle recalls that he was "terrible". He was ready to kill the doctor because Jane Ellen was having labor pains and the doctor did not seem to be doing anything to stop them. Austeene was there too, lending moral support. Floy was content to stay home and let the Cooper contingent take care of the hospital vigil. This was the Good Samaritan Hospital in Los Angeles, where Jane Ellen and Jeff had been born twenty-two years before. Eventually, a little girl was born. They were not disappointed to have a girl. They had no preference whatever as to gender. They had picked out a boy's name—Jeffrey Pixley Cooper—but did not get to use it. They named their little girl Christina because they liked the sound of it and because it made a nice alliterative combination with Cooper. After a few days, Jane Ellen took little "Christy" home to 153 South Gramercy Place to live with Floy, and Jeff returned to the Pennsy which shipped out to the Aleutian Islands on April 23, 1943.

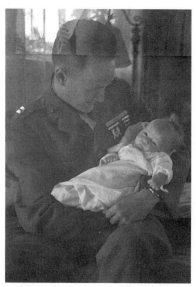

Jeff with his new baby daughter, Christy, in 1943.

Janelle with Christy.

There were two Aleutian campaigns and the Pennsy went out for both of them. On both occasions they went up and crossed the Gulf of Alaska in very heavy seas. That can be a rough piece of ocean and if you have any tendencies toward seasickness they will turn up there. It was quite an experience for the landlubbers among the men, and that included most of them, to be aboard a battleship in high seas. The Pennsy, being made of steel, was mostly underwater. Like an iceberg, all that could be seen above water was a small portion of the total. The ship itself did not move around too much, although it rolled a great deal. This did not mean much to the people below, but to those with stations topside it could get very exciting. The Pennsy had tripod masts and when the men were up in the tops in the heavy seas they could look straight down into the water when she rolled.

There existed an informal initiation for junior officers aboard the Pennsy—informal and illegal, which made it all the more interesting. At the very topmost part of the foremast, which was the highest point on the vessel, was mounted the ship's surface search radar dish. Radar was in its infancy then and it was considered kind of secret. The Pennsy was equipped with both an air search apparatus (called the "bedspring" because it resembled one) for detecting aircraft and a surface search parabolic reflector which was to detect submarine periscopes. It was mounted on a prong at the end of a boom attached to the foremast at the highest point possible and it was pretty remote. It was considered by all that a junior officer was not really one of the boys until he had written his name on the inside of that dish with a grease pencil.

114

To do it right, you had to do it while the ship was underway and out at sea. To escape detection, you had to do it at night. Each would wait until all was quiet on the midwatch some night and then scramble up the pole with the pencil in his teeth. Hijinks on the high seas.

In those days all of the ensigns and the second lieutenant of Marines dined in one mess hall amidships called the junior officer's mess. The rest of the officers dined in the wardroom. There was an old joke that when you came in for breakfast in the j.o. mess and the mess attendant came up, you asked him, "What have we got for breakfast this morning, John?" He would answer, "Eggs, suh. Jus' eggs." When you graduated to the wardroom and asked the same question, the answer would be, "Eggs, suh. Any style." That was the difference between the j.o. mess and the wardroom.

The Pennsy began the war with the notion that officers would dress for dinner. This did not last long. The restriction was lifted very soon and they could "dine" in the uniforms they were wearing at mealtime.

Mostly they drilled. In the morning when they were at sea, if they were not in a war zone, "quarters" would be held on the quarterdeck. Quarters formation was simply a ceremony in which the captain, the executive officer, the division heads and all officers off watch would fall in and be given the plan for the day. They would make their reports as well—how many able for duty, how many sick and other items of importance.

They normally had breakfast at 8:00 a.m. and quarters at 8:30. Immediately thereafter they would set to on the drills for the day which would be laid out by the various department heads as to what they wanted to do. Gun drill, lifeboat drill, main battery drill, signal drill, whatever. One of their famous signals of relief was "FCD" which was Fox Cast Dog and the appropriate three flags. When those flags went up from the flagship it meant, "Cease present exercises." Everyone would sink to the deck and heave a great sigh of relief. They had many jokes about the true meaning of FCD.

On the Pennsy, there was one call they never drilled on and that was "air defense". This call meant, "No kidding here they come!" When it sounded you were instantly in action. They never sounded it unless airplanes were actually coming in. One of the reasons for this was that on average every time they sounded "air defense" on the Pennsy they put about six men in sick bay with injuries. Mostly these resulted from being knocked off ladders. It was a dangerous operation. Jeff was in harbor one time at a battle port, talking with some visiting Australian Navy officers in the wardroom and serving them coffee. The "air defense" call came over the bull horn and the coffee went up in the air and Jeff was over the other officers and up the ladder before the coffee had a chance to hit the deck. What they used to tell newcomers coming aboard ship was that they could learn all the calls by listening to them except one. If you hear something you have never heard before, that is "air defense".

For Jeff, life aboard ship was dull. He had trained all his life as a ground officer and as a naval officer aboard a battleship he was frustrated, especially since the watches were stood by all. Normal watches on a big ship like the Pennsy in a relatively quiet period are "watch-in-four". That means four hours on and twelve hours off. The twelve hours off had to be used to accomplish everything else you had to do. This included all your division work, taking care of your troops and studying and going to class. Whenever they docked, a large number of officers would be grabbed off the ship immediately and sent to special schools such as anti-chemical schools and fire-drill schools where they would be shown the latest systems for doing specialty things. That reduced the watch force aboard ship painfully and those remaining on board had to stand watches closer together. Lack of sleep was a problem that plagued them all, all the time.

The "morning watch" was 4 to 8 a.m. At 8 a.m. the "forenoon watch" took over until after lunch. After lunch the "afternoon watch" came on until 4 p.m. Ordinarily in "watch-in-four", the next watch would be 4 to 8 p.m. In order to make sure they did not get the same watch every time around, they split that watch, called "dogging it". So the "first dog" was 4 p.m. to evening meal and the "second dog" was from evening meal until 8 p.m. They used to call the first dog "the Captain's watch" and the second dog "the Admiral's watch". At 8 p.m. the "first watch" went on until midnight and then the "mid-watch" went from midnight until 4 a.m.

"Watch-in-four" meant that the Pennsy was fully operational and could do almost anything, depending upon its state of training and how many men they had and how long they had been aboard, in five minutes. If they were underway, unaware and unalarmed, and suddenly got a red alert, they could have the guns picking up and engaging targets in five minutes. This was tremendous. There were 2200 men on that ship, jammed in like sardines. When they all moved at once, something had to give. The "man your battle stations" signal was called "general quarters". When that bugle call came over the public address system, before the worded announcement "All hands man your battle stations" came over the air, all the men were responding. They had a live bugler in those days, no taped calls, so the excitement of the moment created some interesting unauthorized variations in the notes. It only added to the excitement.

In port, the Marine officer would stand the deck watch. The officer of the deck was in charge of the ship as a deputy for the captain. Anything that came up went first through the officer of the deck—someone coming aboard, messages coming in on the radio, etc. The officer of the deck would handle these things and see that the proper actions were taken. Everything on a big ship was done by checklist. If you had the deck and the message came in, "Orders from the base captain. Stand by to take on fuel," you would simply go through the files quickly and whip out the checklist and go through the steps. Almost the first item on every checklist was to notify the captain.

One of the most amusing experiences Jeff had came much later in the war out at Eniwetok Atoll. The Pennsy was at anchor, having secured the islands after the battle was won. The signal came from the fleet command, "Stand by to get underway on signal." The officer of the deck was Cliff Cates, who was a roommate of Jeff's at the time and son of Colonel Cliff Cates, one of the most distinguished Marines of modern times who later became Commandant of the Marine Corps. Jeff thinks that when Cliff looked at his checklist, he overlooked item one. So he did everything else except notify the captain. The captain was asleep. Sleep was a very precious commodity in that business and a ship captain hardly got any, grabbing every opportunity that came his way. Something woke him and he saw the palm trees sliding by his porthole. There was no big scandal. Cliff was sufficiently embarrassed at finding the captain charging up in his underwear to find out where his ship was going.

At sea, a Marine may not stand deck watches because he cannot assume control of the ship. Marines stand gunnery watches. The watch to which Jeff was eventually graduated was "sky control". That is the officer in charge of all close-range weapons—not the main battery. The main battery of 14-inch guns was handled by "main control" and they were only brought into action when they had suitable targets. The small guns—5-inch, 40 millimeter, 20 millimeter, 50 caliber—were all under the supervision of the officer on "sky control". Sky control watches were mainly what Jeff stood, concerned with air defense of the ship and general lookout. He stood them "watch-in-four".

The first time up to the Aleutians, the Pennsy went out to Kiska and then out to Attu. They learned about life aboard ship in cold weather. It was not the dead of winter, so the weather was not disastrously cold, just cold. Being topside in the wind and the sea spray with the temperature about 38 degrees is chilly. The men took to wearing balaclavas and learned that they make your head itch badly if you have any hair. The smart ones shaved their heads. Jeff did not, at least not right away.

The Pennsy took on sea water and distilled it for use as drinking and washing water. Up in the Aleutians, there was a little fish that was just the size of the openings in the filters on the ship's water intake system. These little fish filled up the intakes and cut off the water supply. The word went out, and from then on showers and washing were all done with sea water. Many complained but Jeff did not mind. They were issued salt water soap. Jeff considered that since they had both showers and soap they were far ahead of many other people during the war and that it was a joke to complain about the quality of the water.

The Aleutian campaign was kind of frustrating. The Japanese had taken Kiska and Attu and the islands out of the chain reaching out toward Japan. They wanted a place to put their Zero floatplanes, plus they wanted to divert American forces from the Pacific theater. Their taking of these islands was very insulting because this was American territory. The American people were very indignant about the war for the most part. The idea that the Japanese would come in and actually land on American soil was frightening to some people but simply infuriating to the men in uniform. There was not much on those islands—some airstrips and some dockyard facilities and a few people, mostly Aleuts and service people. Some were killed and some were taken prisoner, but not many.

The Pennsy was mainly involved in shore bombardment, although she was also a flagship and that meant that officers from all over the fleet would come in to the wardroom on board the Pennsy to get briefed. Jeff learned much about the conduct of the war from the conferences held in the wardroom on board the Pennsy. The U.S. was sending in light attack bombers against the Japanese positions. Jeff became aware of a senior air officer who was having a hard time getting his pilots to slow down when they made their strafing runs. He told them that when they got there fast and went out fast they did not get enough gun power to the targets on the ground. This seemed obvious to Jeff, who also felt he understood the desire of a young man in a fast plane to go fast.

One of the most significant jobs Jeff was given in the Aleutians was the port deck watch in the harbor at Adak. This was vital because the weather was foul and the ship was riding at anchor with water breaking over the decks and the only way they could get people up and down the side was with a combination ladder and landing net. It amused the junior officers very much to see these very senior officers leaping madly from the gunwale to the net and then up the ladder. Jeff would come to attention very formally and salute these wet and bedraggled senior officers. It was quite a compliment to be given responsibility for the port deck watch. Only four out of about thirty were considered competent for the job: Cooper, Cates, Mahler and Klein. They stood the duty in their rubber boots in the salt spray with the sea sloshing around their ankles, trying to maintain order and keep the boats from crashing.

Three incidents occurred up in the Aleutians which stuck with Jeff. The first was a taste of direct combat, as direct as shore bombardment can get, which was very satisfying. An observation plane was up in the fog when the mist cleared and the pilot found himself looking down on a whole Japanese formation in close order marching across the tundra. He was so excited he practically gobbled across the radio. The Pennsy happened to be in position. They had eight 5-inch 38's on a side, each with a 50-pound shell, and each of those guns could fire a controlled round in five seconds. Eight guns firing every five seconds creates a rumbling like a vast machine gun. These airbursts came in over the marching Japanese column and massacred it. Jeff feels that his participation in this one action is probably the most he did for the United States during the whole war.

The second was something that happened on the beach that was reported to Jeff later. The infantry on the beach had been fighting for several days in the freezing mud. They had the wrong clothes and the wrong boots and they were cold, hungry and exhausted. It was not one of the famous meat grinders, but people were getting killed. They were moving forward across this muskeg area and the Japanese position was ahead of them at the bottom of a forward slope. According to the eyewitness, one sergeant decided he had enough. He was so cold and so tired and so completely washed out that he did not care about death—he simply wanted it to be over. He heaved himself to his feet and walked right in on this Japanese position. The Japanese were all in holes in the ground and he walked right in amongst them stepping from hole to hole and killing the man inside. There must have been 10 to 14 Japanese soldiers, all shooting at him at once. They all missed him, hitting only his clothes. He killed them all. Instead of taking cover or cheering or running back, he sat down on a hummock of moss, put his rifle across his knees and put his head in his hands. He just called off the war. People were screaming at him to get down and come back and he did not. He was not seriously hurt and he did get the Distinguished Service Cross for that, which he well deserved. He was not acting out of any feeling of high heroism or to make the world safe for democracy or to protect God and country, it was just because he could not stand it anymore. He had been pushed over the edge of his endurance. Jeff never learned what happened to him after that. The fighting in the Aleutians was almost over at that point.

The third incident showed Jeff that the Japanese had some humanity, something he and his comrades did not really believe, having learned how they treated prisoners and other disgusting proclivities. The Japanese did, however, have a certain reverence for heroism, especially if it resulted in death. On Attu the men found the wreckage of a P-40 American fighter plane which had gone into a mountain side. The Japanese had taken that three-bladed propeller and cut off two of the flukes and then stuck the other one vertically into the ground and had put a little brass monument on it which translated read, "Here lies the body of a brave young war eagle who sacrificed youth and happiness for his fatherland."

This struck them as a very Western sentiment and they were surprised that the Japanese had done it. Nevertheless, it did not change their attitudes by much, if at all.

Looking back with the perspective of more than fifty years, a master's degree in history and a lifetime of intense reading in world history, Jeff is struck by the ferocity of World War II in the Pacific. The Japanese made a terrible mistake in attacking Pearl Harbor. Admiral Nagumo, who had led the attack there, said, "We have awakened a sleeping giant," and they had. It was the worst possible strategic mistake. If they had simply declared war on the U.S., the Americans would not have had the rage they did at having been hit in the back while asleep at the switch. Pearl Harbor was attacked on a Sunday morning, when people had been out dancing the night before, making plans to play tennis with their wives and attend church the next day. America was asleep. She shouldn't have been but she was not at war and there were a number of peacetime career officers involved there who were really not anticipating anything, despite the way the war was progressing in Europe. In any case, the Americans were *furious*, and this was the motive behind the conduct of the war in the Pacific—rage.

The Americans were really angry, all of them, and the actions of the Japanese as the war progressed not only did not alleviate that rage, it fed it so that it never abated. The Japanese did not operate under the same general code of conduct which bound the Westerners. This code is unspoken, but accepted and venerated by virtue of shared cultural values. One of the pillars of this code is "never beat a man when he's down." The Japanese did not share this tradition and their treatment of prisoners and anyone else at their mercy was unspeakably savage and merciless. The fact of their different cultural mores did nothing to satisfy the rage of the American soldiers when they heard of the Japanese atrocities. They demonized the Japanese. They regarded them as fiends and so were not reluctant to kill them. In fact, they enjoyed it.

The attack on Pearl Harbor was also a military mistake. If they had declared war on the U.S. and then stayed out to the west of Honolulu, the Americans would have had to go out to take action, and if they had been caught on the high seas, the Japanese would most likely have sunk the entire United States Navy. The Japanese Navy was bigger and stronger and faster and heavier than the U.S. Navy at Pearl Harbor. And the U.S. would not have been able to get warships off the bottom of the open sea and repaired like they did in the relative shallow of a harbor. This attack virtually saved the American fleet by not letting us take the war to them.

Time intervened and the entire U.S. war production was thrown into high gear, achieving material success that was unbelievable. Almost before a man could change uniform, the implements of war were coming out of the American factories in enormous quantities. Not just rifles and ammunition, but equipment like warplanes and tanks and brand-new, very good ships that were faster, newer and more technically efficient than the Japanese Navy. This was bad news for the Japanese.

It is interesting to speculate about what sense the Japanese people made of their war news. According to what they heard, every time there was an engagement, it was a great victory for the Japanese Navy. In the beginning, this was often true. But as the war progressed, the tide turned. Now every time an action was reported the engagement was closer to Japan. There must have been some penetrating Japanese who saw something wrong with that. Eventually an awful feeling must have come home to many of them when suddenly they found American aircraft over Japan in quantity. A number of them must have realized at that point that they had been lied to for the previous three years.

War stories

While Jeff was up in the Aleutians, Jane Ellen was busy taking care of Christy. She lived with Floy and they had the assistance of Anna, the German maid Jane Ellen had grown up with. Anna was always there and, according to Janelle "she was wonderful. She had employment with my mother for probably about 40 years." She did the cooking. With Floy lending expert and loving assistance with Christy, Jane Ellen had time to volunteer for both Red Cross and USO work. She hostessed at the USO's Hollywood Canteen, socializing and dancing with the soldiers, sailors and Marines who were lucky enough to get in. More than once, she was mistaken for a starlet and asked for her autograph. For the Red Cross, she drove a station wagon, mostly picking up and delivering various people, both military and civilian.

In late May of 1943, she got a call from Jeff. The Pennsylvania had been hit by a torpedo and was in port at Bremerton, Washington. They would be able to see each other for several weeks while the ship was being repaired. Jane Ellen immediately weaned Christy, whom she had been nursing for three months, left her in the care of Floy and went up to Bremerton.

At Attu, the Pennsy had taken a torpedo port side well forward during a shore bombardment. Jeff did not know they had been hit at the time. They were firing their main battery and being topside when the 14-inch guns let go is to be in the midst of indescribable concussion. They were shooting one gun at a time, which was standard procedure. When something went off forward, Jeff simply thought they had fired again because he was not on the forward command circuit. It turned out they had been hit and the question arose if the ship could remain seaworthy. The captain was a qualified diver. They fitted him out in a diver's suit and lowered him over the side. He wanted to make a decision based upon his own observation as to the nature of the damage done by the hit. He decided to take the Pennsy back stateside to get it repaired. This was good news for the crew, who looked forward to warming up.

The weatherman rode on the flagship—the Pennsy. He was a lieutenant commander in the Navy and he sat in the wardroom playing solitaire and drinking coffee. That's all he ever did. People would ask him if he ever did anything and he would ask what they would have him do. "Have you been topside today? What's the weather like? Right. That's what it will be like tomorrow."

As the Pennsy came in for repair, they came through the Juan de Fuca Strait toward Bremerton, which is a Navy yard near Seattle, and as they approached, the sun came out. This was only the second time Jeff had seen the sun during the entire campaign. The other time was about three weeks earlier on his twenty-third birthday, May 10, 1943, when they were in the midst of a battle way out at the end of the Aleutian chain. That first sight of the sun was something of a shock. This time it seemed a glorious welcome back.

Jeff had the watch and gazed at the sunlight playing on the water with delight. It was made the more magnificent when a pod of orcas came by, going in the other direction. Jeff had only seen one of these before in his life. They were not in every aquarium in the world in those days and to see them wild in the ocean was a marvelous sight. It brought back memories of his lecture to the passengers bound for Catalina when he was a boy. Jeff had developed early on a great capacity for enjoyment and appreciation of the moment. His receptors were and are always open. Despite world war and all the hardship and tragic possibilities attendant, he was able to savor the sun, sea, breeze and wild creatures with a vibrant enthusiasm which startled those around him into a similar mood.

It was a great respite for the men of the Pennsy to be able to stop for a time. Jeff called Jane Ellen as soon as he could to ask her to join him. Travel during the war was problematic and Jane Ellen had a time getting to Bremerton. Also, there was a housing shortage and finding a place to stay was a challenge. They finally got themselves one room in an un-airconditioned hotel by way of begging and bribing and maneuvering. Being able to be together was worth anything. They were thankful to be alive. War marriages were subject to great emotional stress. Every time you say goodby it may be the last time. Consequently, moments together were really treasured. This tended to create solid bases for partnerships. Couples prized what they had and put away pettiness and quarrels over small differences. The war forced them to organize their priorities.

Jeff and Jane Ellen's break in Bremerton lasted nearly two months. Then the Pennsy headed back out to war on August 1, 1943, and did not come back for the duration. She headed straight south to Pearl Harbor where they fitted out to go further and then they moved with the war as it moved westward toward the Japanese Islands. Although he had no way of knowing at the time, Jeff would not be relieved for more than a year, until late in 1944.

As can well be imagined, the armed forces needed rank in a hurry. There was the old argument as between the policy of the Confederacy and that of the Union in the Civil War. In the Union Army they couldn't see putting downy-faced boys in as regimental commanders so they would get political officers who had been justices of the peace or mayors or candidates for congress and they would make them colonels and they would put young soldiers in as juniors underneath them. That did not work. In the Confederacy they made the young soldiers colonels and brought in more youngsters under them. They may not have known what they were doing but they managed better than the Union did, at least in the early stages of the war.

There was no perfect solution to the problem. In World War II, in the Marine Corps, they just bumped people up. Jeff went aboard the Pennsy as a second lieutenant and before he knew it he was a first lieutenant. Almost immediately thereafter, at age 23, he was a captain. He felt awed by the fact but did the best he could and got excellent fitness reports, so it worked out.

The battleship Pennsylvania was issued the job of being a "monitor", which is a seagoing gun platform. You might say that any battleship is that, but the more modern battleships that were arriving with such speed, such as the Iowa and the Massachusetts, were very fast and were given the job of riding shotgun for the carriers. Carrier aviation, coming forth in massive quantities, was the Sunday punch and it needed protection. If the Japanese battleships had got in amongst the carriers, they could have hurt the U.S. terribly, so the new battleships protected the carriers and their precious cargo.

At one battle port, Jeff had the chance to go aboard one of the new battleships to have dinner and exchange notes with a classmate of his from Basic School. This was Augustus Octavius Bacon Sparks, III, also a captain. Jeff was impressed. The ship (perhaps the New Jersey) made the Pennsy look like a relic from the past.

The older and slower battleships such as the Pennsylvania, the California and the Tennessee, could do nothing in the war except ride shotgun for the landing forces—all these massive troop ships laden with troops and artillery and tanks—which were destined to land on the islands. The older battleships could keep up with the troop ships and so they stood guard against air and surface attack and when they got to an island they would swing alongside and blast it with their heavy guns—a technique which worked well, especially after they tried it a few times and learned from their mistakes.

The assaults on Tarawa and Makin in the Gilbert Islands in November of 1943 marked the beginning of the Marine Corps' westward advance across the Pacific. It was the first time a landing was attempted across a reef in the face of opposition. It was also the first time both air and naval gunfire were used to support a landing.

Tarawa was extremely well-fortified. According to the sole Japanese officer

Reprint from Oakland Tribune
March 18, 1945

U.S.S. PENNSYLVANIA KNOWN AS 'SHOOTIN'EST' SHIP IN WAR

By LEIF ERICKSON

U.S. PACIFIC FLEET HEAD-QUARTERS, GUAM, March 16.— (Delayed) — (AP) — The 31-year-old battleship U.S.S. Pennsylvania, peacetime flagship of the United States Fleet, has hurled her 14-inch battery barrage against the Japanese in 13 Pacific amphibious operations.

The "Pennsy" possibly has fired more main-battery ammunition on enemy positions than any other ship in history, and her performance is outstanding in the illustrious record of all the so-called "old" American battleships.

More than 11,000,000 pounds of steel have been thrown at the Japanese by the Pennsylvania's guns, and more than 75,000 pounds of ammunition, ranging from 14-inch main-battery projectiles to 50-caliber machine gun bullets, have gone through her guns.

One of her officers once wrote of the Pennsy: "The old girl shoots so fast and so much that at times she looks at though she's afire."

OFTEN REPORTED SUNK

That may be the reason why the Tokyo radio many times has reported the Pennsylvania sunk.

In addition to bombardment firings in 13 amphibious operations, the Pennsy was in the battle line in the decisive American victory in the night engagement with a Japanese surface force in Suriago Strait, Philippines, October 24-25 last year.

The Pennsy's keel was laid on Navy Day, October 27, 1913.

She began booming destruction on the Japanese at Attu in the Aleutians May 5, 1943. She has treveled more than 100,000 miles in the Pacific in the present war, from the Bering Sea to Southern Australia and from the United States Pacific Coast into the China Sea.

As a result of the Pennsy's work in the Attu invasion her skipper, Capt. William A. Corn, Annapolis, Md., was awarded the Legion of Merit.

As the flagship of Vice-Admiral Richmond Kelly Turner, Oakland, Calif., she led the invasion armada in the conquest of Makin Island in the Gilberts in November, 1943. She blasted the Japanese at Kwajalein, and in the Eniwetok invasion she tossed more than 700 main-battery projectiles at Engebi and Parry Islands.

The Pennsy's present skipper is Capt. C. F. Martin, formerly of Blackville, S.C., who was in command when the broad-beamed old battlewagon turned her guns on the Japanese in the Marianas invasion.

On this mission the Pennsylvania shuttled back and forth from Saipan to Guam. In one stretch her guns pounded the enemy for 16 consecutive days.

Her officers believe that on D-day at Guam, last July 20, she fired more major-caliber shells in one day than any other ship in the war.

LATER CAMPAIGNS

The Pennsylvania was the only battleship to fire on both Peleliu and Angaur in the Palaus attack last September. She was the first battleship to steam into Leyte Gulf in the Philippines. In 37 days of the Leyte campaign the Pennsy's gunners downed a heavy toll of Japanese planes.

On the morning of last January 1 the Pennsylvania was the first to fire on the Lingayen Gulf coast in the Luzon invasion.

Two men have served as the Pennsy's gunnery officers from Attu to Luzon. Comdr. K. S. Masterson, Washington, D.C., served through the Makin invasion. He was succeeded by Lieut. Comdr. Charles A. Burch, Baltimore, Md.

The Pennsylvania's consistent success has been earned by a veteran ship's company. Most of her crew have been aboard the vessel more than two years.

who survived the Tarawa invasion, the Betio islet had been designed "to withstand assault by a million men for a hundred years". Shore and air bombardment lasted three days. When the island was finally taken, after a much longer time and more losses than had been anticipated, it was said that the bombardment should have lasted at least 10 days before landing troops. This was a hard-won lesson, but they learned and naval gunfire got better and better. Another lesson learned at Tarawa was that the U.S. needed better training for both its pilots and its ship's gunners as to target acquisition and pinpointing fire. This led to the establishment of a new, special air and shore bombardment range for training on Kahoolawe in Hawaii.

Jeff got a chance to go ashore at Makin to see the results of the action. They had given the island a "Spruance haircut". Named after Admiral Raymond A. Spruance, the famous haircut referred to what air and shore bombardment prior to landing did to a piece of ground. It rendered the terrain virtually unrecognizable, like standing in a vast field of breakfast cereal. Every direction looked like every other direction. In front of Jeff was broken earth and trash, and to the right, left and behind him. It was a shocking sight.

He also saw how the Japanese committed suicide. They had very long rifles and they were for the most part quite short. They frequently wore tabbies on their feet which were a sort of slipper-sock with a separate sleeve for the big toe. When a Japanese soldier decided to kill himself, he would load his rifle, hold it against his chest, put the muzzle in his mouth and touch off the trigger with his toe. This would lift a hole about two inches across out the top of the head and result in instant death. Jeff learned that the sight of Japanese dead did not affect him at all. He had no mercy, no pity. He knew they were dreadful people in battle and they conducted themselves badly toward anyone they had under their control.

Left: The "Pennsy" got some press of its own later in the war.

One of the Japanese dead had in his papers his pin-up picture. It was not of a girl or a parent or a movie star—it was of a chrysanthemum. This struck Jeff as very telling. He already knew of their different cultural traditions and the idea that a front line soldier would get more pleasure out of looking at a picture of a flower (national symbol notwithstanding) than of anything else really struck him as indicative of the fact that they were very different people from himself. They ate different things and they drank different things and they prized different things. The fact that they committed suicide in great numbers when a battle was lost was also telling.

The stench also struck him. In his reading of history, it was not mentioned much and now it hit him. A battle field on D-plus-3 under the hot tropical sun of the Pacific stank so that it could be smelled before it could be seen. Later on in graduate school a professor told Jeff how terribly a slave ship stank

It was customary for wives and girlfriends to send pin-up photos to their men in the service. This was Jeff's favorite.

when it came into the harbor at Havana or Port Royal. Jeff said he guessed it was pretty bad but it did not compare with a Pacific atoll in World War II.

The next engagement in store for the Pennsy was the attack on Kwajalein, in the heart of the Marshall Islands, in January of 1944. On opening day they had been told that they were going to move in quite close and could expect to take a considerable pounding from the shore guns because the Japanese had been in the Marshalls for twenty-five years. (In fact, the outer islands were better fortified than Kwajalein, in the middle, and it was the best possible strategic pick for that reason. This was Admiral Chester W. Nimitz' decision.)

The Pennsy was destined to shoot the opening salvo. The water was dead calm and it was pitch dark. While they were moving into position, they could hear a big whispering, rustling noise that was difficult to identify. Someone remarked softly that it might be an incoming shell, but the sound was not right. They finally swung sideways and the admiral gave the order over the p.a. system, "Land the landing force!" Eight shells rocketed into the night and as they did, in that great orange glare, back between the masts Jeff could see the largest American flag he had ever seen. It must have been 50 by 40 feet. The captain had rigged it there on purpose. It was not proper to hoist the American flag in the dark, but he had made an exception. Someone got on the p.a. system and shouted, "Reveille, you sons of bitches!" *The Americans had come!*

That was a moment of grandeur. The battery officer on that side took those eight caseheads and had the primer pockets covered with cork and dented the sides to make places for cigarettes (everyone smoked in those days, except, of course, for Jeff who never did anything that everyone else did) and he made eight ornamental brass ashtrays for the eight senior officers aboard ship. Jeff was too junior to get one, but he approved of the gesture. On each ashtray was engraved "Reveille, you sons of bitches!", plus Kwajalein and the date: 1-31-44.

Also on Kwajalein, Jeff saw a beautiful, magnificent aerial hit that he will never forget. The Americans were quick studies and learned from each successive engagement. They had been scraping that island for several weeks with heavy guns and now it was time to go in. All the Japanese fortifications had been stripped of their cover by the shell fire. The island was bare white sand with bare white boxes sitting on it here and there which were the Japanese positions. The Pennsy went in close to provide defense against Japanese anti-aircraft fire in preparation for the U.S. air strike.

The U.S. air strike was delivered by a flight of B24's, four-engine heavy bombers called "Liberators". At that time everyone was very excited by the Norden bomb sight which was supposed to enable a bombardier to put his bomb right where he wanted it. The Pennsy went in there, standing by with her 5-inch guns to shred any remaining anti-aircraft defenses which might remain. (It turns out there were none. The preparation had been done well.)

Off in the distance, Jeff saw a formation of twelve B24's which had formed up in a single column, one after the other. They came in directly upwind so there would be no problem with wind deflection.

Another pin-up Janelle sent to Jeff was this photo of a portrait of Janelle painted by her friend, Doris Smith

127

They flew dead center into the eye of the wind, down low and slow. They were not too worried about Japanese anti-aircraft fire and there was no fear of any Japanese air power. As they approached, Jeff was looking at them through his binoculars and he saw the first aircraft open its bomb bay. The doors swung open and the bomber continued its majestic, straight-line approach toward the island. Then he released.

Each of those airplanes carried one bomb and it filled the whole bomb bay. Huge bombs. Their individual weights may have been 2,000 pounds or more. When the bomb separated, the sailor next to Jeff said, "My God, what are they dropping, P40's?" The first bomb

Sergeant George Sandona.

arched beautifully against the bright blue sky, and went straight over and down right inside the defense gun revetment on the beach. It was perfect.

Jeff saw the flash (there was no sound yet)—a big, blue-white flash and then a great cloud of black smoke. And then out of the top of the cloud came this double cannon—six-inch guns—turning end over end in the air and then dropping to the beach. Perfect.

Jeff went ashore the next day and took photographs of that anti-aircraft position and it was like an ant hill which had been opened with a knife. The passages were all half gone and the bottom had filled up with sea water. That was a beautiful bombing strike and those watching were impressed and heartened by the accuracy of the aircraft and the successful implementation of the mission.

The best rifleman in the detachment to Jeff's way of thinking was Sergeant George Sandona of Cle Elum, Washington. A tall, slim Italian, 29 years old, Sandona had enlisted in the Marine Corps on January 17, 1942. An accomplished hunter and collector of firearms, Sandona always kept his M1 in first class shape. Jeff found that this rifle shot exactly right for him, so he borrowed it each time he went ashore. He did this for two reasons. First, the Japanese would shoot first at any man carrying a pistol because this signified an officer and they were naturally interested in killing officers whenever possible. Secondly, Jeff had been shooting since he was a boy. He had won medal after medal for his shooting in the ROTC and had proven his excellence with a rifle in numerous hunting situations. He considered himself a rifleman above all and he was itching to put his proven skill to the best possible use in the war. That meant killing the enemy, one on one. He has always regretted not being in a position to do what he felt he could do best.

Sergeant Sandona was none too happy to be called upon constantly to give up his rifle to Captain Cooper for his shore patrols. He had no choice in the matter, but he needn't have worried about the care Jeff would take of the gun. They both appreciated excellence.

On Kwajelein Jeff had his first face-to-face lethal confrontation. He was often sent ashore to observe the results of the Pennsy's gunfire and to bring back reports on beach conditions in general. Twice he was sent ashore in charge of burial parties. On Kwajelein, he happened to be carrying Sandona's rifle, as well as a .45 caliber Peacemaker which he understood from reading a prominent gun writer of the day (who turned out to be wrong) to be more reliable than the 1911 Colt. At one point, Jeff and his patrol had taken cover when a Japanese soldier appeared, trotting toward them carrying a Japanese-type 97 automatic rifle without being aware of their presence. Jeff drew his pistol, aimed and fired one-handed, using the sights. His shot hit in the center of the man's chest at a range of about ten paces. The soldier fell at once without any outcry, kicked a little with one leg and then lay still. Jeff and his patrol stayed under cover and moved away from the area, so he had no chance to gather more information. The incident did not strike Jeff as particularly significant and he went on about the business of leading the patrol.

Sergeant Sandona kept a diary about the movements and activities of the Pennsylvania which has served as source material for this book.

The Pennsy went north up to the Eniwetok Atoll for it's next mission of shore bombardment. There Jeff had a close call. He had been ordered to go ashore on Parry Island to observe the action of their shells on the beach. While he sat out on the fantail of the Pennsy, out beyond close range, he held Sergeant Sandona's rifle and watched the approach of the LCI (gunboat) which was coming out to pick him up. The LCI was between the Pennsy and the beach and its orders were to come to the ship, starboard side aft, and pick up Captain Cooper.

Things went to hell, as they mostly always do in battle. It was very hard to see anything. There was an unusual amount of black smoke and the destroyers were shooting into the beach and there was a lot of debris being blown around and the wind was blowing from the beach out to the Pennsy. Jeff could hardly see the approaching gunboat. Then it got hit.

Jeff did not know what hit it, but it was mounted with rockets and they all started to explode and the gunboat looked like a 4th of July display as it came around slowly, turned and headed out toward the Pennsy, afire and bursting in all directions. Jeff was concerned about its coming alongside because it looked like it would blow up completely and kill everybody. It began to run out of rockets as it continued its approach.

The skipper of the gunboat, who was a JG in the Navy, was sitting in the wheel bucket up on the stern, surrounded totally by observers, of which Jeff was supposed to be one. The skipper was standing in the midst of all this, still in control with the wheel in his hand, while the boat just blew apart. It was listing badly as it came alongside and it was a mess. A friend of Jeff's who was deck officer at the time, up on the bridge, said he looked down from the bridge into the gunboat and it looked like a meat market.

They threw lines across and Jeff volunteered to organize the rescue because he was on the quarterdeck. He got a working party out there and they made the LCI fast to the Pennsy before it sank and started getting the wounded up over the side. There was, of course, not much they could do for the dead. Jeff took hold of the skipper and got him up over the side. He was covered with blood. Jeff took him down to his quarters and administered about two ounces of bourbon. This was strictly illegal but Jeff figured he could use it. They cleaned him up, got medical attention for his wounds, which were relatively minor, and then he went on up to report to the captain. Timing really is everything.

In those days, liquor was forbidden aboard ship, but it was more or less tacitly understood by the higher command that every officer was entitled to one bottle per operation. An officer could smuggle a bottle aboard in various ways and as long as he kept it out of sight and kept a lock on his safe, he would not be bothered about it. But one could not have two. In any case, that's how Jeff came to have bourbon available for the skipper of the LCI, who was understandably appreciative.

That afternoon, the commander of the landing forces ordered Parry Island be secured by sundown—no excuses. The troops moved down the atoll and the sun began to set. The tank commander took over. His people were designated by colors, geometric figures and numbers. So Red Square One was the squadron leader of the first unit. Jeff got on the air and listened. He heard the leader calling for positions from the various tanks.

"Red Square Two, how are you?"

"Sir, I don't think I can move. I think my starboard tread is broken."

"Okay. Three?"

"Sir, I can't train my turret. It's jammed."

"Four?"

"I haven't got any ammunition, sir. I've run totally out of thirty caliber and I only have four rounds of 75."

The tanks were expended, but the skipper wasn't because he had been supervising and not shooting. So he told them to cover him, he was going in. He got a storm of protest over this, but went in anyway. He went from around the left side along the beach all the way down to the end of the island where he turned and came back up the other side of the island. He didn't talk at all while he was doing this. When he came back on the air his voice was considerably higher in pitch.

"Okay, give me some light. I can't see.......*Not on me*, God damn it!"

He was pretty upset, but he did make it. Jeff never did catch his name but he admired his spirit.

On March 12, 1944, the Joint Chiefs of Staff endorsed a plan for the invasion of the Mariana Islands, key to Japan's "Inner South Seas Empire". This was to include the taking of Saipan, Tinian and Guam, in that order.

When the Pennsy left Eniwetok to go west, the "sleeping giant" was fully awake and his might was terrible to behold. Jeff went up to take over the watch at 8:00 a.m. and as he took position at sky control he looked around and saw what looked like the entire United States military underway. As far as he could see there was American military power. In the middle of the formation were lines of carriers, a double line of about six to eight carriers. Between them were modern battleships to protect them. Outside, more modern battleships surrounded by high speed cruisers. Then on out were the destroyers and then the Pennsy with other transports and heavy battleships for more protection. The sea was covered.

There is no way to recreate that impression for a person who has not seen it. It cannot be reproduced on the screen. There is no way to convey the massiveness of it. In the movie *Patton*, the general was supposed to have got up to the line in Sicily and said to the man next to him, "You see that? Compared to war, every other human experience is trivial." All Patton saw was 20 or 30 trucks and 16 tanks, but Jeff knows what he meant. Jeff's platform was about 50 feet above water level and he could see American military might vanishing over the horizon for 360 degrees. It made him feel like shouting, "Alright you little bastards. I bet you wish you hadn't started this!" This was the all-time greatest steamroller and it is not likely that anything like it will ever be seen again for the rest of human history. Moments like that are not experienced much. Jeff, young as he was, was fully capable of understanding and appreciating the magnitude and significance of what he saw.

"I will always thank my father and my mother for cultivating in me an ability to appreciate. The ability to appreciate is what makes life worthwhile, and you owe it to your children, and they owe it to their children to cultivate this quality. If you can appreciate, there is almost nothing in the world that does not have its grand side. The world is grand."

— JEFF COOPER

In April of 1944, the powers that be decreed a holiday in Australia and it was a memorable one. The Americans had saved Australia from the onslaught of the Japanese. The Japanese never landed on Australia, but they were right across the straits in New Guinea and they were coming forward, victorious everywhere in the beginning. The Australians were very much aware that they had stood in peril of their lives until the Americans arrived. Saviors are always popular, and there were other things.

In the first place, all the Australian men were off fighting, either in the Western desert or in Malaya, so the shortage of men who were neither very young nor very old was acute. In the second place, American men generally had manners that Australian men paid no attention to—such things as opening doors and lighting cigarettes and holding a woman's chair and ordering for her. In addition, the clinching point was that every American who landed in Australia was granted a year's ration ticket. Things were scarce in Australia as they were the world over. Cigarettes and silk stockings and clothes were good for trade, but the real clincher was soap. The Australians were allowed something like one bar of soap twice a year, but every American had a full ration. So the joyous joyfulness of liberty in Sydney was just as one might imagine it. Then they all packed up and headed back to war.

At Saipan, the shore bombardment commenced at 0540 hours on June 14, 1944. The Pennsy had launched her spotting aircraft and they were cruising along low and slow, near the beach, looking for targets for the ship's guns. One lone Japanese pilot picked up the Pennsy's OS2U and decided to take it out. He was flying the very latest, hottest and fastest version of the Zero. Instead of being clever and coming in behind the American aircraft and murdering it from a range of about 100 yards, he decided to dive on it from high and to the right. This was not a good plan, but he was probably very junior, the Japanese having lost practically all their experienced pilots at Midway.

This pilot came in with a high deflection shot from several thousand feet in about a 60-degree dive. As he came down, the American pilot saw him and kept his course, knowing the Japanese pilot would want to get closer before opening fire. At exactly the right moment, the American started a slow turn to the right, coming more and more directly under the Zero. The Zero pilot was lured into deepening his dive, pushing his stick forward to 65, 70, 80 degrees. Just when the American thought the Japanese was going to open fire, he made a hard right and the Zero flew right into the water. He just could not pull out. All the time he was on his way into the water for the last few seconds, the rear gunner on the observation plane was shooting at him with a twin 30. He got credit for killing that Japanese in the air, but to Jeff, that is not what it looked like. He thinks the American pilot just flew the Japanese pilot into the water and the gunner in the back just sprayed him as he went down. In any case, it was a fine piece of work and Jeff saw it very clearly from his position sky aft.

At one point in the fight for Saipan, the Pennsy was in formation with a number of other vessels, destroyers and a couple of escort carriers. Escort carriers are not full battle carriers, but they can transport aircraft. In this case, they could deliver planes but they could not receive them. The aircraft were P47's (Thunderbolts), called "Jugs", and they could get off the carriers, but could not land on them. At this time, a decision was made to refuel the destroyers. Destroyers have enormous horsepower and use up a great deal more fuel proportionately than battleships, so in operations, whenever there was a window of opportunity, the destroyers would be called alongside the battleships for refueling—a complicated operation. About the time this was well underway, air defense was sounded. "They are coming in from Iwo!" (Saburo Sakai, the great Japanese fighter, was flying from there at the time. He had been reactivated even though he was blind in one eye because the Japanese were desperate for pilots.) So, the Japanese were coming and the Americans had to cut the destroyers loose and get free.

The flat decks of carriers are always the first targets of any naval aviator. In effect, the Pennsy was fairly safe. The skipper of the carrier nearby had the kind of decision to make that shows why he wore four stripes. What to do with the P47's? Saipan was not fully taken and the airstrip was in question. If he launched the planes, they had no sure place to land, but if he did not, would they survive the incoming attack?

He decided to go. The P47's started launching into the air. It turned out later that the Marines on the beach were in the midst of fighting over the airstrip and a couple of them reported the surprising experience of shooting at Japanese and having American aircraft land right across their line of fire. The P47 squadron leader came in, put his wheels down, ran the whole length of the strip, could not stop, cartwheeled into the bushes, jumped out of his plane, ran for a hole and dived in.

The P47 squadron did not take any serious losses. The majority of the planes made it and so did the carrier. Jeff did not hear of any American pilots being killed in this action. The carrier was under heavy bomb attack, but this was post-Midway and the Japanese pilots just were not very good. Once the U.S. got the upper hand in the air, the Japanese were on their heels going backward. This happened with the Germans against the Russians on the Eastern Front and it happened with the Germans against the British on the

Western Front in World War I. As Erich Hartmann said about the Eastern Front, when he went to war the Germans had better aircraft, but they did not know much about fighting. However, the Russian aircraft were so inferior that the Germans were able to take their measure and build up invaluable experience. By the time the Russians got some good airplanes, the German pilots had 30 and 40 and 50 victories, whereas the Russians had 30 and 40 and 50 *hours*. The consequence was that the fighting became very lopsided. That happened in the Pacific after Midway. Admiral Nagumo knew what Midway had meant. He committed suicide on Saipan.

It was on Saipan that Jeff had his second personal lethal engagement. This time he had left the Peacemaker in his locker and carried his 1911 Colt along with Sandona's rifle. He and his radio crew were trying to locate the flank position of a battalion they were attempting to contact. Jeff crawled up on a broken palm tree in order to see better and what he saw was a clump of brown helmets below and to his right. One of the Japanese soldiers saw Jeff just as Jeff saw him and he turned in Jeff's direction, raising his rifle. The slope made his turn awkward. Jeff does not remember racking the action on his pistol, and it may have already had a round in the chamber. Jeff shot one-handed from a fully extended arm, at fairly close range. Jeff recalls the soldier's rifle being tossed upward upon the impact of the bullet, but again he did not stay to observe since there were many more Japanese then Jeff and his radio crew wished to engage in a fire fight. Jeff dropped off the tree trunk and moved away. The war continued.

Then there was the tremendous Tinian shot. The Americans had taken Saipan, the island to the north, and now they were getting ready to land on Tinian, the second island of the Marianas. In order to support that landing, all the artillery was moved down to the southern tip of Saipan. (There is a luxurious Japanese golf resort there now.) They placed the guns so that the smallest were farthest forward and the biggest were at the back because they had longer ranges. The smallest guns were 75 millimeter pack Howitzers, about the size of an ATV. They have short barrels, 3 inches in diameter and they are about 2 ½ feet long. The men at the extreme south end of Saipan had a battery of pack Howitzers. They were right at the edge of the sand, practically in the water.

Jeff was on watch topside and knew they were going to register their guns. They were going to fire onto Tinian to check their zeroes, so that when the landing took place the next day, they would know exactly where their shells would land.

The first gunner fired his ranging shot and it arched into the air and turned over and started down. It must have gone right through the overhead ventilator for the main Japanese ammunition depot for the whole north end of Tinian. That's the only way Jeff can explain what happened. Jeff saw the puff when the Howitzer fired and when that shell came down there was an incredible white flash, like a piece of sun. No sound, because he was several thousand meters off shore. The flash hurt his eyes. Then there was a great mass of black smoke and then the traditional mushroom cloud, straight up and roiling over and over into the sky and then spreading out at the top.

The thing that hit Jeff was the lack of sound. Then, across the water from the direction of the cloud, came this arc of white. It was the sound wave on the water. It looked like high surf—all white—and it raced toward the Pennsy. The destroyers were inshore of the Pennsy, standing watch, and Jeff saw one of them heel over when the wave hit it and then the wave came on. Jeff gritted his teeth and went up on his toes and put his fingers in his ears and waited and whew! It hit him. Very effective. He could just imagine that artillery second lieutenant turning around and saluting and asking, "Will that be all, sir?"

The Tinian operation was masterminded by Colonel Clifton Cates, father of Jeff's roommate. It was, as far as Jeff knows, the only perfect set piece of action of the Pacific War. Everything went exactly as planned—and that never happens. Like death and taxes, another sure thing is that a battle is not going to go as expected. Tinian, however, did.

The Pennsy moved on down to Guam, the third and final objective in the Marianas. By this time, shore bombardment by naval gunfire had been honed into an effective and terrible weapon. Most Japanese did not survive it, but those that did later said it was more terrifying, destructive and demoralizing than anything.

At one point in the reduction of Guam, Jeff had the night watch. They were on "watch-and-watch" at the time and everyone was staggering with exhaustion. The mission for the night was to make life miserable for the Japanese defending the beach. That did not mean continuous shelling, for that would deplete the supply of ammunition too rapidly, but it did mean keeping them from sleeping or moving.

What they did was wait until full dark and fire a star-shell which would go over the beach and suddenly become a junior-grade sun. This would catch any soldiers who were out in the open for any reason—food, water, ammunition. As soon as the star-shell lit they would follow up with an air burst of high explosive, shredding the ground with five-inch splinters. When that drove the Japanese into the ground, they would fire white phosphorus, a terrible weapon. It explodes and fires a shotgun full of pellets of burning phosphorus which cannot be put out because they contain their own oxygen. They come down in pieces from the size of a finger to the size of a fingernail and they burn through just about anything. When they burned through the various Japanese overheads they would set people on fire and when the men would come running out the Americans would fire the high explosive again.

This was cruel. It was a terrible war and Jeff and the men around him did not regret their parts a bit. It had to be done and doing it well was immensely satisfying. Admiral Nagumo's prophetic words were more true than anyone knew.

On the day of the main attack on Guam the Pennsy was located on the north of the Orote Peninsula which projects out from the island and flanks the landing beaches. This meant that the Japanese up on the peninsula could shoot into the flanks of the landing forces, assuming there were any Japanese left there who could shoot. So they put the Pennsy on the left flank of the landing and turned it so that every gun it had, all batteries, were all going to open up against the peninsula at the same time.

Later on at Quantico, Jeff met a Marine officer named Tom Witherspoon who was part of the first landing wave. When the signal went out to land the landing force, the Pennsy commenced firing. The main battery and the port side 5-inch, and the forward and aft port side 40's all opened at once with one awful thunderous crash and the ship was totally immersed in flame and smoke. Witherspoon looked over in alarm and thought the Pennsy had been blown up.

On that occasion, Jeff had a startling experience. When they got into position, he turned loose with the 20's. He was "sky aft" and had command of the after short-range weapons. They were shooting right into the beach. The guns were air-cooled and spring-recoiled and they got red hot. A too hot gun will not work and may even burst. The drill for the gunners was when the barrel looked ready to become incandescent, one man put on his asbestos gloves and ripped the barrel out and threw it into a water tube, maintained right next to the gun. Jeff was not aware of this.

He jumped up on an ammunition box with his megaphone to tell the starboard aft short-range guns to commence firing. Just as he was about to sound off, the gunners pushed this hot barrel into this tube on his right. It instantly boiled all the water in the tube and the boiling water burst out of that tube and struck him right across the back. All day long, debris had been landing around them and he had a bad split second. He was afraid to look down and see his intestines down around his ankles. He was blistered across his back, but it was no worse than that.

In the landing on Guam, after Witherspoon thought the Pennsy had been blown up, the first wave to hit the beach consisted of LVTA's (Landing Vehicle, Tracked and Armored). These are what they used to call "Amphibian Tanks" although they were not tanks because they did not have enough armor. They did have a turret and they were rifle-proof. They could only be hurt efficiently with something heavier. The gun on the top was a 37.

The LVTA's hit the beach and their orders were to find a hole and get down with their turrets just showing and support the incoming infantry. One kid got the bit in his teeth and charged forward shooting. He charged right through the Japanese defensive position and went right on up and inland and Jeff could see him from the ship with his binoculars going forward amidst smoke and fire. He almost made it to the top of the ridge and he just stopped. He just charged right into the teeth of the enemy until he was killed. He was disobeying orders, but he was doing his best to win the war. That is true heroism. He and the tank squadron leader on Parry Island would not have been faulted if they had stopped their actions earlier, but they chose to go forward, get on with it, make a difference. "Above and beyond" or not?

"Above and beyond the call of duty." In later years, Jeff and Colonel Bud Reynolds would often debate this issue. Bud maintained that there was no such thing—that if you can do anything to further your cause, that is your duty.

In terms of sheer hazard, the greatest number of deaths in Jeff's immediate presence aboard the Pennsy were "industrial accidents". People would fall down hatchways and get caught between two moving parts, etc. He saw one young man get brained right in front of him not more than three feet away. He missed his hold going down a hatchway and hit his head on the combing. It did seem a sad way to go.

Jeff got more and more nervous as the time approached for him to be relieved, hoping that if he got killed it would be more on purpose and not because someone dropped a helmet on him from fifty feet up. Accidental death seemed unrewarding, especially with supreme acts of heroism all around.

A good friend of Jeff's from his youth, Ed Stanton, was killed in the landing at Salerno. He was an infantry officer, a captain. When his landing craft hit the beach, the ramp refused to go down. Ed leaped over the side and raced around to see what he could do and at that point the ramp came down and drove him into the sand. He was killed stone dead right then. This was a lamentable way to die in action. Jeff knew he could not choose, but he hoped that if death came his way it would be in the midst of leading a charge with Sergeant Sandona's rifle hot in his hand.

August 21, 1944. One of the most remarkable pictures of World War II. An aerial view of the Pennsylvania as she fires her twelve 14-inch guns at the Japanese airfield on Orote Peninsula, Guam.

Home again

T he Pennsy was at the battle port of Efate, in the New Hebrides, when Jeff got relieved. It was summer of 1944. He did not know anything about rotation, but the policy was that a man who was on a forward battle station was entitled to be transferred back to the States after two years of continuous active duty. Jeff got his orders after two years, but it took six months for his relief, Captain Lessick, to find him. They used to make jokes about this in the wardroom.

"What's that out there?"

"I'm not sure, sir, but I think it's a whale boat with a Marine in it."

"What's he doing?"

"Looking for Captain Cooper, sir."

Jeff would take part in an action, come back, reload, go out to another action, come back, reload, and all the time Captain Lessick was trying to find him. This was not as easy as it may seem because a captain did not rate any special treatment and he couldn't just whistle up an air taxi to a forward battleship. And putting Lessick on a destroyer and sending him to find Jeff would interfere with the war. So, it took six months. This meant that Jeff had 30 months of continuous active duty and he fought in many actions. He had certification for six major battles, and that did not include any number of minor aerial and submarine confrontations.

Jeff spent as little time as possible briefing Captain Lessick and then he went ashore at Efate with his kit bag and his trunk and his orders. He was immediately assigned to Transient Officer's Quarters—a rather loosely organized concentration camp. This was no place anyone wanted to be. On the bulletin board was the name Maynard Chance. He had been in Jeff's battalion in high school! Jeff looked him up and he came down, picked Jeff up in his jeep and signed him out of the camp.

Chance's quarters seemed like paradise. He had his own house on stilts on the hillside, complete with palm trees and green grass. He was in charge of reassignments. He was a Marine First Lieutenant at this time and he managed to get Jeff on a ship going home. It was heading for San Francisco, a voyage that would take six weeks. Jeff's orders stated that he was due thirty days' leave until he was to report for duty at Camp Pendleton in Southern California.

Jeff does not recall the name of the ship that took him home. During that six-week trip, they did nothing but drill. This was the only way to keep people from going crazy. There were about 300 enlisted men on that ship who were being sent home, having served their time in the Pacific. They had Marine pilots, sailors and some Army people, but nobody had been given any authority. It was obvious that someone had to do something with the men, but nobody knew who or what that was. Jeff discussed it with the Executive Officer, who was a two-striper who turned out to be junior to Jeff. So, he deferred to Jeff's authority. Jeff jumped up on an ammunition box and took command of the passengers, under the general supervision of the captain of the ship.

Jeff set up and supervised drills and signed orders. Another thing nobody knew was that there was an elaborate welcome home program set up in San Francisco waiting for them. Jeff learned of it as they approached the end of their journey, but he had other plans. When the ship came up under the Golden Gate Bridge, a patrol craft came out to make contact. Jeff was all dressed and packed. He decided to improvise his own abandon ship drill. He jumped up on the rail and hailed the patrol craft and went aboard and asked them to take him to Pier 7. (This was somewhat irresponsible because he was relinquishing command without having anyone to relinquish it to. But he had not been assigned command in the first place and these details did not seem to matter in the excitement of homecoming.)

Jeff whistled up a taxi (surprised that there was one), got to the airport and called home. He was told to come to 500 North Rossmore and Jane Ellen would meet him there. He arranged for his trunk to be shipped and then found passage on a DC3 bound for Los Angeles and took off. They landed at the Burbank airport. There were no freeways in those days and the airport limousine went from Burbank to downtown Los Angeles right down Rossmore Avenue. Jeff got dropped off across the street from his house. He could see the three red stars in the front window. Gold stars signified service men who had been killed. Red stars signified men on active duty and Austeene had two sons and a son-in-law in service. Austeene met him at the door and, being a romantic herself, had arranged for Jane Ellen to wait for Jeff upstairs. It had been more than fifteen months since they had last seen each other.*

Jeff and Jane Ellen had been married for more than two and a half years and had a baby daughter, yet they had spent not much more than six months of that marriage together. Now they had thirty whole days completely to

*NOTE: See: "The Trip Home" in *Another Country* by Jeff Cooper.

themselves. This was heaven. It occurred to Jeff that being given thirty days of leave in the middle of a war was unbelievable, but he took it. He could sleep in! The greatest hardship on Jeff and everyone around him for the last 30 months had been exhaustion. As his leave began, he thought he would sleep 12 hours a day every day. He was surprised that he caught up on his sleep and felt well-rested with just one round-the-clock snooze.

For thirty days, they played. They left Christy with Floy and made their base of operations the house at 500 North Rossmore. They went up to San Ysidro and spent some time at a resort there. They played tennis and swam and danced and dined and made love and talked and made plans.

Jeff, ever an eager student with an immense capacity for taking in and analyzing information, was eager to discuss and dissect his war experiences from top to bottom. He was disappointed to find that everyone at home seemed to have been warned to change the subject whenever a returned military man started to talk about the war. He also found that when he *could* turn the talk to war, most people were not interested—they could not readily comprehend what he was talking about and they had lived through their own hardships at home. Jane Ellen was a good listener, but not many others.

The other thing that struck him was how irritating it was to hear someone say, "I know about that battle. I was in it." He knew first hand that amidst the smoke and the noise and the utter confusion, one could only *know* a very small portion of any battle. It really amazed him now to reflect on the major battles of antiquity when there were no radios. How could Alexander maintain control of his troops in a battle where the opposing forces extended from horizon to horizon and all he could see was dust? He determined that for the rest of his life, he would visit battlefields of all sorts whenever possible to see for himself how things must have looked to the participants. Like Jack and his real estate development, Jeff wanted to see the ground before passing judgement on the validity of any historical documentation.

Jeff had orders to report to Camp Pendleton, near San Clemente in Southern California. Housing was in short supply and they had to find a place to stay. Fortunately, Jane Ellen's Aunt Estelle and Uncle Walter Pixley (Floy's brother and sister-in-law) had a small summer house in Laguna Beach, several miles up the coast right on the Pacific Coast Highway, and they loaned it to the young couple indefinitely, until Jeff received a more permanent assignment.

They packed up their belongings and their daughter and moved into the small Laguna house. Jeff drove down to Camp Pendleton and reported in. He was assigned to Tent Camp Three, on the northern edge of the base, which was a training establishment where veteran officers were given the job of teaching junior officers (who had just come out of school) how to teach their people.

This assignment had appeal for Jeff. He was accustomed to leadership and training from his years of ROTC and his recent 30 months aboard the

Jeff, Janelle and Christy settle in to life in Laguna and duty at Tent Camp Three.

Pennsy. He was still frustrated that he was not able to use his skill with the rifle to shoot enemy soldiers, but if an infantry assignment was not forthcoming, then teaching was acceptable. He could live with his wife and daughter in relative comfort and safety and could make use of what he had learned to assist others. This was okay.

The command at Tent Camp Three ran on the war-time schedule of ten days on and one day off. The work started at 7:00 a.m. and the general in command, "Speed" Caldwell, made sure that the scheduled activity of the day began precisely at 7:00 a.m.—not forming up or getting ready. It was a fetish of his. All senior officers had fetishes of one sort or another. If rifle practice was the order of the day, rifles had to be firing at 7:00 a.m.. This meant that Jeff had to leave Laguna at a very early hour. He and Jane Ellen had only one car, so he carpooled whenever he could. Jane Ellen would get up in the black dark of the morning of the winter months in Laguna, get Christy up and packed into the car, get Jeff to work and then drive back.

There was not much socializing to be done in Laguna in the middle of the war. Their small loaned house was a wood structure on the ocean side of the highway. It was not far from the small center of town and Jane Ellen would put Christy in her stroller and walk to and from the grocery store.

When it became apparent that Jeff would stay awhile at Tent Camp Three, Jane Ellen went house-hunting and found a small rental house at 612 Puente

Street in San Clemente. At that time, this little house was quite isolated, but much closer to Camp Pendleton, so life became much easier and relatively pleasant. Jeff was familiar with the area around San Clemente from his father's association with Hamilton Cotton. Also, the Rasmussen family were relatives of Jeff's and their home in San Clemente served as quarters for General Caldwell.

General Caldwell was never Jeff's commanding officer, but he was a friend of the Rasmussen's and Jeff and Jane Ellen socialized with the Rasmussen's and as a result, they came to know the general and he took an interest in Jeff's career.

Art and Neil Rasmussen were close in age to Jeff and Jane Ellen and were Jeff's cousins. (Art had gone elk hunting with Jeff in college.) Their parents, Lucy and Neil Sr., owned the home in San Clemente. Lucy was a member of the well-to-do pioneer *Californio* family of Dominguez. Little Christy, nearing two years old, took to referring to Lucy and Neil with one hyphenated word, "Wucy-Bampa", and this became one of the earliest of the many Cooper family memories to be enshrined in family lore.

The various shortages they all had to endure because of the war were not arduous. They made do with what was available and were able to laugh about attempts to make meals out of some rather odd combinations. One common and continuous shortage was fresh meat. The butchers made the most of this and stories were told by young wives to their husbands about the lecherous suggestions some of these enterprising tradesmen made as to what they would like in exchange for a pork chop or two.

They were happy. Jane Ellen made the most of her role as wife, mother and homemaker and Jeff enjoyed his work. He was not getting shot at and he could spend every night at home with his family. The hours were long and the work was hard, but this was heaven compared to most of the alternatives.

Jeff was head of a training section on how to teach. He had never been formally trained in how to teach, but there were plenty of books on the subject and they were not hard to get. Jeff was a senior captain, about to make major, and he had four officers working for him—three captains and a first lieutenant. They would hold school in the classroom, teaching the second lieutenants in the class how to teach their troops to do things. They had all sorts of exercises—mainly small unit infantry exercises—attacking pillboxes and things like that. There was a lot of shooting and Jeff loved that. They did not shoot much with the pistol, mostly rifle, machine gun and mortar. They used the M1, which was a joy to Jeff. So he taught and he shot and he loved it.

Nothing lasts forever. "Speed" Caldwell recognized Jeff's ability as a teacher and put him on the list for Command and Staff School at Quantico. This was where they would send company grade officers (lieutenants and captains) to teach them how to be field grade officers (majors and colonels). When Jeff got the assignment to Tent Camp Three, it was supposed to last for about six months. That's not how it turned out. After only a little more than three months, the Cooper family had to pack up and move to Quantico, Virginia. It was early in 1945.

Moving across the country in war time was not exactly like taking a Conestoga wagon across the plains, but it was not simple and not without its challenging complications. They shipped what they could and packed up the "old" station wagon—the 1941 Ford in which they had nearly perished three years earlier. There were no special seats for children in those days, so they built a sort of nest for Christy in the back seat with pillows and blankets. Christy was a trooper and a good little traveler. Each morning, they would ask her what she wanted to do that day. She would reply, "Go bye-bye!" Jeff and Jane Ellen were concerned that the long trip over questionable roads in a car with no air conditioning would be a hardship for their two-year-old. Christy just continued to say she wanted to "go bye-bye" and enjoyed the scenery from the back seat.

They got caught in a major storm in the vicinity of St. Louis. The sky turned pitch black. The rain poured down. They came to a bridge over a river where the water was rolling across the pavement. Jeff was all for pressing on and after they got across, the bridge washed away behind them.

Bad weather, bad roads and various shortages aside, they made it to Virginia, and Jeff reported in as a student officer at the Command and Staff School. They had no place to stay and found that there were no military quarters available to them. They ended up in a small motel across the river from Fredericksburg called Brown's Motor Court.

This little motel was run by a Dutch family named Verberg. They were very congenial and had a large number of adolescent daughters who did various chores around the motel. Christy had long, blond hair and the Verberg girls delighted in practicing new "do's" on her whenever they could. Every time Jeff returned from the base, there would be Christy with a different hair style.

Brown's Motor Court was not convenient to the base, so they moved as soon as they found closer quarters. What they found was the upper story of a two-story home in Fredericksburg. They had one bedroom, a kitchen and a sleeping porch for Christy. The ground floor was inhabited by two maiden sisters. Christy, just beginning to maneuver through the intricacies of language and etiquette, discovered the name of one of the sisters and used to call out to her, "Yoo-hoo, Ann Harrison!" Thus was born another of the Cooper family anecdotes.

It was now early summer and the heat and humidity hit Jeff and Jane Ellen like a hot, wet towel in the face. The sodden heat of the Tidewater region in summer is legendary. Air conditioning was not common in those days, so they adapted as best they could. This meant washing down with a cool, wet washcloth, soaking the sheet in water, lying naked on top of the sheet and turning the fan directly on their bodies in order to sleep at night. There were

Jeff and Christy.

no ceiling fans and they had to keep screens on all the windows because of the innumerable bugs. Being born and raised in Southern California, Jeff and Jane Ellen were not used to the thick, oppressive heat. Jane Ellen did not complain, but she found it hard to believe that anyone would choose to live in such a climate.

Bug problems were also new. Cockroaches had invaded and conquered the kitchen in their second floor apartment. Jane Ellen waged war with them until she secured a tenuous victory—one which needed constant vigilance in order not to suffer a setback. All homemakers in cockroach country are veterans of this war.

And then there were the fleas. Little Christy developed a rash and Jane Ellen took her to the base clinic for their first experience with socialized medicine. The only doctor available had no experience with children. He discovered Christy had a mild sore throat, but had no idea what the rash was. Jane Ellen suggested chicken pox, but the doctor said, "Ah, no. I saw a case of that once and it didn't look like this." He sent them home with some nose drops. The rash persisted.

Jane Ellen remained concerned, but the doctor seemed to think there was nothing to be done. While in the grocery store one day, Jane Ellen started a conversation with a young woman who turned out to be a nurse. She took one look at Christy and diagnosed flea bites. She suggested they get rid of the mattress on the sleeping porch on which Christy had been sleeping—it had come with the apartment. They got rid of the bed and the mysterious rash went away, never to return. When the landlady, who was a sweet southern belle who did not appear to know much about housekeeping, came for one of her rare visits, she told Jane Ellen her dog had used that bed on the sleeping porch. She also told Jane Ellen that she had decided to sublet as often as she could because the apartment had never been so clean and free of cockroaches.

The one bug they enjoyed was the firefly. Fireflies don't qualify as pests and they lend a certain charm to the soft, warm nights of Virginia in the summer. They also enjoyed the bounties of a small garden, something heat and humidity actually encourage. They could hear the tomatoes growing. Jane Ellen was beginning to take up cooking in a more serious way now and decided that fresh was best whenever and wherever possible. She learned how to make an authentic Brunswick stew (a traditional southern dish made with squirrel and lima beans) from Ann Harrison and her sister.

They were still in Fredericksburg in August of 1945 when Japan surrendered and the Pacific war ended. As the school wound up and Jeff was finishing his classes, he was assigned to the G2 staff of the Third Corps, which was scheduled to go in to the south island of Japan, part of the plan to invade the Japanese islands and win the war. This was understood by all to be a rough undertaking. They estimated there would be one million American dead and twenty million Japanese dead. The plan was to give the islands the "Spruance haircut", land and conquer—the strategy that had worked time after time in the islands of the Pacific. Jeff understood that the best he could hope for would be an incapacitating wound. If he got seriously wounded and made it out to a hospital ship, he might make it. Otherwise, survival was not likely. He prepared as best he could for the worst. Then the atom bombs were dropped.

The dropping of the bombs and the ending of the war was an overwhelming, awesome experience. There was joy unbound. The sun shone on everyone after long years of unrelenting sacrifice and the unspoken danger of loss hanging over everyone's head. Men suddenly realized they were no longer in immediate danger of death. Women suddenly realized that their husbands were coming home and staying home and that their children would have their fathers. Life had unlimited possibilities after all. Celebration was the order of the day.

Word went around that there was going to be an enormous party at the Shoreham Hotel in Washington, D.C.. Jeff and Jane Ellen got a sitter and drove up with Marge and Mike Ryan (later General Ryan) to the party. They piled into the station wagon for the hour-long ride to the city. As they approached Washington, it struck them that all the lights were on! They had been subject to blackout for so long, this was a sight to see. At the Shoreham, it was elbow-to-elbow, with stars and stripes in every direction and good will unrestrained. Victory was sweet and relief was enormous.

Peacetime military life

With the end of the war, Jeff's orders were immediately changed since the Third Corps was not going to invade Japan. What to do with a recent graduate, grade of major? Jeff had aced out his intelligence training, which was odd since he had never given military intelligence any thought at all until he ran across it in class. In school he had been briefed on the four general staff categories: personnel, intelligence, operations and supply. He took full credentials in all of those, but he aced the two exhaustive exams in intelligence. The decision was made to keep Jeff on as an instructor in military intelligence. Jeff questioned Colonel Hogaboom (later General Hogaboom) about this because he had never seen an intelligence section at work and did not even know what it might look like. The colonel said not to worry, that Jeff would learn. He was right. There is no way to learn anything quite as well as to have to teach it.

If there is such a thing as a "natural-born teacher" Jeff was it. His intelligence, curiosity, remarkable memory, enthusiasm, use of logic and ease in front of any audience was motivating to even the most unenthusiastic student. He developed his own style: never talk down to any audience, treat even the most inane question to a politely delivered lucid answer, use the force of logic, demonstrate principles with numerous examples, corollaries and anecdotes, let students discover things for themselves, expect the best of your students, show them how and they will be motivated to deliver their best. Jeff excelled.

When Jeff got his assignment to the G2 section of the Command and Staff School as an instructor he was given quarters on base—Quarters 424 up on the top of the hill not far from the BOQ 17. The house was not luxurious, but it was comfortable. Still no air conditioning.

Jane Ellen settled in quickly and began to feel more at home. For the first time in their marriage, they had their own house (albeit owned by the mili-

A natural-born teacher.

Above: Quarters 424 at Quantico.
Left: Janelle in the back yard of
Quarters 424 in winter.
Below: Janelle and Christy in the
yard of Quarters 424.

tary) and she really began to relish her life as the wife of a Marine major and mother of a pretty, blond toddler. They began to entertain and enjoy warm friendships with their contemporaries, most of which last to this day. One of the other military wives decided "Jane Ellen" was too cumbersome a name among friends, so she shortened the name to "Janelle" and that name has stuck ever since.

As was customary, a woman was hired to help with the housekeeping several days a week. This was Anna, a large black woman who was the living image of the advertising character known as "Aunt Jemima". She lived further south and would come up on the train to work at the base.

Anna was friendly and helpful and would often look after Christy and assist with the entertaining as well as the housework. The house had a room referred to as "the maid's quarters" and Anna would sometimes spend the night there. True to form, bed bugs invaded and Anna got bitten. Janelle had the base maintenance people get rid of that mattress too and the problem went away. The septic climate was heaven for insects and all entertaining had to be done indoors, or at least behind screens.

Both Jeff and Janelle have fond memories of their months at Quantico just after the war. Their good friends included Mike and Marge Ryan, Bill and Mary Flake, Jane and Herbert Woodbury, Tab and Marie Collins, Howard and Vonnie Rice and more. A typical party would be drinks, followed by dinner, followed by more drinks, all the while engaging in lively conversation on all topics under the sun.

Jeff became famous for his "mysteries". These were delicious drinks usually made with lots of fresh fruit juice, rum and a liqueur. Several of these before dinner would loosen up even the stodgiest of people, and there were none among the Coopers' friends.

Jeff had given Janelle the famous cookbook by Escoffier, the renowned French chef. She also had taken a cooking class in Washington from Dionne Lucas, another famous chef, and subscribed to Gourmet magazine. Encouraged by Jeff's rather sophisticated palate and appreciation for her efforts, Janelle began to experiment with more and more exotic dishes. At one party, she decided to splurge and serve pheasant. She also made *crepes aux champignons* with lots of cheese on top. The pheasant took longer to cook than anticipated, and everyone relaxed with "mysteries". When they finally sat down to dinner, people were feeling very happy. Anna had stayed to help serve. As Anna held the dish, Janelle tried to serve the crepes. The cheese strung higher and higher, Anna lowered the dish, Janelle stretched her arms as high as they would go and still the cheese would not break free. Anna started to giggle and so did Janelle and the entire party dissolved into hilarity. All in all, a memorable evening and a great success. As Janelle commented, "Those Marines could put it away, but nobody fell on his face. You'd never find them under the table. Never."

Janelle and Harriet Rich with some of the first of the many Cooper family feline companions.

At dinner one evening at the Woodbury's, Jane served Mexican food. Jane was a Westerner, but Herbert Field Woodbury II was from the East. The meal was particularly spicy, much to the delight of Jeff and Janelle. Woody, however, gamely did his best but had tears streaming down his cheeks the entire meal.

Most all of these good friends were Marine majors and their wives. Officers really only associated with other officers of equal rank or one grade up or down. Thus majors would associate with captains, majors and lieutenant colonels, but did not mix much with lieutenants or colonels. It was just not done. Even so, at cocktail parties such customs relaxed somewhat and, as members of a school staff, the instructors of Command and Staff School all had fairly intimate social acquaintance with the entire group.

At one cocktail party, Colonel Hogaboom made a statement that Jeff remembers to this day. He said, "There are two transcendent experiences in a man's life that surpass anything else he may ever know. The first is when the one girl in the world says yes she will, and the second is when he stands on a hill, exhausted, bloody, hurting, covered with grime, with a gun in his hand and watches strong, brave, armed men flee in terror from his presence." Without a war you cannot get the second, and the sexual revolution has destroyed the first. So, according to Colonel Hogaboom's thinking, no young man of today can ever really live with the stops all the way out. When you stop to consider what may have replaced these transcendental experiences of 1945, not much comes to mind.

Jeff was teaching military intelligence and military history. Since Quantico was not far from several of the major battlefields of the Civil War, he included tours of them in his instruction. He also developed a presentation on the battle of Gallipoli, which was the Old Testament of amphibious war. It was the source from which the Marine Corps devised the theories of amphibious war which made it possible for the Allies to be a success in the Pacific.

When the British were thrown off of the Gallipoli Peninsula in World War I, it was assumed that proved that under modern conditions of machine guns, barbed wire and rapid-fire artillery, the idea of attacking from the sea against a defended beach was ridiculous—out of the question. Winston Churchill took a terrible pounding after World War I because Gallipoli was his idea and it failed. The Marine Corps came to the conclusion that this was an entirely mistaken concept.

In the landing on Gallipoli, the Allies violated 6 of the 7 important principles of amphibious warfare. If they had only violated 5 of these principles, the attack would have been a success, in so far as the Marine Corps could analyze it. So the Marine Corps formulated the basis of the theory of amphibious warfare and made it its own in spite of the resistance of other countries and other elements in the United States. When the Marines went to war in 1941 they had the doctrine and they made it work. Jeff taught this. He had a four-hour presentation from eight in the morning until noon telling people about Gallipoli.

The Marine Corps schools had the finest imparting system that Jeff has ever known to exist before or since. They had almost unlimited manpower. If Jeff wanted a chart, he would go down to the chart room and they would build it for him. If he wanted films, they had a film library. If he wanted a projector, one would show up for his use. He could turn his eyes away from the class and say, "If you will just examine the beach here....." and the lights would go out and an image would appear and an orange light would point out what he was discussing in detail. He would turn to the class again and the lights would come on and the image would fade out and they would get right back to the lecture. Technically, it was marvelous.

Standing ovations are common today—one sees them all the time and participates in them as well. In those days, they were not common. In Jeff's tour at Quantico, he knew of two standing ovations. They were not for politicians nor entertainers. They were in response to presentations. One was for a presentation given by Colonel Victor H. "Brute" Krulak (now Lieutenant General Krulak, retired) and the other was for a presentation of Jeff's. Krulak was in charge of a group of instructors who

Janelle on the left with good friends Tom Witherspoon and Jane Woodbury.

151

Lieutenant General Victor H. "Brute" Krulak, retired, was a Lieutenant Colonel when Jeff served under him at Quantico.

traveled to other military colleges and presenting the theory of amphibious warfare. On this occasion, they went down to the Air Force University at Montgomery, Alabama. They gave a full two days, starting at 8:00 a.m. on Monday morning and finishing at 5:00 p.m. on Tuesday afternoon. There were about eight officers involved in this effort. Jeff was in charge of the terrain portion.

When Jeff finished his four hours on Gallipoli, he got a standing ovation from the audience of mostly majors and lieutenant colonels. This was a fine sensation. He was a fairly new major at the time.

When the entire two-day presentation was over, they could see that the Air Force had been waiting to pounce. They had not said much and there had been very little discussion during the presentation. When they got to the end and Krulak asked for questions, a grey-haired senior colonel got up and said, "Colonel, I am most impressed at your presentation and I think all of us here very thoroughly understand *how* one conducts an amphibious operation. The question we have for you sir, is *why?*" The Air Force felt that there was no need for it since we had bombers. Krulak was just waiting for that like a tennis player waits for a high lob to come down at center court, and he put the answer across with absolutely unassailable reason. When he was done, he said, "I think that answers your question, sir." And that audience of skeptical officers all got to its feet and applauded. Those are the only two standing ovations Jeff ever heard of in his military experience.

Brute Krulak made a lasting impression on Jeff and they have remained friends to this day. Krulak is very short, and had to get special dispensation to get into the Naval Academy because he was under height. He cultivated a soft, unostentatious manner of speaking that concealed a razor-sharp intellect. It was common knowledge that you had never been chewed out until you had been chewed out by the Brute. This happened to Jeff and he has never forgotten.

They had an annual problem called the Advance Base Problem, where a team would work up a three-day presentation, complete with slides and sound and all the bells and whistles. This particular problem involved landing on the Canary Islands. Krulak was a lieutenant colonel and Jeff was a junior major. Jeff asked him at one point if he needed anything more and Krulak replied that he needed to know the height of the escarpment on the eastern shore of the island of Lanzarote, one of the islands of the Canaries. Jeff replied that as far as he could tell from the photographs, it varied. Krulak said he had to know exactly. Jeff replied, "Well sir, how would I find that out?" That was the wrong thing to say.

A few minutes later, when the tongue-lashing was almost over, Krulak said, "Cooper, you are wearing a gold oak leaf on your collar. Don't you ever, ever, *ever* ask anybody how to do your job again." Jeff did not resent this. He felt Krulak was absolutely right and admired him for pointing it out so forcefully.

"I met Jeff first in Quantico when he was an instructor at the Marine Corps Educational Center. He was an unusual instructor in that he was extremely penetrating. He did not accept an idea at face value. He went after the facts......He was a good speaker who always had his work done......He became a very skilled intelligence officer. His greatest interest gradually became teaching and he had a great flair for it......Jeff was not an ordinary man, not an ordinary Marine. He was acknowledged as about as intense as any Marine could be.......He was serious about his profession."
– LT. GENERAL VICTOR H. KRULAK

Around Thanksgiving of 1945, Jeff suffered a severe fracture of his right elbow which indirectly led to the development of practical pistol shooting, for which Jeff Cooper is perhaps most famous. He was running to catch his ride to the office when he slipped on some ice and landed on the heel of his right hand, telescoping his right elbow joint. This was a very severe injury, but they did not know how bad it was at first. The doctor on duty assumed the elbow was dislocated, so he had some corpsmen try to relocate it. This was excruciating. The head of the radius had broken into six pieces which were sitting inside his arm like six pieces of broken glass. The doctor immediately gave Jeff sodium pentothal and knocked him out.

The injury required surgery and fortunately Jeff had a very fine surgeon. No nose drops this time. This left him with no knob at the end of his right elbow, in a cast and in considerable pain, so he stayed in the hospital for several weeks. They gave him a shot of penicillin every four hours to fight infection and morphine for the pain. He gradually became addicted to the morphine, a condition which was no secret to the staff.

For awhile, Jeff was in the same room with Colonel Lew Walt, later General Lew Walt, who commanded I Corp in Viet Nam and became legendary. He was in for treatment of a gunshot wound. When you are lying in bed, waiting for your next shot of morphine, you get to be very chummy with the guy in the next bed.

Lew Walt told Jeff that there was nothing in life he liked as much as killing Japanese. To say that today would cause shock waves and a storm of protest from all sides. Walt had been a football player for the University of Colorado and when he got involved in the war in the Pacific he was a battalion commander. He got one of his Navy Crosses by maintaining his command after he had lost the use of both arms. He'd been shot in one, or received a shell splinter, and a tree fell on the other one. So he had both his forearms taped to his chest and his telephone taped under his ear and aides helping him move and he went ahead chasing the Japanese up Guadalcanal. He said, "What would anyone expect me to do, quit? I had been training those boys for months. I knew every officer intimately. I knew every NCO by first name and

I knew most of the privates. I had told them what to do and how to do it and they were doing it! You wouldn't expect me to let go of the operation now. I had my teeth in the Japanese butt and I was not going to let go!" Jeff thought Walt was quite a man.

Morphine does not actually kill pain. It produces euphoria, which makes a patient less concerned with the pain he still feels. That is its danger. When Jeff would get a shot of morphine, he still hurt but he no longer cared. He enjoyed the pattern of the ceiling tiles and liked the bustling of the nurses and was fond of the doctors. His addiction was obvious, but there was nothing else to do.

Right around Christmas of 1945, the doctor decided to let Jeff continue his recuperation at home and go "cold turkey" off the morphine. The thing that upset both Jeff and Janelle immensely when they understood what had happened was that neither one was warned about drug withdrawal. It was bad.

Jeff was not seriously addicted, but still it was bad. Jeff could not stand conversation, or the sound of the door closing, or any of the sounds or events of normal living. It was the opposite of euphoria. With euphoria, everything is good and with withdrawal, everything is bad. It was impossible for Jeff to be nice. He simply had to get up and leave the room whenever anything at all happened. Janelle was bewildered and hurt. Little Christy must have felt the same. This lasted, in addition to severe headaches, for about four or five days and then faded slowly.

In later years, Jeff would discuss his experience with doctor friends of his. He learned the difference between addiction and habituation. Addiction is a chemical necessity which one has nothing to say about and which can be cured. Habituation is the mental desire to extend euphoria and one cannot "cure it"—one simply has to rise above it by the power of will. One can handle narcotics habituation by mental power, but mental power or self-control is out of fashion today and rarely alluded to. Jeff's experience of becoming habituated to morphine gave him a certain advantage in understanding addiction and withdrawal and mental power over a habit. As is his wont, he has made the most of this knowledge and put it to use in his teaching.

After the initial healing period, it was obvious to the medical staff that Jeff had to use his right arm and elbow joint in particular in order to avoid losing its use permanently. The layers of adhesions were numerous and they had to be pulled loose. Jeff underwent extensive physical therapy that was extremely painful. One nurse was not quite strong enough to work his elbow with just her hands. She would put her arm behind his elbow and place her shoulder against his wrist and shove. This made him feel like shrieking, but he held out. She could tell when he had enough when the sweat broke out in big beads on his forehead and his face turned a pale shade of grey. It occurred to Jeff that playing more tennis would be good therapy for his arm, but when he tried it he could not manage the overhand serve. It was simply too painful.

Early work with the service auto pistol at the F.B.I. range.

By coincidence, Quarters 424 overlooked the swale in which the FBI shooting range was located and Jeff and Janelle could hear the crackle of small arms fire from their porch. This interested Jeff very much. He was not getting much shooting practice with his teaching duties and the range was right there. He made inquiries.

At that time the FBI was a guest of the Marine Corps and consequently had to be polite because the Marine Corps owned the land. Jeff was told that he could have use of the range if he wanted to pretend he was a student at the FBI Academy. As a Marine on full duty at the Command and Staff School, he could not very well sign up for classes, but he could audit. He would not take tests or receive any type of certifications, but he could participate in whatever instruction his regular duties would permit. So he signed up for various courses, got out on the FBI range and learned a great many things.

Jeff, having used the .45 automatic for years, wanted to use it on the FBI range. The FBI used revolvers exclusively. They told Jeff he could not use his .45 because their courses were not designed for it. Jeff suggested they ignore that fact and let him run each course as best he could. If any problems resulted, they could handle each as it came and no harm would be done. Jeff prevailed.

This produced a certain amount of consternation. One of the phases of the FBI course of fire which was known as the PPC (Practical Pistol Course) was the firing of five rounds at short range, reloading the pistol and firing five more. Obviously, the self-loading pistol was a great deal easier to use that

Getting more proficient with the draw.

way because one simply slapped in a new magazine. This gave Jeff a distinct edge because he could use the allowed time to shoot more slowly and concentrate more carefully.

The head coach said, "You can't do that. It's not fair." Jeff was a guest and was too polite to argue so he offered to shoot five rounds, put the pistol back in the holster, take five loose rounds from his pocket, load the magazine, put the magazine back in the pistol and shoot the additional five rounds, all in the allotted time. He did. The time allowed was so long that it was not difficult for Jeff to do this.

This irritated everybody because it became clear that certain advantages came from the use of the auto pistol. The auto pistol was scorned at the time for being unreliable. What Jeff learned was that it was a matter of complexity, not reliability. Understanding how the auto pistol works, making sure the pistol you have in your hand is of high quality and maintaining it properly very nearly negates the reliability factor. This fact was apparent to Jeff, but slow to become accepted by more than just a few.

Jeff's use of the auto pistol continued to irritate the FBI. He started entering all sorts of police-type tests and exercises and would come out way ahead. Partly this was because he was a good shot, quick and well-coordinated and practiced in the art of concentration, but mainly because he was using a very superior weapon. It was not only superior in mechanical operation but delivered much more power, which Jeff assumed would be much more effective when striking a human target.

That got it started. Jeff became very much interested in shooting the automatic pistol in what he calculated was a realistic fashion, rather than target shooting. He suspected that using the .45 to shoot targets was like using a Ferrari to pull a plow. The .45's best use would be in combat.

In turning his attention to pistol shooting in the context of the FBI, it occurred to Jeff that if one were called upon to use a pistol, there was a good chance that it would still be in a holster. The military people did not agree with this because they felt that if you know there is going to be a fight, you will have plenty of warning—if not days then minutes. The military taught nothing of drawing a pistol from a holster. Jeff saw that the use of the pistol had the potential to be used against sudden lethal violence at short range and that presupposed that the pistol might not be in one's hand.

Teaching himself how to draw and shoot from a holster had the added advantage for Jeff of constituting effective therapy for his damaged arm. It was also fun. True to form, it was also unique. After drawing, it was still the form to shoot one-handed from the "FBI crouch" position. Other developments came later.

Located at Quantico along with the schools was the Marine Corps Equipment Board. One of the officers assigned to this board was Captain Howland "Howie" Taft. Howie was an experienced tournament pistol shot and he had a distinguished pistol rating with the military and had used his weapon to some extent during the war. He had been a middleweight varsity wrestler in college and was lithe and strong. Howie and Jeff got to know each other well and began a long friendship. Howie was intrigued by Jeff's activities over at the FBI range and they began to shoot together and push the limits of what was the norm up to that point.

Jeff became utterly fascinated and dedicated to the study of defensive pistolcraft. He and Howie began to do everything out of the leather. They discovered that the 1911 pistol really was the way to go. It was the most efficient and controllable duty sidearm available and they could make it do whatever they wanted it to do, once they learned how. They traded first places in all the competitions and left everyone else in the dust, muttering.

In the fall of 1945, Jeff and Janelle decided it was time to add to their family. The war was over, Christy was growing, friends were abundant, teaching was rewarding and life was good. They discussed it and agreed that a three year span between children was just about ideal. No two in diapers at the same time and very little sibling rivalry. Their planning matched their luck and soon they were expecting their second child in June of 1946.

Janelle has always referred to their second child as their "socialized medicine baby". In the wee hours of the morning of June 9, 1946, this second baby started to arrive and Jeff packed Christy in the car and drove Janelle to the little family hospital on the base. The main hospital was too heavily involved with veterans and their health problems, so a small wooden building close by was dedicated to "family care." Jeff dropped Janelle off and went home with Christy to wait.

There were two nurses on duty. They prepped Janelle and put her in a bed and left her alone to await further developments. No one called the doctor. When Janelle, having had the experience of one birth already, felt that it was time, she called for the nurse. Nothing happened. She called again. Again nothing. Finally a nurse popped her head in and said, "Why didn't you use the buzzer?" Janelle hadn't seen it and nobody had bothered to point it out to her.

They wheeled her into the operating room and stood over her. One nurse asked the other, "Have you ever delivered a baby before?" "No. Have you?" "No." Before Janelle had time to become really concerned, a doctor she had never seen before strolled in and delivered their second baby, another girl, this time brown-haired.

They had decided on Jeffrey Pixley again for a boy's name. For a girl, they had decided to use Austeene's middle name, Paralee. Again, they had no middle name chosen and did not see the need for one. Again, they were delighted with their healthy new baby and did not consider her gender a disappointment in any way. They decided to call her Parry. They took her home to meet her three-plus-year-old sister and now there were four.

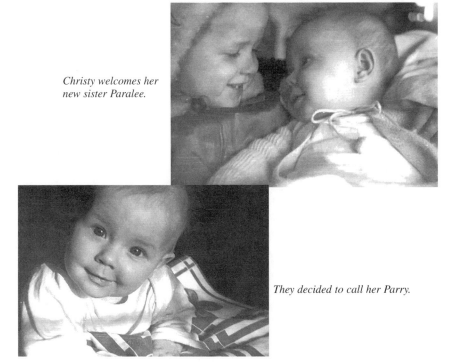

Christy welcomes her new sister Paralee.

They decided to call her Parry.

More peacetime military life

Life was very good for the growing Cooper family on the base at Quantico in 1946, 1947 and 1948. Jeff was teaching and shooting and doing well at both. Janelle was busy as a homemaker, wife and mother. The group they socialized with was composed of highly motivated, intelligent, gung-ho Marine officers and their wives. They played tennis and had dinner parties and explored some of the countryside. They saw a lot of movies, both because it was a convenient form of entertainment and because they had a certain connection to the film community in Hollywood. Heinie had by this time married a successful actress whose stage name was Claire Dodd—we always knew her as Aunt Ann.

For some reason, it was difficult to get good babysitters. On one occasion, Janelle discovered that a sergeant's wife was available and she asked her to stay with the girls for the evening while she and Jeff went to Washington. When Janelle stopped to call home, she got no answer so they left the city and headed back to the base right away. The babysitter had found the liquor cabinet and was passed out on the floor. Fortunately, the girls were fast asleep.

The base theater was within easy walking distance of their quarters so Jeff and Janelle started taking turns going to see the latest feature film while the other stayed home with the children. This entertainment neatly avoided the babysitter problem. It did leave them, however, with a noticeable void in their choice of cultural events since most of those took place in Washington.

They enjoyed their children. Jeff has always maintained that infants are not his cup of tea, but as soon as a child was able to carry on a conversation, he took an interest. As his girls got old enough to talk and go for walks, he took great pleasure in their company. They bought Christy the latest tricycle which they called "The Red Racer" and she pedaled at high speed all over the neighborhood.

Most of their friends were also raising families. Lieutenant Colonel Gordon

Heinie's second wife, Ann. Her stage name was Claire Dodd.

Janelle gets in a little target practice.

Janelle on a Sunday morning breakfast ride.

Christy's "Red Racer" under the Christmas tree.

Gale and his wife lived just across the street and had a boy named Donald who was the same age as Christy. They played together and went to each other's birthday parties. The Ryans had children who played with the Cooper girls. Jeff remembers Brute and Amy Krulak's children who were small boys in short pants. One of them went on to become Commandant of the Marine Corps.

General Shepard was the base commander and he was a Virginia horseman. His idea of a great good time was to have breakfast rides on Sunday mornings. Brute Krulak would go along on these rides although he was never comfortable on the back of a horse. His legs were not long enough to get a good grip on the body of the average sized horse and he was understandably uneasy up there.

Besides "mysteries", Jeff perfected all kinds of mixed drinks—that was the custom. Having his superior officers to dinner was part of Jeff's social obligation and he remembers fine times with them all—Colonel Stonecliff, Colonel Baer and others. Quarters BOQ17, just up the street from 424, had a big ballroom and often had organized dances, so Jeff and Janelle could keep up their skill in dancing.

> *"The Marine Corps was small and close knit. We socialized with Jeff and Janelle quite a bit. Janelle brought charm to the scene in addition to her beauty."*
>
> *– LT. GENERAL VICTOR H. KRULAK*

Although Jeff was not an enthusiastic player, they played tennis. Janelle got quite good and at one point took second place in the ladies' base tennis championship.

162

of his detachment and gave and received orders. He had not shot scores of enemy soldiers single-handedly or stabbed anyone with a knife or strangled anyone with his bare hands. Mainly he did what he was told. When he looked at his fitness reports after the war he had his share of "outstandings", but he did not come away with any tremendous feeling of personal pride in accomplishment.

It was obvious to Jeff that with 100 more majors than billets, medals won in action in World War II would count heavily—they would have to. Others counseled him to simply stay around and retire at the proper time and go play golf. This did not appeal to Jeff. So he pondered his future with a distinct uncertainty.

Jeff's tour of duty with the Marine Corps schools was up in 1948. He was assigned to a special operation—a task force that was so secret that when he asked about it up in Washington he was immediately hushed. He was not supposed to know about it. Task Force 128. It did not deserve that degree of secrecy.

Task Force 128 was a multi-purpose Naval amphibious exercise going from the East coast of the United States, through the Mediterranean, through the Red Sea to the Persian Gulf. The purpose of the expedition was to chart the Arabian side of the Persian Gulf, especially with regard to water supply, in case the U.S. had to operate there. This was amusing because nobody ever suggested that the U.S. would make war in the Persian Gulf! The task force was put together with a Commodore—that is a four-stripe naval captain given the temporary rank of one star in order to command a task force—and was composed of a jeep carrier, a couple of destroyer transports, a command ship and some destroyers. This task force pulled out and headed east.

So Jeff was assigned again as Marine liaison to the Navy. He was an obvious choice because of his duty aboard the Pennsy, but he would not have chosen it for himself. He was a Marine and he understood and appreciated the fact that there is a world of difference between the Marine Corps and the Navy. Of course he did as he was ordered.

The task force was to be away for several months and Jeff's subsequent orders were to be attached to Amphibious Group 2 in San Diego. So, while the Red Sea assignment got underway, Janelle made all the arrangements to leave Quantico, move herself and their two little girls and all their belongings to San Diego, find housing and set up housekeeping. She also had to find a second car.

These tasks which fell directly on Janelle's shoulders were enormous, the kind that break up marriages and cause others to seek psychotherapy. Janelle simply went about it. She was absolutely intrepid, courageous and totally uncomplaining. Other men with assignments that took them away sometimes had problems on the home front that interfered with their performance of duty. Not Jeff. He could always rely on Janelle and the fact that she could handle anything that came her way with intelligence and efficiency, leaving him free to do the task at hand.

Janelle found a fairly new, one-story home on Point Loma and settled in there with five-and-a-half-year-old Christy and two-year-old Parry. She also bought a modern, space-ship type car called a Hudson. Cars had undergone a considerable transition due to war time technological advancements. The new models were touted as "cars for the new age." They kept the 1941 Ford station wagon, but now added a new, forest-green beauty to their garage.

The staff of Task Force 128 was composed of a Naval officer in command (Commodore Rogers), a Marine officer (Lieutenant Colonel Piper) as his chief of staff, and an assortment of Marines and Naval officers because it was essentially an amphibious operation. They were going to study the beaches and go ashore a good deal. For troops they had a Naval Underwater Demolition Team—the ancestors of the Seals—and a Marine reconnaissance company which was useful for whatever they were going to do beyond the water's edge. They also had some air support on the jeep carrier.

So Jeff went off to the Mediterranean and saw some more of the world. They put in at such places as Gibraltar and Naples and Athens, all of which are interesting liberty ports. In Naples, they got a chance to see the ruins of Pompeii, and Jeff went over to Capri to swim in the Blue Grotto. He'd done it before as a child. In Greece, they put in to the harbor of Piraeus at Athens just as the mist was clearing and the sun began to shine on the Acropolis— a magnificent sight! In Piraeus they picked up some more units to go with them on the expedition, including a big carrier with an admiral on board. Jeff had the opportunity to look at ruins not only in Athens but also in Corinth, which is a very interesting place to visit, especially for one steeped in Greek mythology as was Jeff.

He also had a chance to go north and put in a couple of days with the American Advisory Group which was involved in the frontier war between Greece and Macedonia. Jeff hardly touched down, but he came away with an entry in his file as having experience in irregular warfare which figured in a later assignment. When he found out about it, Jeff thought it was rather like walking down Wall Street and receiving a certification of qualification as an investment counselor.

They went from Athens to Smyrna in Turkey where Jeff acquired a severe case of dysentery. It was so severe it was nearly fatal. He had come back aboard ship feeling all right and had to go on watch at 8:00 p.m. as they pulled out to sea. He began to feel bad during the watch and at midnight, when he was relieved, he stumbled below feeling miserable. He had developed a case of explosive dysentery, dehydrating rapidly with both vomiting and diarrhea. He could not keep anything at all down and the condition worsened. In a Naval force one never asks for help except during working hours because everyone is exhausted and sleep is precious. At sunrise, Jeff finally got some medical attention. The ship's doctor squirted something like ether down his throat to paralyze his gag reflex so he could pour some water into him. The doctor told him he would have had only a few more hours, perhaps four or five, before he would have died of dehydration. This was not an ordinary form of what is known in Latin America as the "turistas". It may be that it was a form of cholera. In any case, he recovered rapidly and hardly missed a day's duty.

When they got to Egypt they went through the Suez Canal. They did not go ashore at either Alexandria or Cairo but proceeded down the Red Sea. Their equipment began to show signs of distress. It turned out that the prevailing wind moved down the Red Sea from north to south at almost exactly the cruising speed of the formation, which was about eleven knots. This meant that while they were underway all of their flags were hanging still. They were in effect in a "dead calm". It began to get hot. They went all the way down past Mocha and Jeff called attention to the fact that this was where "mocha" coffee comes from. They did not put in at Aden but went around the horn and headed east along the south coast of the Arabian Peninsula.

The ship's doctor ordered that all officers wear dark glasses on watch top-side. It bothered Jeff because he had never worn any kind of spectacles in his life and having something resting on the bridge of his nose gave him headaches. The order was probably a good idea because the kind of harsh glare they were subjected to could cause problems. It was a severe salt haze, permeated by a hot sun which made no particular point of origin of light. It was just a blast of silver blowing into their faces.

For purposes of personal hygiene, they ordered that all crew members wear sandals rather than shoes. They found out right away that one could not stand a four-hour watch on a steel deck in sandals unless one had grown up doing it. So they received permission to wear shoes while they were actually on watch and they would then take them off for the rest of the day.

The formation wandered through the straits of Hormuz and on up to Qatar and Dahran and then to Kuwait. They were supposed to explore the coast of Arabia for purposes of determining the feasibility of landings. They would put people into the water and go ashore and determine if that location provided a good landing site and if not, search for some place better. It was August and the heat was intense. They decided on a work day which began at 4:00 a.m. and concluded at 11:00 a.m. This put them in the water doing their various chores in the dark of the morning when the heat was not too bad. The only time anyone was comfortable was in the boats in the early morning with the waves sending a fine sea spray into the air around them.

In Kuwait, which was a village and not the metropolis it is today, they would cruise around on the beach. Once, they were invited to dinner with an important sheik. They all went ashore with the Admiral in the lead. They entered a tent where a feast of mutton and rice had been prepared. The sheik sat at the head of the rug on the floor and his honored guest, the Admiral, sat at his right. To the sheik's left was Colonel Piper and so on down the line on either side. A whole roast sheep was placed on the rug directly in front of the sheik. He reached out and plucked the eye out of one of the sockets of the sheep's head and handed it to the Admiral. He took the other one for himself and raised his hand in a sort of toast or salute to the Admiral and popped the eye into his mouth. Jeff was fairly adventurous in his eating but he was glad not to be the Admiral. The Admiral sat there in his whites with his ribbons and wings and stars and popped the other eye down without turning a hair. That is obviously one reason he was an admiral.

It was the theory at the time, and it proved to be true, that when people are in extreme heat such as the Persian Gulf in August the best thing for keeping them healthy is physical conditioning. They began to have the young men, the Marines and the UDT's, exercise strenuously every day from the time they assembled in Virginia until they got through their assignment in the Persian Gulf and were headed back. They played medicine ball and did various types of calisthenics. They never had a case of heat exhaustion although they were working out in the direct sun. The Marines wore helmets but the UDT's wore nothing on their heads and they all came out fine.

By contrast, the aging boozers among the men died. The military officers seemed to be in fair shape, but the civilians had a bad time. The merchant ships were being manned by middle-aged to elderly old salts who did not stay in shape and who were powerful drinkers and they lost seventeen dead in the Persian Gulf during the course of their mission. There was nothing much to be done about it, except down in the bowels of the ship they had a photo lab which had to be kept as cool as possible. The ship's air conditioning had almost completely collapsed and what was working was diverted to this lab. Jeff would go down to this lab to look at photos and have to step over cots. Merchant sailors were in effect dying from heat exhaustion down in the coolest part of the ship.

Commodore Rogers, obvious to everyone, was verging on a mental breakdown, showing acute paranoia as one of the symptoms. He was so continually placing officers under arrest that he was running out of officers to be in charge of the officers who were under arrest. When an officer is placed "under hack", he is still on duty, and another officer of equal or superior rank must accompany him everywhere, wearing a pistol. The officers all started having to guard each other. At one point, Jeff was in charge of a Lieutenant Commander in the Navy, (the same rank as Jeff as a Marine major), at the same time that he was in charge of Jeff. While this was happening, they had occasion to go off and look for breaks in the escarpment which led from Kuwait up into Iraq. They went off in a desert car to accomplish this while each was under arrest and in the other's custody. The entire situation was nerve-wracking.

The Commodore would come up to the bridge and ask, "Where are the destroyers?"

Izmir, August 3, 1948. Left to right, Piper, Hagenah, Cooper.

"Over on the other side of the Gulf, sir."

"What are they doing there?"

"That's where you sent them, sir."

"I never did anything of the kind!"

They would then pull out the order in writing and when he would see evidence that he had written an order, signed it, and then forgotten he had, he would simply grab the paper, crush it in his hands and throw it over the side. He was pretty far gone and it was trying on everyone.

On the way home the issue came up regarding how to report the mental failure of Commodore Rogers to his superiors. It occurred to the other officers at about the time they were going through the Straits of Gibraltar on the way home that they ought to put him under arrest. He was getting violent. He was throwing people out of his state room physically and destroying reports. He had gone over the edge. The other officers held a conference. There was a way of placing a commanding officer under arrest, but it was a terribly dangerous thing to do, as it should be, and it was frightening. If one was wrong in this, the results could be disastrous.

Colonel Piper was the man to do it, because he was number two. Jeff was glad he was not in that position. If they had displaced Commodore Rogers, the Admiral would have had to convene a court martial and try Colonel Piper and the rest of the officers for mutiny. Justification would have been a hard thing to prove.

Colonel Piper decided that if it had been wartime, he would place Commodore Rogers under arrest and take his chances with the court martial. But, since it was peacetime and they were due to make it home in seven or eight days, he declined to do it. Jeff could not wait to get off that ship. His nerves were stretched. Almost at the moment they tied up at the dock at Norfolk, Jeff was gone. He had stored the station wagon in Virginia so he immediately headed west across the continent to make sure he was out of earshot before any courts martial were discussed. He joined Janelle and Christy and Parry in the little house on Point Loma in San Diego, California and did not look back.

Jeff and Janelle were happy to be back in California and pleased to be stationed in San Diego. San Diego has always been one of the most pleasant duty stations possible, and today it is one of the most pleasant large cities in the United States. They took advantage of the beach and the zoo and the balmy weather and appreciated the lack of bugs. The only fly around was the one in the ointment as Jeff was still attached to the Navy, assigned as intelligence officer to Amphibious Group 2.

Amphibious Group 2 did not even have ships assigned to it on a permanent basis. When a mission was decided, a force would be put together and the command would be put in charge. They worked out of a command ship. It was an AGC, which was in effect a liberty ship supplemented with a forest of radios for intense communications all over the world.

In early 1949, Amphibious Group 2 was assigned some ships and some men and sent to the Aleutians to find how best to operate in sub-Arctic conditions. This was another several-month assignment and, like the Persian Gulf, was interesting but not fun. Red Sea in summer. Gulf of Alaska in winter. Jeff learned first hand about both extremes.

As intelligence officer, Jeff had a certain amount to do with the civilian press. These people were junior newsmen who came aboard the AGC and were supposed to be put up and taken along on the expedition. In Jeff's eyes, they were totally insufferable. Military courtesy was deeply ingrained in Jeff and while he did not regard the Admiral as a particular hero, Jeff felt the man in charge should be treated with proper

Parry and Christy on Point Loma.

respect, addressed properly and not taken lightly. On one occasion, one of the newsmen got furious about something and burst into Admiral Fischler's cabin without announcement. He began calling the Admiral names so Jeff grabbed him by his shoulder, spun him around and booted him right through the door and onto his fanny in the passageway. That might have become a highly publicized "incident" today, but at the time it seemed to Jeff to be the only proper thing to do.

They all had trouble with the weather. The AGC was not very big, perhaps 10,000 tons, and it

Major and Mrs. Cooper.

tossed around on the sea like a cork. A lot of people went down with seasickness. Mealtime proved to be tricky. Down in the wardroom the only way to keep one's feet was to hook an arm around a stanchion. The ship was alternately 45 degrees up one way and then 45 degrees up the opposite way. In the morning the mess boy would come in and hand Jeff a plate of scrambled eggs and toast and then leave to get the coffee. By the time Jeff got the eggs onto the toast to make a sandwich edible with one hand, the mess boy would put a cup of coffee in his other hand, making him incapable of eating or drinking.

That ocean in the Gulf of Alaska between Puget Sound and Anchorage is one of the roughest waters in the world. It produced waves Jeff could not believe. When he stood on the bridge and saw whitecaps a few yards away higher than his head, he knew he was in heavy weather.

They went to Kodiak. Being winter, it was almost always dark. It would get light enough to see around dimly for about five or six hours in the middle of the day, but the rest of the twenty-four were black. Jeff seemed always to be on the bridge wearing foul weather gear with sleet blowing into his face. It was not as cold as it might have been, not below zero, but being topside in a Naval vessel in high seas with the temperature around thirty degrees and the wind around thirty knots is cold enough.

The most fun Jeff had was playing chess with the weatherman, who had lots of time on his hands. Jeff never got really good at it, progressing to a 2½ on a scale of 1 to 10, but he was good enough to have fun.

171

Amphibious Group 2 completed the Aleutian assignment. They reported that UDT's can work in cold water. It was hard on them and they got extremely uncomfortable, but nobody died. They returned to San Diego.

Jeff was unhappy with his professional life. He saw no place to go. He felt he was at a dead end as a Marine officer. He had missed his chance for an infantry assignment, had no medals to show for the big war and had no new war on the horizon. He saw no place for himself and he was getting more and more frustrated.

One day, Jeff was out romping with the girls. He was lifting Christy out of the back of a truck when some little kid crashed into the back of his knees with a tricycle. Jeff could not drop his daughter on the street so he held her up and went down full force on his right knee on the pavement. He shattered his right patella like an eggshell. He was completely out of action and hospitalized with his leg in a cast. Now he had ample time to consider his future.

Austeene had remarried. She had chosen for her second husband a handsome bachelor in his forties who was eleven years her junior. His name was Warren Watkins. She had known him prior to Jack's death and perhaps well because Jeff remembers hearing Jack accuse Austeene of having an affair with Warren. Austeene's reply was that she did not do that sort of thing. Warren owned and ran a candy manufacturing company in Los Angeles he had inherited from his father.

Heinie and Phyllis were both married and raising their families in the Los Angeles area. Heinie and Ann had a daughter they had named Austeene (known as "Heidi"), and Phyllis and Art Balinger had a son, Keith. (Phyllis also had another son, Tony, from her second marriage—to screenwriter Niven Busch). Janelle's parents both lived in Los Angeles. All of them wanted Jeff and Janelle to "come home" and settle into civilian life. Warren offered them a modest home on 8th Street rent-free to get started. Janelle had planned a third child for arrival three years after Parry's birth and, right on time, their third baby was due in September of 1949. They considered where they would want it to be born and thought about the hardships constant moves brought upon military families.

When Jeff regained the use of his leg and was declared fit for duty, he resigned his commission. Looking back, he considers this a mistake. It may or may not have been. He certainly gave it careful consideration. At the time, he did not realize that his "warrior mentality" might be out of place in civilian life. He contemplated his options, discussed it at length with Janelle and made his decision to look around for something to do as a civilian.

CHAPTER

17

Korea

J eff and Janelle left San Diego and moved to Los Angeles into the small, two-story house on 8th Street owned by Jeff's stepfather. Christy was six years old, Parry was three and baby number three was on the way. The house was relatively old, but conveniently located just down the street from Wilton Place Elementary School, where the girls would be going to school. At age 29, Jeff set about looking for gainful employment.

This was a very difficult period for both Jeff and Janelle and neither looks back on it fondly. Memory fades more rapidly when it comes to the unpleasant experiences in life and the details of this period of about one year have not remained clear in either Jeff's or Janelle's mind.

Jeff was not trained to enter any civilian profession. Although he had a college degree and had been highly successful as a teacher in the Marine Corps schools, he was not officially certified as a teacher and besides, teaching did not pay well. His degree in political science did not lead to any particular professional slot. His skill with firearms was not readily marketable. The fact that he was widely traveled, mature, well-read, sophisticated, cultured and intelligent did not translate into immediate job opportunities.

He found, as many had found before him, that the only entry-level positions which required no particular training yet still promised the opportunity to make enough money to support a growing family were in sales. Jeff gamely tried several of these, insurance and cars among them. He was a dismal failure. He was constitutionally incapable of ever being a success as a salesman. He felt there was no reason to tell someone else what he should have. He thought people should know what they want without being told and to treat them otherwise was insulting. This was not a winning attitude in any sales force.

" I first met Jeff not too long after Ginny and I were married, when he was between wars......he lived on Eighth Street with Janelle and the girls. He tried selling life insurance with New York Life. We were one of his first sales. We did not buy very much but he took us to Perino's for dinner to celebrate and I'm sure the dinner cost much more than the commission. He went the day before, 'cause he knew how to do these things, and ordered dinner with the chef. We still have that policy."

– CHARLES ARTHUR

As unmotivated as he was at selling products, he was more inept at selling himself. For any job supplicant, selling oneself is a very useful skill, but Jeff found it difficult if not impossible to blow his own horn and ask for consideration. He still does. It is not that he has no pride or confidence in his own abilities, quite the contrary. It's just that he feels accomplishment should speak for itself and anything else is undignified.

Money became tight and they had to squeeze pennies. Janelle's upbringing came in handy now because she had lived with Floy, who knew how to make the most out of every nickel. Frugality came easily to Janelle, but Jeff was discouraged, believing he was letting Janelle and his girls down.

The brightest spot in this period was the birth of their third daughter on September 12, 1949. I was born in that same Good Samaritan Hospital where Jeff, Janelle and Christy had all entered the world. They decided to name me Theresa both because they liked the name and to honor Jeff's Great Aunt Tess, Louise's sister. (Aunt Louise had died in an auto accident in Arizona in 1945. Miradero had reverted to the City of Glendale. Theresa Virginia Dean, "Aunt Tess", had been provided for financially in L.C. Brand's will and she lived for many more years in a high-rise apartment building in Los Angeles, near the famous Farmer's Market.)

It occurred to Jeff and Janelle that "Theresa" might be shortened to "Terry" and that this might make distinction from "Parry" difficult. They overcame this problem by tacking "Linda" onto the front of their new baby's name with the idea that I could drop that name later. They started calling me Lindy. Jeffrey Pixley was the name they had still kept in reserve in case of a boy, but again they were not unhappy with a girl. Another healthy baby was fine, whatever its gender.

Linda Theresa "Lindy" arrives in September of 1949 in Los Angeles.

174

Jeff and Janelle socialized with Heinie and Ann and Phyllis and Art, plus various other friends from their youth who were still in the area. Janelle was very busy with three children, although she did have some part-time help in the form of a young student who acted as a live-in "mother's helper". Austeene took over as social chairman and arranged dinners at the Los Angeles Country Club and did what she could to help Jeff find employment. She meant well but her constant attention amounted to hovering and it did nothing to help Jeff's mood. Jeff was also not impressed with Austeene's second husband, discovering him to be not at all intellectual and finding that he compared most unfavorably with Jack. Jeff missed his father acutely.

When North Korea decided to invade South Korea in the early summer of 1950, Jeff knew immediately that his place was back in the Corps. He was a reserve major and signed up right away, making sure they knew he was ready to go wherever and whenever they needed him. The first thing he discovered was the Marine Corps had no need for reserve, field grade, intelligence officers. What they needed were captains, sergeants and lieutenants in large quantities. They did not need a major whose specialty was intelligence, G2, small wars and military history.

Jeff was determined to play a part in the Korean "police action" so he flew back to Washington, D.C. to find out what was going on because nobody seemed to know in Los Angeles. He started looking up people in the telephone book. He found several officers he had known from the war and the one he contacted first was Colonel Deakin. Deakin had been a company officer at Basic School when Jeff was a new second lieutenant. Jeff called and Deakin asked him to dinner. Deakin asked Jeff if he knew Bob Cushman and Jeff told him he did, that Cushman had left the Pennsy when Jeff had gone aboard. Deakin said he thought Cushman would like to talk to Jeff. Jeff said he was willing and got on the phone with Cushman, who invited him to his house. It amused Jeff to find that Audrey Cushman was very impressed with his Hollywood connections. When she found out that Rita Hayworth and Lana Turner and Randolph Scott had all been entertained at 500 North Rossmore, she was very excited.

Bob Cushman was then a lieutenant colonel. He asked Jeff if he had ever been to Australia. Jeff said yes. Cushman then said he thought they could use Jeff's services. It turned out that Cushman was a branch director for the Central Intelligence Agency. He told Jeff to go home, get ready and come back to work. Jeff was to report to Cushman's office and there was much work to be done there as well as overseas.

It was now necessary to move Janelle and three children all the way across the country and find another place to live. Again, housing was in short supply, but Jeff managed to find a brand new house in Arlington, Virginia which he purchased. It was ready for the family by January of 1951.

Janelle was all for it. Years earlier, when Jeff had told her that he was going

Another new home (the white house on the left). This one was at 3808 30th Road North, North Arlington, Virginia.

into the Marine Corps, she thought it was something like the Foreign Legion. She had no military tradition or background in her family and she had to learn everything from the ground up. ROTC was a highly integrated and acceptable part of both her high school and college experience, but it was not something she really knew a great deal about. She had enjoyed their stay in Quantico and the friends they had made, so she had nothing but good thoughts about the Marine Corps. She also understood Jeff. She knew that his interests lay in military matters and she knew how miserable he had been for the last several months. If there was a war, Jeff felt it was his duty to be in on it and Janelle felt the same way.

> *"Having been exposed to the military in a time of war, I could not help but feel that the whole concept of protecting the country, providing security for the country, the men making it possible for the women and children to not be in harm's way, was a very attractive one and I was always very sympathetic and liked the people in military service. They seemed to be worthwhile. I don't think that I had a sudden realization that Jeff was unduly preoccupied with fighting and war and weapons. It just kind of came with time, and the fact that he wanted to get back in because of Korea seemed to me to be perfectly natural."*
>
> *– JANELLE COOPER*

In January of 1951, Janelle and her three daughters, aged sixteen months, four and a half and nearly eight, boarded a night flight bound for Washington, with a stopover in Chicago. She held me on her lap, thinking I would sleep, but no such luck. I squirmed and struggled and thrashed around the entire

176

flight, robbing Janelle of any rest. In Chicago it was very cold and by the time Janelle had walked to the terminal, unpacked warm clothes and dressed the girls, she had missed the connecting flight to Washington. They were soon booked on a later flight, but Janelle had no way of informing Jeff because the new house did not yet have phone service.

Their original flight was turned back to Chicago because of engine trouble. This was the flight that Jeff was monitoring. In the meantime, the flight they did catch landed in Washington. They were cold and tired and had only the address of their new home. It took quite awhile, but Janelle finally found a cab and got herself and the girls into it with all their luggage. Just as they got started, Jeff came around the corner in the trusty old station wagon. They made the transfer and went home.

The house was a nice, new two-story and waiting for them was Anna, from their days at Quarters 424. Janelle was very glad to see her. Anna took charge of the children and Janelle collapsed into bed for a well-deserved night's sleep.

The new house was in Bellevue Forest, and was to be their home for the next two-and-a-half years. The builder lived next door. His name was Phillips. He and his wife had two children, Donna and Billy, who played with the Cooper girls. Jeff and Janelle always had music in their house—music of all kinds with the singular exception of country and western. On one occasion, they were playing a classical record when Billy came over. His comment was, "Oh, that's that *other* music. There is country-western music and then there is that other music."

Jeff reported for duty in temporary offices by the reflecting pool. It developed that Bob Cushman, who was now a full colonel, had brought Jeff aboard under somewhat deceptive circumstances because they wanted someone who knew Australia. Jeff did not really *know* Australia, but it could be said that he had been there. When Jeff reported for work he found that Cushman was about to leave the CIA. Now that there was a war on, he had to fight it. Cushman went back to regular duty as a regimental commander and Jeff was left more or less stranded amongst a bunch of spies. Again, an infantry assignment had eluded him.

They stayed in the house in Arlington and Jeff was sent on one tour after another, most for months at a time, without ever being able to tell Janelle either where he was going or what he was doing, either before or after the fact. He still won't talk about it to anyone, not in any detail. Even though the Korean War is now history and the world has changed and many of the people Jeff served with are dead and the rest would most likely not care, Jeff will not discuss the details of what his assignments were during his attachment to the CIA. His reasoning is simple. He took an oath of silence on the subject and to him his word must be above reproach. It makes no difference that circumstances have changed to the point where such disclosure on his part could do no harm. He will not budge. *He gave his word and he will not take*

Left: Jeff's pilot in southeast Asia, "Dutch" Brongersma. Below: When Jeff sent this photo to Janelle, he wrote on the back, "This is the other side of the 'office' where I spend considerable time."

it back. This stubborn and perhaps excessive adherence to principle is characteristic of Jeff and is a large part of both what appeals to his admirers and what exasperates his detractors. Compromise does not appeal to him.

What he was doing was devising and participating in various operations designed to unsettle people in the rear of the Chinese armies so that the Chinese would have to divert troops from Korea to look after insurgencies at their back door. Jeff had his somewhat phony specialty in small wars which he had received as a result of his thirty minutes in Macedonia, when he was on his way to the Persian Gulf. He did, of course, read all he could get his hands on regarding such activity and the CIA had it all. He read and learned

These operations were not as successful as the CIA hoped for because of the peculiarities of Chinese society. The Chinese that the CIA were able to recruit were all incipient warlords and their ingrained idea of the way to wage war was to march on Peking at the head of an army with their banners waving. This was not the way. Whenever they tried it, the communist armies knocked them off easily.

The CIA wanted their recruits to infiltrate the populace and do dirty work behind the lines. But Chinese society was too stratified. Chinese officers could not act like peasants. They very definitely did not want to. Even had they wanted to, they would not have known how. Among other obstacles, they could not speak the correct dialect. Jeff's activities did inconvenience the Chinese, but not to the degree desired. Many of the people Jeff worked with were killed very quickly.

Jeff spent most of his time in Washington, D.C., on Saipan and in Bangkok. He also touched down in Korea from time to time. During this period he learned to fly. He did not get to be an accomplished pilot, but he did a lot of flying in a DC3 and his pilot was quite ready to let Jeff have the controls after he had told him what to do. Jeff learned to do most things that could be done in that plane except navigate in the dark.

He spent quite a bit of time up country in the boonies and he discovered that back country food in Southeast Asia, at least where he was, was good. It was a great deal more to his taste than the food served to him in cities where they were trying to cater to Westerners. Back country food was all rice-based and he liked rice to begin with. He would always ask for *cao paht. Cao* means "food" and also "rice" and *paht* means "fried". What he would get would be a bowl of brown rice with little pieces of miscellaneous edible tidbits mixed in and a fried egg on top. Delicious.

In back country "bars" they had a diverse supply of Western beverages. They had champagne, whiskey and often Guinness. When Jeff would ask for a Guinness, the people around would all laugh. Guinness, being an acquired taste, had been sold to these people as a sexual restorative. They laughed when this fairly young man seemed to be seeking aid from this beverage. Jeff did not learn the cause of their laughter until later.

Another interesting thing to Jeff was the *kwai*—the water buffalo which is domesticated in that part of the world. They were a common sight. They were usually managed by little boys. The small boys would learn to live with the buffalo and the buffalo would get used to having them around and as long as they were around, the buffalo were quite manageable. If anything happened to his boy, a buffalo would become quite antsy. They would kill people quite regularly if they were left without their boys in charge.

Jeff learned that the orientals in that part of the world were very fond of teasing the *farang* or "franks" (Westerners). Any chance they had to panic an Anglo with a snake, real or fake, they would do so with glee. There was one young man with Jeff's command who had to be sent back to the States because he could not stand this. He was terrified of snakes, and the more he reacted the more they teased. Every time he went to bed, he would find something like a coiled rope strategically placed for maximum effect.

Jeff had a remote base in the mountains and he needed a man to take charge. He was sent a man who seemed to have all the right credentials and had one of the best resumes Jeff had ever seen. He was a former Marine major who had been a professional boxer and had also earned a PhD. Jeff figured that as soon as this new man understood what was needed, he could be sent to the remote location with Jeff's full confidence. This was done.

Jeff soon began hearing rumors that things were not as they should be. He arranged to drop in on that remote base unexpectedly and found that his recruit had gone completely native. He was sitting with crossed legs on the

Jeff's caption for this picture read, "Me and the boys." Jeff is third from the right.

In Bangkok.

Staff car – a Riley, made in Britain.

floor with a turban on his head and dancing girls all around. He had decided to become the "white king" and had proceeded accordingly. Jeff admired his vision but could not keep him on.

Jeff had some contact with the French and the subject of drugs came up. Jeff asked the colonel whose base he was visiting if his troops had trouble with opium and he said no. He said the troops got liberty once in a while and they would go to the big city and get completely bombed out on opium. Then they would come back and get back to work with no ill effects. Jeff found this quite interesting because of the reputation opium had for being powerfully addicting.

It was a very interesting part of the world and Jeff took it all in. There were plenty of tigers, snakes, enemy troops of all descriptions, sometimes fighting against Jeff's command and sometimes against each other—and overall was the opium trade. This started in the mountains where the local peasants would sell the sap to a collector. He would take it to a distributor who would take it to a market and sell it to a transporter who would take it to a big city. Each time the product changed hands its value would go up by a huge percentage, so that the peasant barely made a living but the dealers overseas made millions. The authorities regarded it as a harvest problem. The last thing they wanted to do was eliminate it. They wanted to profit by it. They would make sure the traffic was interrupted just enough to make money for them but not enough to discourage the trade entirely.

During Jeff's service in Thailand he had his third experience with face-to-face lethal violence. He was up near Chiang Rai, traveling on the road in a Land Rover driven by one of the constabulary people. They were not in a battle zone and they were not expecting any action. As they drove along, a non-descript-looking oriental stood up in the ditch alongside the road and fired a burst from what turned out to be a 9 mm Sten gun. Three of his bullets struck the car—one low, one high and one squarely through the door, passing just in front of Jeff. Jeff shouted at the driver to stop the car. This was probably foolish since they had no idea what they were faced with, but Jeff got mad and his first instinct was to flatten the gunman.

Apparently their attacker had emptied his weapon because he stayed on his feet and attempted to change magazines. The range was fairly long— about 25 meters. Jeff fired from the car, which had skidded crosswise in the road. He fired one round from his .45 auto, again with one hand and again using the sights. Then he and his driver dove for cover, one on each side of the road in the ditch. They assumed that there were more people involved so they remained under cover for long enough to discover that the gunman was alone. As Jeff eased up onto the road he could just see the sole of one foot back where his target had fallen. He and his driver quickly ran back to where the man lay, the driver quickly went through his pockets for papers and Jeff took the Sten.

The two of them got out of there quickly and Jeff never did acquire what he thought of as a satisfactory analysis of the situation. He believes that the opium traders felt that Jeff's outfit was infringing upon their territory and sent one man to knock off a *farang* as a warning. The man they sent was most likely a troublemaker whose demise was not entirely undesirable. Jeff of course was not interested in the opium trade, but they did not know that.

With this third personal kill under his belt, Jeff concluded that the big-bore pistol is a reliable man-stopper when its shot is well-placed. He also concluded that hand-held, full-auto fire is a waste of time. Time has taught Jeff that neither of these conclusions is infallible, but as general rules they still apply.

Jeff had a friend who was a very senior policeman, one of the bodyguards of the dictator. This friend did a very smart thing. His salary was not much, but he had several Mercedes' and mistresses and country houses and all that sort of thing. In that part of the world at that time a police officer making an arrest was entitled to half the monetary value of the haul as assessed at headquarters. One night this friend left a party Jeff was attending at about 10 p.m. and came in the next morning with about $35,000.00, tax-free. His trick was not to take anyone with him when he made arrests. He was a hard man and a brave man and a pretty good shot. (Jeff did a certain amount of recreational shooting during this period and had seen him use his .357.) When he made a haul, he made it himself. His other friends said he would not last long this way and that opinion seemed true to Jeff. He has often wondered what became of him.

Footboxing was another local custom that intrigued Jeff. He liked to see how the combatants could box using both hands and feet and he went to see the local matches whenever he had the chance. Jeff concluded that using the foot is a waste of time. He figured that anytime a boxer took one foot off the ground on purpose, the other boxer could grab it and sling the first man clear out of the ring. This was not the custom, but Jeff saw no reason it could not be done other than the dictates of custom. Footboxers insist this is not true, but Jeff remains unconvinced. It's possible that too much practicality would abolish the sport altogether.

Jeff became very fond of the 3.5 inch Bazooka because it had such a wonderful effect upon the upcountry chieftains. When he got off an airplane, Jeff carried this thing, slung over his back, with the two pipes, unjoined, and one bomb down his leg. He would proceed to tell the head man that in addition to so much ammunition for his Mausers, he would also receive one of these and then Jeff would put it together and demonstrate it. Jeff would blow up truck beds and such and they thought this was great. Then he would make a great show of giving the chief the Bazooka—without bombs. This was his ace in the hole when negotiating.

Jeff also learned a great deal about the social conventions of the Southeast

Still in Bangkok. Jeff's caption for this picture read, "This lad on the left is from the U.S. Embassy. His expression typifies the State Dept's attitude toward the whole show."

Asians. They are generally much more relaxed than the Arabs or the Hindu. The Thais were sort of slaphappy. They laughed at almost everything, very much like the Zulu as Jeff would learn later in Africa. Jeff taught one Thai to parachute. When they threw him out of the airplane once, his line stuck so they had to haul him back in at some trouble and danger. When he got back in the plane he broke up in hysterical laughter and then fainted.

One of the recruited Thais got involved with a girl he wanted to marry. The family said he first had to do his required six months as a monk. He had to join a monastery, shave his head, take the begging bowl, wear the yellow robe and go out and have the citizenry feed him. He would be forbidden from eating anything between noon and sunrise of each following day. He joined the monastery. He was not a bad guy but he was full of mischief and he disrupted the entire group of monks. After a few weeks, they turned him loose and agreed to count his service as the full six months. He got out and married his girl. This you would never find among the Hindu. The Thais are more light-hearted and tend to see the humor in life.

Jeff learned enough military Mandarin to conduct the range exercises. He had a good ear for language and had been exposed to many foreign tongues since his first European trip at the age of six. He found it did not take much effort on his part to duplicate sounds and he knew enough of inflection and rhythm to do well with just about any word he tried the first time. In addition,

The Cooper family, May 1953.

he found he could remember sounds just as well as things he had read. This facility was to become even more useful later on.

It was an interesting tour. It did not do Jeff much good career-wise. He got into several clashes with his superiors in Washington. He learned early on that speed is very important in guerilla warfare. By the time Washington cleared him for an operation it was often too late to matter. He developed the habit of telling them he would be proceeding with such and such an operation unless he heard otherwise. By the time they could get the necessary committee together to decide whether or not what he was proposing was approved and communicate their decision to him, the operation was over. This did not make Jeff a lot of points. He got pulled back on occasion for not being as well-disciplined as they would have liked. Jeff disagreed. He had learned from Krulak that a military man should be given a mission and told to accomplish it and not be told how. The government in Washington did not play that way.

At one point, Jeff arrived in one of the capitals in the region and not more than three days later a conspicuous double agent was found face down in the bay. Jeff immediately got all sorts of clandestine compliments on this "hit" in which he played no part.

Looking back on his Korean War activities, Jeff feels they accomplished some good. They scared some people to death and embarrassed some others who needed it and did the best they could to disrupt the Chinese communists. They gave good value for the money. They were not expensive. As he puts it, "I don't think I cheated the taxpayers during this time. I gave it my all and we accomplished a certain amount." Jeff is not sure how much of a secret their activities actually were. All the intelligence services of the world keep good track of each other.

All the time Jeff was traveling in and out of Washington on various assignments, Janelle was left alone with the girls for several periods of many months at a time. Jeff would leave and then come home again and then leave again, all unexpectedly for Janelle. This made it impossible to plan anything, but being the mother of three children is time-consuming, challenging and demanding and Janelle kept busy. She planted another garden and again they entertained often. Washington was a busy place and many of their old friends came through on their way to overseas assignments.

In Los Angeles, Austeene had wanted to get Janelle more involved in the society scene and had encouraged her to join the Junior League. Acceptance into the Junior League was much like being accepted into a social sorority—one had to have connections. One had to know existing members and be sponsored and then approved. Jeff's sister Phyllis was a member and she became Janelle's sponsor. Janelle's membership was approved just about the time she moved to Arlington.

In the Junior League, members were required to do a certain number of hours of volunteer work. Janelle worked with children with cerebral palsy in an Arlington clinic. She disliked it. It was more depressing to her than anything else. She worked as an assistant to a woman who had charge of about twelve children with various degrees of handicap. Janelle was competent in her role as assistant, but on those occasions when she had to be left completely in charge, Janelle felt her limitations strongly. She learned that this was not her calling.

At this time, Jeff and Janelle had their first experience with post-World-War-II commercial transactions. Up to this time, they had always made choices and paid cash, as had their parents before them. Because of the severity of the cold on the east coast in winter, they had decided Janelle needed a fur coat. They chose a beautiful beaver coat (which Janelle still has) and told the saleslady to wrap it up. She asked how they wished to pay and they said they would pay cash. She asked if they had an account there and they said no. She asked if they wished to open an account and they said no. She excused herself and called a supervisor. The supervisor came up to them and said, "I understand you wish to open an account." They replied that they simply wished to buy a coat. The supervisor explained all the conveniences of their various payment plans. When Jeff and Janelle insisted, she had to call in a male supervisor. He also tried to get them to open an account. They finally got the coat. They also had a lesson in the history of commerce. At that time, if a tradesman sold a high-ticket item for cash he made no money because all possible profit was in the interest on the payments. This still holds true today but not as strictly. The practice was new then and nobody had figured any profit at all into any purchase made with cash.

Janelle's brother Jay had gone on to receive his PhD from Stanford and had begun a career as a geologist with an oil company. He had worked for a time in Ecuador where he had met and married his wife, Consuelo. They had begun their family and had a boy just older than Parry and another boy just older than I. Jay had occasion to do some research at the Smithsonian Institute for Creole Petroleum, so he took the opportunity to stay with his sister and her family in Arlington. Janelle put him upstairs in the master bedroom and she stayed downstairs with the girls. They really enjoyed this time together catching up on family news and adding details to the events of the last several years.

"I stayed with them for.....a month and there I became fairly well acquainted with Jeff.....and I was very much impressed with him. The more I spoke with Jeff and observed him the more admiration I had for him because every time I would bring up a subject, something that I had happened to touch on or something that I knew something about, he knew more about it than I did. He always knew everything about everything and could recall all this....."

– JAY GLENN MARKS

During these years, Jeff and Janelle decided to begin for themselves the old Cooper family tradition of giving a large Christmas party each year. In the Marks household where Janelle had grown up they did not have parties. On the other hand, Jeff had seen first hand how well his father's punch had worked in creating the proper holiday spirit in his guests, so he perfected the Zombie punch. Janelle took this opportunity to experiment with fancy hors d'oeuvres and a tradition was reborn that was to last for almost twenty years.

Jeff and Janelle made another decision as well at this time. They decided that their family was complete with three daughters. They did not want a son at this point because he would have three older sisters and they thought that would not be a good situation for a boy. They thought it would be difficult for him to be a single male with three females. They also thought their family was big enough. If they were going to be able to give enough attention to each child, three was manageable. So Jeffrey Pixley Cooper was not to be.

The parking situation in Washington is ghastly and always has been. Jeff discovered that there was a little section at each of the main buildings in the downtown area for very small cars. One could not get any of the regular cars into these spaces, but Jeff found that he could get a parking permit if he had one of these new little "sportscars". He checked with a friend of his, Regan Fuller, whom he knew to be crazy about MG's. Jeff found one available, a light blue convertible, and bought it. From that point on Jeff was driving that MG from Arlington to the reflecting pool and back under all sorts of conditions and finding it to be great fun. An MG in traffic was very agile, which he liked, plus he now had a place to park.

One day, a flyer was dropped into his cockpit, advertising the MG Car Club which was meeting that weekend in Georgetown. Jeff decided to go over and check it out. He liked what he found and was soon heavily involved in the sportscar scene.

The people in the MG Car Club all assumed that if you were interested enough to join the club you would naturally be interested in racing. Jeff found himself being pushed into learning how to drive his car fast. He and Janelle started to go to as many rallies as they could, as well as meetings. They became good friends with George and Jean Stathers. George was the "den mother" for what became known as the Lavender Hill Mob and at all hours

186

Christy, Parry and Lindy complete the family.

of the day and night people would be standing around in the Stathers' garage while he fiddled with screwdrivers and pliers. George was a genius and had a marvelous ability to improvise, taking a car that would not run and getting it to move, seemingly by magic. Jeff thought this was a gas.

Jeff's first race was at Allentown, Pennsylvania. He buzzed up there one weekend and saw all these people going round and round on an airstrip course marked by pylons. He shouldered his way in, put his foot down hard and realized that he could do it! He was flying past people like they were standing still! It turns out they were not racing, just checking the course. Jeff was encouraged anyway.

Airstrip racing was a great way to learn to race, especially to take a corner at high speed without killing yourself. If you missed a turn you just spun out

Jeff and his new MG.

Driving this little car around Washington was fun.

It was a tight squeeze, but the whole family could fit.

Jeff's first Porsche.

Racing his new Porsche.

onto more concrete without crashing into anything, except perhaps a hay bale or two.

This activity opened up a whole new group of congenial people for Jeff and Janelle to socialize with. They were generally spritely and fun. Janelle remembers "top-downing" in the summer—driving from their home in Arlington up into Maryland to see a summer theater presentation—as well as various rallies and races.

The time came when Jeff's MG simply would not go fast enough. Dick Thompson was at that time the senior hot driver for the Lavender Hill Mob and he got a Porsche. He went up to Bridgehampton and just wiped everybody out—not so much because the Porsche was the fastest car but because Dick Thompson was a very good driver. Jeff saw Dick driving that Porsche around that course, usually at 45 degrees to the line of march with all four wheels smoking, and he said to himself, "That's what I have to have."

So Jeff went up to New York and bought himself a Porsche. It was a beautiful jade green with tan upholstery *and it cost $3,500.00.* This was beyond belief. A car at that time was $1,000.00 and an expensive car was $1,500.00. Jeff was queasy at the thought of spending so much money, but he wrote the check and drove away.

When the Korean War was over in 1953, Jeff had come to the realization that he was not cut out to be a civilian. He had been nothing but a soldier since he got out of college and now he was thirty-three years old. So he said, okay, let's be a Marine. They had good friends and numerous interests and three children and life was good—let's stay for more.

At that time, the Commandant of the Marine Corps sent out a special letter thanking all those who had leaped to the colors when the Korean War began and saying he hoped they would consider the possibility of staying on. Jeff put in. The word came back that they could not use him. There were simply not enough jobs. Jeff was a lieutenant colonel and that rank is essentially a battalion commander. The Marine Corps had hundreds of light colonels and only about 24 battalions. Jeff did not have sufficient FMF experience as a company commander or platoon leader to qualify as a fully experienced infantry officer. He had all kinds of specialist jobs but not the jobs they wanted and besides, he was too senior. What they needed was staff sergeants and lieutenants. Jeff got a very nice "Thanks but no thanks" letter back.

"Jeff was just one casualty of a very large number. At the height of the Korean War, we had about 400,000 Marines and they wanted it back to 95,000. There is a lot of sadness connected with that."
— LT. GENERAL VICTOR H. KRULAK

That was that. He reverted from active duty to reserve status, inactive, and moved his family back to California to take another stab at civilian life.

190

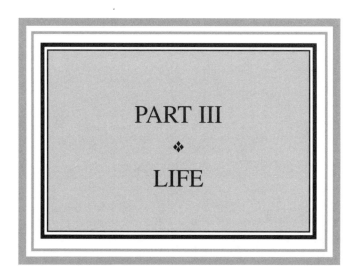

PART III

❖

LIFE

Civilian Life

J eff and Janelle and their three girls were lucky to have the Los Angeles house on Eighth Street available to them again rent-free, through the generosity of Warren Watkins. Having no job to hurry to the West Coast for, they took their time getting there, taking the opportunity to see some new country and visit places of special interest along the way. It was late summer of 1953. Janelle drove the Hudson and Jeff drove the Porsche and the girls took turns as to who got to ride with daddy in the fast little red coupe. (Jeff's Porsche had been clobbered in a disputed left turn in Arlington so he had it repainted in Italian racing red, a color he stuck with through all subsequent Porsches.)

They took a northern route, visiting the Badlands and Mt. Rushmore in South Dakota. Jeff was particularly interested in walking the battlefield of Custer's last stand. Here they added another brick to the great wall of family lore—the fact the I was so blasé about this famous battle that I slept through it.

They also did some exploring around Jackson Hole and Jeff caught his toe in some barbed wire. The subsequent fall resulted in a few broken ribs and Jeff had to drive the rest of the trip in considerable discomfort.

Back in Los Angeles, life took on the suspicious look of the bad year before Korea. All the problems Jeff had in finding his niche in civilian life cropped up again. He went back to New York Life, but his prior record was not good enough for them to want to hire him back for another try. He took a job selling cars for Joe Coberley, who had been a fraternity brother at Stanford, but Jeff's personal opinions of the various cars were strong and had little or adverse bearing on the sales thereof. He had no trouble talking cars with customers, but selling is a different skill and he didn't have it. He followed leads and answered ads and tried various things, none with conspicuous success.

Having been bitten by the racing bug, Jeff continued to enjoy rallies and races and the people involved. In an uncharacteristic stab at limiting ex-

The Hudson and the Porsche taking a break during the summer trip across country, 1953.

The girls enjoy the Badlands. . .

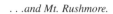

. . .and Mt. Rushmore.

penses, Jeff sold the Porsche coupe and acquired a Porsche Roadster. Where the coupe was a luxury tourer and expensive to keep up, the Roadster was Porsche's entry into the inexpensive car market. It was not cheap, but it was less than the coupe, without many frills. Still it drove with the characteristic Porsche charm and he had lots of fun with it.

Jeff discovered that Los Angeles did not have a Porsche club of any type, so he founded the Porsche Owner's Club of Southern California. He and Janelle organized and ran rallies and put out the club's newsletter, starting them on a trend of newsletter writing and publication that continues to this day. Jeff went so far as to lay out a plan for a grand Golden State Rally which was to make a complete circuit of California starting and finishing in Hollywood. This plan never came to fruition, lacking the requisite funding and promotion.

Jeff had definite skill at auto racing although he was too big and had started too late in life to make a serious attempt at a career. He had good eyesight, balance and reactions and he learned the tactics of racing from watching the winners. He once fell in behind Dick Thompson at Andrews Field, about three car lengths back. He saw that he and Dick were following the same line through the turns except that each time they exited a turn, Dick would pick up another length on Jeff. By the end of the race Dick was the entire length of the long straightaway ahead. That gave Jeff much food for thought.

He found that the Porsche Roadster was in great demand. He went out to a race at Riverside and put a "for sale" sign in the window of his car and a man bought it before the day was over for more than Jeff had paid for it. With his proceeds, Jeff bought another Roadster and had much fun with that one too—also bright red.

The Porsche Club had two more or less official mechanics, Ferdi Hannig and Ewald Olbrich. These men were Germans who really knew their Porsches and kept the club members' cars in excellent condition. Jeff discussed Porsches with them and also picked their brains about their experiences in Nazi Germany during the war. It turned out that one of them had been a member of the SchutzStaffel (SS) and his telling comments to Jeff centered on his re-energized pride in his heritage and homeland, brought to life by Adolf Hitler.

The culmination of Jeff's racing experience was the second place he took in a national auto race in Glendale in 1955. The circuit was on the airport grounds—no mountains, just flat terrain with pylons marking the course. Jeff had done quite well in practice and was feeling confident. The field of contestants numbered about 30 and included drivers from all over the United States.

The starting lineup was a row of three cars, followed by a staggered row of two cars, followed by another row of three cars and so on. The starter was Al Torres, who had a unique style with the green flag. He would run up and down the line making sure everyone was ready. He would wave to friends and

Jeff's first Porsche Roadster.

fiddle with a toothpick and shuffle with papers and then—pop! He would drop that flag with no warning. This meant that the competitors had to be on their toes. They had to have their revs up and their clutch pedals under control and be paying attention.

When Al popped that flag, Jeff was ready and he roared off the line. The driver of the car two rows ahead, who was directly in front of Jeff, was not ready and Jeff nearly drove into him. Jeff had to stand on the brakes so hard he killed his engine. The whole field went roaring by him, heading into turn one, while he was re-starting his engine.

Jeff finally took off and despite the inauspicious beginning had a fine time. He went sailing through the entire field from rear to front until he got to the number two position behind Dale Johnson, a test pilot for Northrop who was the leading Porsche driver on the West Coast. Jeff and Dale had the same car. Jeff just could not pass. Dale was the better, more experienced driver. Jeff rode about a length back for the remainder of the race while the two of them lapped the rest of the field.

Dale kidded Jeff later and dubbed him "the red baron". The drivers had no uniforms in those days and Jeff wore a red helmet with black goggles and a black leather jacket with a black fur collar. Every time Dale looked in the rear view mirror, there was this vision in black and red, one length behind.

Eventually Dale pulled ahead in traffic and they finished the race with Dale in the lead by about 100 meters. Jeff really enjoyed himself and was proud of his accomplishment. Both his father and his Uncle Les would have been delighted to have been among the spectators that day.

Jeff did a little teaching with Dan Gurney during this period as well as some announcing on the podium at races. Clubs would organize teaching sessions and ask various drivers to undertake the instruction. Jeff and Dan did one session together out on the north side of El Mirage Lake near George Air Force Base. They would take people out one-on-one, drive the course they had set up and then let the student try to imitate what they had done. Introduction to driving at high speed can be shocking. Two of Jeff's students had to vomit when their rides came to an end.

Jeff remembers Dan Gurney well. Dan was ten to fifteen years younger than Jeff and Jeff believes Dan to be the best driver that he has ever personally seen drive. Dan never won the World Championship, but that may have had more to do with the politics of racing than with skill. On one occasion, Dan won a race in a rented Volkswagen. As a promotion, VW invited all the biggest names in racing out for an informal race of Volkswagens around a course in Nassau. Dan lapped everyone on the course, and these were international drivers. He was very, very good.

Dan's good friend was Skip Hudson, who appeared to Jeff to be an equally good driver. Jeff once saw Skip do a piece of driving that certainly put him on a par with the best. Skip was knocking around the Riverside raceway at a Corvette competition, asking for a ride. Someone finally broke loose with a stock Corvette that Skip had never seen before. They made him start dead last since he had not qualified. He not only went through the entire field in two laps but he lapped the entire field before the race was over. His talent was definitely in the rare category.

In late 1955 a most promising career opportunity came along. It was a

Above: The "Red Baron".
Right: Dan Gurney was a friend.

Heads of the new Los Angeles International Motor Raceway, announced today for construction near Ontario, are pictured looking over plans for the course. From left, Jeff Cooper, engineer; Kermit Pollack, president; Rudy Cleve, assistant race director. Plans for a multi-million plan were revealed

—Herald-Express Photo

The proposed raceway got lots of press.

Construction of a multi-million dollar racing plant, the Los Angeles Motor Raceway, will begin immediately near Ontario, it was formally announced today.

The plant, to be built on a 470-acre site just 32 miles east of downtown Los Angeles, is designed to accommodate almost any type of motor-driven vehicle.

HERALD EXPRESS

International News Service   Associated Press   United Press   Dow-Jones

TUESDAY, MAR. 6, 1956

L.A. Motor Raceway Revealed

chance to work for the Los Angeles International Motor Raceway. A group was put together, complete with a financial backer, to design, promote, build and launch a premier, multi-million dollar international auto racing facility near Ontario to serve all of Southern California. Jeff signed on as an advisory consultant to Quinton Engineers through the recommendation of Clair Peck, another fraternity brother.

This was a real breakthrough for Jeff. He was finally doing something he liked with a congenial group of people. He leapt into the design and promotion of the track with enthusiasm, traveling to events and speaking to groups. He was paid a decent salary and began to feel that he had found a good place for himself at last. Things began to look up and Jeff was very encouraged.

After several productive months, the financial backer changed his mind and pulled out. The race track plan had to be abandoned. This was terribly discouraging. At the same time, Jeff and Janelle were feeling smothered by Austeene who demanded more interference in their lives than they could comfortably tolerate. Austeene would happily have taken over their entire business, social and private lives and she attempted to do so. The less successful Jeff was at landing a good, solid, financially lucrative position, the more Austeene felt obligated to intercede. It got so bad that Jeff lost his temper with his mother on one occasion and slapped her. This was shockingly out of character. It was contrary to his personal code of conduct and his vision of himself. It was the signal that it was past time to get away.

Big Bear Lake, California had always been a haven for the Pixley family. Janelle had spent all her summers up there as a child and young adult. Floy had made the trip many times on burro back with the infant Janelle in her arms. Jeff had begun to visit while he and Janelle were courting and had also come to love the blue lake with its tall pine forests and surrounding mountains. They packed up and moved there in the summer of 1956. They knew that finances would be tight, but they felt the living expenses would be cheaper and that the small community in the San Bernardino Mountains, 100 miles east of Los Angeles, would be an ideal place to raise their three daughters, now 12, 9 and nearly 6 years old. They thought Jeff could write or teach or something, as long as it was away from the big city.

They found a summer home in the hills around Boulder Bay, just past the dam, which rented inexpensively. When the owners defaulted on their payment, Jeff and Janelle were able to buy the three-bedroom, two bath, two-story house for less than seven thousand dollars. The house needed some work to make it comfortable year round for a family of five. They bought the two lots next door and added two more bedrooms, an additional bathroom, a large fireplace and living room/library and an office for Jeff. They settled in and lived comfortably there for the next nineteen years. Jeff refers to this period between 1956 and 1975 as "the era of Porsches and ponytails", but it was much more.

April 1, 1956. The entire Cooper clan gathered on the back lawn of the house at 500 North Rossmore. From left to right, front row: Heinie and Ann's son Johnny, daughter Heidi and son Brandy, Parry, Aunt Tess, Phyllis and Art's son Keith and daughter Shelley, Lindy. From left to right, back row: Heinie, Ann, Art Balinger, Jeff, Christy, Janelle, Phyllis, Warren Watkins, Austeene.

Above: The house on Robin Road in Big Bear. The structure on the left is the stand-alone garage.
Right: On the front porch of #8 Robin Road. Jeff, Parry (holding Alexander), Janelle, Lindy and family friend John Lyon.

Writing, developing doctrine

Kermit Pollack had been the pro-
moter for the Los Angeles International Motor Raceway. He had become
fond of Jeff and impressed with his potential. When the track failed to mate-
rialize, Kermit wanted to do something for Jeff. He was friends with Bob
Petersen, the Southern California publisher, and so he arranged for an introduction between Bob and Jeff. The result of this first meeting was *Sports Car
Annual*, Jeff's first book. It was one of Petersen Publications' entries in their
paperback *Trend* books series. The *Sports Car Annual* listed and described
the various sports cars available at the time (1957) and included numerous
photographs Jeff had taken at various races and rallies.

One chapter in the book described how to enter a race, negotiate through
traffic and what line to take through corners. Jeff had learned his cornering
technique from following Dick Thompson. When he put what he had
learned on paper, he submitted it to Sterling Moss and Carrol Shelby and a
few other known drivers he had met through the years. He incorporated
their suggestions and the basics of cornering were committed to print for the
first time.

Sports Car Annual was a modest success and Petersen was sufficiently
impressed with Jeff's abilities to keep him in mind for future productions.

In 1957, Janelle's brother Jay and his wife and children, fresh from
Venezuela, had the opportunity to spend five or six months taking it easy
while Jay was between job assignments. They decided to rent a house in Big
Bear, just a few blocks from Jeff and Janelle. This was a happy time for
everyone since the two families, Coopers with three girls and Marks with
three boys, got along famously and were able to spend time together.

At this time, the Volkswagen people asked Jeff to test out a new van-type
machine they were introducing. Jeff knew that Jay spoke fluent Spanish, shot
well and liked the outdoors. Jeff suggested to Jay that the two of them take a

trip down into Baja California for purposes of testing this vehicle. Jay agreed and off they went.

They first stopped in Ensenada where Jeff wanted to look around the town and Jay went fishing. Jay went out on one of the live bait boats and caught several big barracuda. They put these in the back of the car on ice and drove inland. There were a lot of dove flying around and Jay suggested they shoot some for dinner, to go with the fish. Jay, who was an accomplished bird hunter, shot down several dove under Jeff's analytical and appreciative eye.

Janelle and Jay were happy to be in the same town for awhile.

While the dove shooting was underway, along came a drunk Mexican with a big .38 in a holster on his hip. He had heard the shooting and wanted to know what was going on. He bragged to the two "gringos" in Spanish about what a great shot he was and gave them a rather haphazard demonstration on some hillside rocks. Jeff and Jay complimented him on his shooting and he, in the characteristic off-road Mexican tradition of hospitality, invited them to his home for dinner, saying his wife was a great cook. They accepted this offer and offered in return the fish and the doves for provender. They had a delightful meal and visit and that's the way the trip developed.

> *"We got along just fine......he appreciated what knowledge I did have in my head and could relay to him about life in South America....He would nod his head and you could just see him fitting that back into the background of knowledge that he already had, tucking that information away so he could use it sometime in the future."*
>
> *– JAY MARKS*

The Volkswagen developed gear trouble and would not operate in anything but neutral and third gear—no first or second. They were on their way home and spent the night halfway between Ensenada and Mexicali in their sleeping bags, parked on the dirt road. At midnight, Jeff woke Jay up and said he was in terrible pain. It seemed to them both that the symptoms indicated kidney stones. They had a first aid kit and Jay gave Jeff a shot of morphine and then drove like mad for the hospital in Mexicali, with Jeff writhing around on the floor in the back. The car would not go slowly, so Jay drove as fast as the car would go and Jeff bounced around in the back amidst all their gear.

Along about daylight as they were approaching the border Jeff said he felt much better. All of that jolting and jarring from the ride probably loosened the kidney stones. By the time they reached Mexicali, Jeff decided to skip the hospital and get back to Big Bear and check in with the family doctor. Doctor Barney Godwin said Jeff must have passed one hell of a stone. Jay was very disappointed that their adventure had to be cut short, but it was a great few days.

Jeff, who had skied in his youth, wanted his girls to learn how, especially now that they lived at 7,000 feet and had snow in the winter months. He met Tommi Tyndal, a promoter from Bohemia, who was putting together the premier ski resort in Big Bear—Snow Summit. Jeff and Janelle became good friends with Tommi and his wife Jo and joined the original group of investors in the new venture. This gave the entire family gold investor cards which provided them with free lift tickets for life.

Because Snow Summit only operated in the winter months, Jeff thought it would be a good idea to make some use of the grounds during the summer months. He came up with the idea of putting on a pistol shooting event in conjunction with the local annual festival known as "Old Miner's Days", held in August of each year. The idea was that this event would draw a crowd, publicize Snow Summit and make a little money for the ski operation. Jeff had learned a few things about promotion while working for the Los Angeles race track.

So Jeff created, planned and administered the First Annual Leatherslap, which was a straightforward "quick draw" contest, presumably on the old western motif of pistols slung low in holsters and shooting from the hip at man-sized targets at short range—one-handed, of course. Between shooting

Learning to ski.

Relaxing at the lodge at Snow Summit.

with Howie Taft at Quantico in 1953 and the First Annual Leatherslap in 1957 Jeff had hardly fired a shot. The idea for the contest just came to him because it seemed an interesting and fun way to help Tommi promote his new ski resort.

The First Annual Leatherslap got a lot of attention. Jeff even went down to Hollywood and appeared on television in buckskins to advertise the event. Nearly two-hundred people signed up as competitors. It was a good thing Jeff's idea was a simple one because nobody knew how to administer or score a match. Still they all had a lot of fun. The winner was a Los Angeles cop named Don Nowka. Jeff was up against Don in the final bout but Jeff made

Jeff in his promotional togs.

a false start and called it on himself. He ended up second. That was the first of many lessons on how difficult it is to both administer and compete in the same match.

The local people who had participated in the Leatherslap decided that it was so much fun they could not wait another year for another contest. They wanted one once a month. They organized themselves into a club called the Bear Valley Gunslingers and decided to vary the kinds of matches they would put together in order to present a different kind of challenge each month.

Due to Jeff's influence, they remained true to the concept of practicality. Jeff searched every source available, including historical records, to keep presenting different kinds of contests to the competitors. Several matches recreated actual events, as far as they could be determined. One such was the famous gunfight at the OK Corral. That one was over so quickly that the original participants were shown to have been no match for the gunslingers of Southern California in the late 1950's!

This was the proving ground for what is now known as practical shooting. It was one massive research project with Jeff as the professor. Self-funded, it drew research volunteers from all over the southwest and continued for many years. Experimentation was the name of the game and whatever won consistently was put under the microscope, analyzed, emulated and embraced as doctrine.

It did not, however, pay bills. Having three children in the local schools, Jeff and Janelle made friends with all the local school administrators and

Some of the early competitors. Jeff is in the middle.

teachers and Jeff got taken on as an occasional substitute teacher at Big Bear High School. When it became apparent that Jeff knew a great deal about guns, Petersen commissioned him to write two more books for the *Trend* series: *Custom Rifles* and *Handguns Afield*. Jeff also wrote articles for *Car & Driver* magazine. This helped to pay the bills while Jeff delved more and more deeply into the study of practical shooting.

Jeff searched all over the world as well as he could in papers and magazines and various publications to see what kind of shooting was being done in other countries. Jeff brought all that he learned together into his "field laboratory". One of his most popular exercises was the Mexican Defense Course, which he borrowed from south of the border.

> *"We were very closely associated during those times and that was when Jeff was developing his sidearm techniques. I was fascinated by the way that developed and how Jeff kept pulling things together and working out new refinements to the technique and pulling information and insights in from the people he was connected with. I noticed that everyone who came to work with Jeff at that time went away respecting him. That is one thing that he commands is—respect."*
>
> *– JAY MARKS*

Jack Weaver on the right, with Colonel C.F. "Bud" Reynolds, a family friend who often helped out with administering the matches.

Jack Weaver vs. Thell Reed--a classic bout.

Jack Weaver demonstrating the "Weaver Stance".

Above left: Thell Reed, probably the fastest of the top six. Above right: Janelle became a master at scoring matches. Below: Five of the top six competitors in the early days of practical pistol shooting. From left to right: Ray Chapman, Elden Carl, Thell Reed, Jeff Cooper, Jack Weaver. Missing is John Plahn. Jeff dislikes this picture because they are all violating two of the basic safety rules.

They learned many things. One of the first things they discovered was that the police service revolver on which all American law enforcement and civilian competition was based was only good for certain kinds of matches. When they started to vary the courses of fire and mix them up they found that the service revolver was harder to use well than the service automatic. This realization was delayed because one of the greatest champions of those early days of practical shooting was Jack Weaver, and he was a dedicated revolver man. Jack was so good with his revolver that he trounced just about everybody, no matter what gun they were using. This did not have to do much with reloading, he simply shot better. He used a .38 Special with a light load and he was masterful. It eventually became obvious beyond a doubt that a man with a revolver was not really competitive when up against an equally good shooter with an auto pistol.

They learned that two hands are better than one. This is a main component of the now famous "Weaver Stance" that Jack came up with entirely on his own. Jack came to the Second Annual Leatherslap in 1958 and won it easily. The Weaver Stance, with its balance and isometric control, is simply easier and better. Jeff tried to compete against Jack with all the techniques he had been taught in the military and at the FBI ranges. He could not beat him, so he decided to join him. Jeff studied Jack's two-handed hold and stance and adapted it to the auto pistol and incorporated it into his own shooting. Jeff was an eclecticist and always profited by what others developed but perhaps did not appreciate or carry far enough. He lived by the axiom that "a fool learns by his own experience—a wise man learns by the experience of others." After Jeff perfected the Weaver Stance for himself using the auto pistol, Jack never beat him again.

As the competitions progressed from year to year, six men consistently traded places amongst themselves for top awards in every match. They were simply the best and set the standards to which every other shooter aspired. These were Jeff, Jack Weaver, Elden Carl, John Plahn, Ray Chapman and Thell Reed. In order not to discourage other shooters, the Bear Valley Gunslingers instituted an informal class system of A, B and C and awarded trophies in each class. This was a concession to making people feel good about whatever level of competence they attained without reaching the top. Jeff regrets its introduction. It did not prove anything. It was a forerunner of the unfortunate methods we use to reward almost everything today, with almost no regard for what is actually the best. As long as everyone feels good about himself (or herself), who cares about excellence?

The matches were always held on either a Saturday or a Sunday. Janelle would assist and she eventually became a master scorekeeper, devising the best ways to score various types of matches. Christy, Parry and I would patch targets and blow up balloons and run up and down hills. There was always a Deer Shoot in the fall which was a timed walk up a small canyon at Snow

Dancing after a match. From left to right: Janelle, Ray Chapman, Parry, Elden Carl.

Summit where the shooters had to pick out deer targets at various heights and distances and place two shots carefully but quickly on each target and then move to the next. I would spend the entire day behind a large pine tree with a roll of masking tape. About every 30 minutes a shooter would come up the canyon, take shots at the two targets for which I was responsible and go on. As the shooter and the scorer came back down, I would call out the score and sit back down behind the tree. Ah, the carefree days of my girlhood!

After each match, everyone was invited back to our house for food and drink and fellowship. We had wonderful times and I look back on those days with nothing but pleasure. The shooters and their wives and children came from all walks of life and were all ages, shapes and sizes. Some came and left and were never seen again. Others came often, came early and stayed late and became lifelong friends. Elden Carl and Ray Chapman were like members of our family and would normally spend the Saturday night after a match in our guest room. Elden was a great dancer, and he and mom would often clear the living room for a dance or two. Ray always had a new Corvette and he would let me take his car into town! For a small town teenage girl, this was heaven!

A big step in the progress of Jeff's study of practical shooting came when they decided to form a league. Big Bear was just one place and for many interested competitors it was simply too far to come every month. The idea became reality with the formation of the Southwest Combat Pistol League. "Combat pistol" meant that they were all shooting imitations of actual combat situations. Any community that had enough interested participants could form its own club which could then affiliate with the league. Individual clubs

The Weaver Stance against the one-handed method. Jeff is on the left. Guess who won.

could have all the matches they wanted, but once a month each club would host a "league match" and members from other clubs would come to compete. There would be club championships and an overall league champion. That was the birth of the Southwest Combat Pistol League. Jeff was the founder, organizer, chairman, secretary, program master, president, treasurer and everything else, with Janelle's efficient assistance. He was very glad to turn over these various jobs as the league grew.

When the league tried to incorporate, the Secretary of State for California objected to the word "combat" in the title. They removed the offending word and incorporated as the Southwest Pistol League, which is what it is still called today. Jeff was the first president. This was another job he was happy to pass along to someone else when the time came. It was a lot of hard work.

So Jeff shot and studied and saw what worked—what kind of gun, what kind of holster, what systems and techniques. This was the birth of the Modern Technique of the Pistol. He was predisposed and fully capable of putting it all together, understanding its significance, putting it down in writing and teaching it. He began to put some of it down in the form of articles for *Guns & Ammo* magazine, a Petersen publication.

> *"When I first met him in about 1958 we were looking for fresh young authors for Guns & Ammo magazine. I had heard about him in Big Bear and about the Leatherslap. I liked his writing and his approach. His passion is what makes his writing good.....he believes. Passion, knowledge and dedication come through in his writings. His writings are from the heart, based on his study. He is terribly disciplined."*
>
> *– TOM SIATOS*
> *PETERSEN PUBLICATIONS*

Raising children

Life in Big Bear was very good. Jeff was doing a lot of shooting and learning and writing, a little teaching and a good deal of child rearing. Jeff and Janelle were of like minds on how to raise their children, and their united front on all important issues was an anchor of security for their girls. They believed in strict, consistent discipline. They agreed on what was right and wrong and they imparted this with firm and unwavering consistency, always backed up with lots of love and support. Both were also always logical and reasonable, so that if one of us was inclined to question a rule or lesson, they would explain the why of the issue in clear, understandable terms. They almost never had to resort to the old exhortation, "Because I said so, that's why!" I remember asking a lot of questions, especially after I went away to college. I never failed to receive an answer that made absolute sense. There was very little rebellion or conflict in the Cooper household. Parental word was law, but it was law with intelligence and logic and almost impossible to argue with. I know there were disagreements, but I don't remember any of these as important. As an adult, I know they were excellent parents, thoughtful and dedicated. They seem to me to have been always right, at least about everything that was and is really important. That gives me a feeling of security so complete as to make me think I'm invulnerable.

Jeff taught us to shoot and took us hiking and made sure we all learned to ride horses and ski and swim and play hit-the-bat.

> "(Uncle) Jeff has always loved outdoor activities. He loved to organize hikes. He would also organize (foot) races around obstacle courses. These were great as long as I beat Parry. When I lost, my day was ruined."
>
> – STEVE LUNCEFORD

Janelle, Parry and Lindy enjoy some horseback riding.

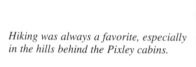

Hiking was always a favorite, especially in the hills behind the Pixley cabins.

Jeff followed his father's lead in making sure that we all sat down to dinner together and discussed all manner of things. There was only one conversation at a time around our table, but anyone could lead the discussion or introduce a topic. We talked politics and history and world events and local events and our own personal concerns. We went to movies together and then came home and criticized what we had just seen, from the casting to the cinematography. We listened to music together and discussed what we had just heard. Our favorites included many classical pieces, many mood pieces by Percy Faith and Martin Denny, lots of folk groups like the Kingston Trio, the Limelighters and Joe and Eddie, several vocalists like Doris Day, Jo Stafford, Andy Williams and Tony Bennett and many more.

Jeff had a huge library and whenever any of us expressed an interest in anything, he would pull out a book on the subject and, like his father before him, say "Read this." We had a complete set of encyclopedias and while I never read them from cover to cover, I read much more of them than I was asked to or needed to for homework assignments. I also read every Edgar Rice Burroughs book we had several times.

Jeff used to read to me on the couch in front of the fireplace, even after I was old enough to read for myself. We went all the way through The Lord of the Rings by J.R.R. Tolkien and all of the Hornblower series by C.S. Forester. I treasure memories of my father's very expert renderings of various characters in these books. He made those stories live in a very special way and I was enthralled.

The rule for living that Jeff discussed with us was this: *Understand the problem. Pull your weight. Appreciate.* What I took away from these discussions was the idea that "understanding the problem" involved reading and learning and being aware of and keeping informed about what was going on in all aspects of life. It meant forming a broad understanding of all of life's challenges, from why we are here to what kind of taxation schedule would be best for the community to what method to use to remove splinters. Understanding the problem requires constant study, analysis and the application of reason and logic to gathered information. It never ends. It's not easy, but a goal to reach for.

"Pull your weight" referred to the obligation every human being has to make his own way and not be a burden to anyone, neither to any single person nor to any group or government entity. The best way to live is to take care of yourself—solve your own problems, produce for yourself and reap your own rewards. Self-reliance and self-discipline were the guideposts.

"Appreciate" is the admonition to enjoy! Enjoy the good things in life, both large and small. Make good things happen and revel in them. If you do all these things, you will be well on your way to a full and productive life which you will be able to look back upon with pride. Always remember happiness is the by-product of achievement.

Jeff and Janelle have always been extremely proud of the fact that all three of their girls excelled. In Big Bear, there was an annual local beauty contest where they crowned the "Snow Queen". It was modeled on the Miss America pageant, although there was no talent portion. The contestants, mostly seniors at Big Bear High School, would parade in front of a panel of local judges in bathing suits, ski wear and formal gowns. At one point, the master of ceremonies would conduct a short interview with each contestant. Christy, Parry and I all won for our years. We were all also head cheerleaders. Christy and I were valedictorians for our graduating high school classes and Parry was in the top three of her class. We all went on to receive college degrees. We know we have our parents to thank for good genes and a wise, healthy upbringing which made us nice looking, athletic and intelligent. How can you miss doing well in school when you have a walk-

Janelle was a superb athlete.

Christy shooting. . .

. . .and as Snow Queen of 1960.

Parry shooting. . .

. . .and as Snow Queen of 1964.

Lindy shooting. . .

. . .and as Snow Queen of 1967.

215

ing encyclopedia for a father and a library at your fingertips? The Pope's blessing carried on into our generation and we were lucky.

"I remember being impressed that all the Cooper girls knew their Greek alphabet. It was posted by the breakfast table."
— *VIRGINIA DEAN ARTHUR*

"I remember Jeff saying that he was going to raise his daughters the same way he would raise sons. 'They are going to be hardy. They're going to know everything I know. They're going to be able to survive in the wilderness—and yet they are going to have their mother's femininity.' "
— *DORIS SMITH VISSCHER*

Our family attracted many people who were missing something in their own lives and who found some element with us that they could hold on to. Many of these people are still friends today and look back with gratitude on what influences they picked up from the Coopers.

"In August of 1960 I signed up for the Leatherslap.....and won it. That is when I met Jeff.......Jeff told me they had monthly shoots and invited me to come up......he had this beautiful, wonderful wife who was more impressive than he was and kids that were just outstanding.....The Coopers really raised me. My own family was a disaster. The Coopers were the first family I ever knew that was a unit where the parents related to the children the way they should and vice versa. I soaked that up. I'll never forget that hike we took. I stayed overnight after a shoot. The next day we hiked up to the top of a peak. That was the first time I can remember doing anything as part of a family. Those impressions stayed with me. I'm not sure I would be happily married right now if it had not been for those impressions......"
— *ELDEN CARL*

"Another early recollection was being in your home. I was about 15. Jeff offered me a small glass of Tequila—but it was drinking with thought rather than just drinking. We talked, which should be translated as he talked and I listened, about how Tequila was in reality the indigenous drink from our part of the world and should be known to us as part of our cultural heritage. We talked about the origins of Tequila and that there were so many different qualities of the beverage. We talked about how Tequila could be compared to Scotch and other more reputable drinks. It was this wide interpreta-

tion and analysis of an experience which was different and very satisfying to me. I don't recall anyone else really doing that before (and not enough since). I really enjoyed listening to Jeff—and enjoyed the Tequila because of knowing more about it."

"I cannot ignore the fact that I was essentially a fatherless boy, and that of all the men I knew, Jeff was my ideal father image."

"Jeff was and is a natural teacher. He enjoyed ideas and the imparting of them. And his ideas were tailor-made for a young man—guns, cars, beauty, courage and in general how to fashion a life satisfying to the mind, spirit and body."

– CLIFFORD DOUGLAS

Jeff continued to race his Porsche Roadster after the family moved to Big Bear, but not for long. He finally traded in the Roadster for another coupe, a 356 SC—bright red. Although he no longer raced formally, he drove the road from San Bernardino to Big Bear as if it was a race course and he finally came to a sort of stand-off with the local California Highway Patrol. They knew about him, could never catch him, so decided to let him alone. He realized he was too impatient to teach his daughters how to drive, so he left that to Janelle and the high school driver's education classes. He did, however, go over lines and cornering and techniques with all of us and we learned by watching him. On special occasions, when we caught him in the right mood, he would let each of us drive the 356 into town. That was a treat we did not take for granted.

Jeff also found time for two other activities during the Big Bear years. Since his daughters were all cheerleaders and he liked exercise and the outdoors and football, he offered to run the lines during the games. So while we were leading the cheering section for the Big Bear Bears, Jeff was running up and

Jeff's final Porsche – his 356 SC.

Jeff plays the heavy in yet another of the presentations of the Bear Valley Players.

down the field with the down markers.

He also joined an amateur theater group, taking parts when available and especially enjoying playing the heavy. In one play, he played the part of a murderer who did his victim in with a knife. Being interested in violence and weaponry of all sorts and a student of history, he objected to the director's original idea that he thrust the rubber stage prop into the victim's stomach once and then have the victim fall dead. Jeff said that was unrealistic. So, he devised his own method and convinced the director. When the scene finally came, it was wonderfully gory and effective. Jeff taped a vial of red food coloring inside the sleeve of his shirt and had the victim pull the top off when his back was to the audience. Jeff's thrust was to the lower abdominal area with a tremendous ripping motion up toward the solar plexus—in effect a disemboweling motion. The actor playing the victim got the top off the vial of food coloring and as he fell, the "blood" ran down the back of Jeff's hand, still holding the rubber stage prop knife, and dripped onto the stage. The audience gasped. Marvelous.

While Jeff shot and studied and wrote and taught, Janelle became immersed in various civic activities. She joined the PTA (Parents' and Teachers' Association), eventually serving as its president. She was carnival chairman for the "Moms-N'-Pops" organization, which supported school activities. She was active on the hospital board, a group attempting to bring the first hospital to Big Bear Lake, and she was the founding president of the Bear Valley Republican Women's Club. In this last capacity, she put out another newsletter called the Trunkline, typing it on a master stencil and running copies by hand.

Both Jeff and Janelle were and are dedicated individualists, believing in the power of individual achievement. As such, they have been and remain members of the conservative branch of the Republican party in American politics, it being the most rewarding to and appreciative of the individual. It should come as no surprise that their children agree with them, as do most of their friends. Jeff's writings on almost all his various topics have included his ad-

218

vocacy of individual freedom and responsibility, it being interwoven into the fabric of his consciousness. When we discussed politics at our dinner table it was inexorably tied to right and wrong, so our political views are strongly held and an integral part of our personalities.

One thing we did not have was television. Jeff and Janelle agreed that it was a distraction, a time-waster that gave almost nothing in return. So while we were growing up, there was no television to keep us from our athletic activities or our homework. The good things that television has to offer are easily substituted with books or other printed material. The bad is better left unseen. This was another reason the Cooper girls did well in school.

Janelle continued her self-taught education in culinary achievement with Jeff's encouragement. Janelle's meals and various specialties have become legendary. Jeff was and is an enthusiastic gourmet and when he tried his hand in the kitchen, as he often did when we were growing up, the result was always interesting and mostly delicious. His specialties were ethnic egg dishes on Sunday mornings, not to mention exotic drinks. He was also a master griller on the back yard barbecue.

One area of education where we lacked formality was religion. Jeff had no formal religious upbringing in his home and neither did we. We belonged to no church and attended no single church regularly. I went to a few Sunday school sessions at the little Community Church and attended Catholic mass

Jeff and Janelle party with some of their many good friends in Big Bear.

219

The Cooper family in December of 1958.

with several of my friends and boyfriends on various occasions, as well as sermons at the Methodist church and the Baptist church. Jeff discussed the precepts of the various religions with us, but we did not take our moral lessons from Bible teachings or sermons from any minister or priest. Our moral guides were our parents and what they said was law.

Every few months, two fresh-faced young men in slacks, white shirts and ties would come to the door and ask to speak with "Mr. Cooper". These were the latest proselytizers from the Jehovah's Witnesses. Jeff would never invite them in because that would interfere with the other activities in our household, but he would sit on the front porch with them and discuss religion and various ethical and moral issues until their eyes would start to spin in their heads and they would politely take their leave. We deduced that sending the first-timers out to speak with Jeff Cooper was that church's trial by fire. Once they had a thorough discussion with him, they could take on anyone else and it would seem easy.

Jeff and Janelle continued the Cooper Christmas party tradition in Big Bear for all the nineteen years they lived there. These parties were always lots of fun and were looked forward to by all of us and by everyone lucky enough to get an invitation. Jeff would mix his potent Zombie punch and all the guests were handed glasses as they entered the front door. Janelle would have a table laden with wonderful things to eat, normally including mountains of cold shrimp with a spicy sauce and all kinds of hot hors d'oeuvres that we would

220

help to cook and pass among the crowd. There was much music and dancing and merriment. As I got older, I got to stay up later and later, but I don't remember ever being able to stay awake until the end of the party. The last party-goers drifted away in the wee hours of the morning and we would spend the next day cleaning up and getting the house back in some semblance of order. We had a thick, gold-colored shag carpet and would often find various edible things in it for days after one of our famous parties.

While Jeff was not particularly successful financially, he knew he was amassing the necessary experience with pistols to build something important. He was not making money, but he had some inherited income which he supplemented by teaching and writing. Janelle also inherited money from relatives' bequests from time to time and this helped considerably. The Coopers were never destitute, but things were lean at times. This did not hamper them in raising their children, who have been a source of pleasure to them.

> *"We thank God and good fortune and (we'd like to think) a little bit of intelligence on our part that we have had nothing but success in that regard."*
>
> *"The happiest part of anyone's life is that period between the time the youngest child can take care of himself and the oldest child goes away to college. That's a short time. That period we look back on with great satisfaction."*
>
> *– JEFF COOPER*

Shooting, writing, consulting

J eff continued to shoot and study and write. He won the overall pistol championships for the years 1959, 1960 and 1961. This gave his writings additional clout as it became obvious that here was someone who could put his money where his mouth was. He documented what was developing as far as the techniques of practical pistolcraft, interspersed with his personal philosophy on every individual's right and obligation to defend himself, his home, his loved ones and his country. This struck chords with people all over the world. Petersen's publications have always had wide distribution, including overseas, and Jeff began a voluminous international correspondence that continues to this day.

Another book project came along. Jeff was asked by Tom Siatos, the editor for *Guns & Ammo* magazine, to pick the best that had appeared in that magazine over the past five or six years and put it together as an anthology with the proper credits to the appropriate authors and then to fill in where there were topics which were not covered with his own work. This became the pistol section of *The Complete Book of Modern Handgunning*. Someone scraped all the attribution off so the edition that got to print credits Jeff with all kinds of things written by others that Jeff not only did not write, but often did not agree with. That left a bad taste in his mouth, but he held no grudges and continued on.

In 1960, Jeff and Janelle's eldest daughter Christy was graduated as valedictorian from Big Bear High School. She was accepted to Stanford University and went away to college, living in the same freshmen dorm Janelle had lived in more than twenty years earlier. Although Jeff was busy, he still did not have what anyone would call a steady job and Christy's entrance into college led him to consider the possibility of his obtaining a graduate degree and perhaps going on to become a college professor. He loved learning and had never stopped and he found he liked writing and enjoyed imparting knowledge to others. He pondered the possibilities for a while.

In late 1961, Jeff made a characteristically unusual decision. Having fought through two wars without feeling any particular distinction, he wanted to do something that offered a dangerous challenge in a combative sense. He was 41 and perhaps a little of what is known as "mid-life crisis" came his way. He felt that peril, not variety, was the true spice of life and he wanted to seek some out while he was still young enough and fit enough to do so.

He had been told in his youth that the Rio Balsas in the interior of southern Mexico was a "river of no return"—you don't come back from there. This had always intrigued him. The Balsas trench was an area that was essentially unpoliced to which fugitives gravitated. In Mexico at that time if you committed a crime in one of the small villages you simply got out of town. The authorities would not chase you far, but you had to go somewhere. Where you went was to the Balsas trench. The Rio Balsas thus had a reputation which lost nothing in the recounting as a place one does not go. Jeff also discovered that no one had ever followed the Rio Balsas from its source southeast of Mexico City to its mouth in the Pacific Ocean about 200 miles up the coast from Acapulco—a total distance of some 400 miles. He resolved to get an expedition together and kayak the length of the Balsas.

He was gone a total of seven weeks in January and February of 1962. If Janelle thought Jeff was a little mad to do this she never said so, and she supported him as always. Parry and I were still living at home and I remember

Jeff and Janelle at the Bon Voyage party before the Rio Balsas trip, 12-31-61.

Mom worried a great deal. Communication from the interior of Mexico was not possible and we went many weeks with no news at all.

Jeff had wanted to recruit a group of eight, one reason being that he knew watches would have to be stood to protect their camps. He also insisted on having a medical doctor along and so he convinced our family doctor, Barney Godwin, to accompany him. The group that finally started out numbered only four, and one of these dropped out early on so they continued with only three. Standing watches with only three people in a camp was difficult, but they persevered.

They were of course all armed and conspicuously so. Whenever they would stop and local people would gather to exchange hospitality, Jeff would be sure to demonstrate for them his skill with his pistol. This was designed to discourage any possible predation upon their little expedition and it seemed to work.

There in the backwoods of Mexico is where Jeff learned to make the very best salsa—in a *blender* of all things. There was no vehicular traffic, but some enterprising blender salesman had penetrated the country, most likely on horseback, and convinced every housewife with access to a generator that a combination of onion, garlic, tomatoes, chilies and a little salt whirled in a blender for a few seconds was the best way to make the best salsa in the world. Jeff and Janelle use this recipe still.

There were not enough participants and not enough supplies and there were many portions of the river that were impassable to kayaks. They exhausted themselves with many unplanned portages and other obstacles. The expedition was not as successful as Jeff had planned or would have liked, but it was a true adventure. He had taken off into the unknown and endured a certain amount of hardship and some danger and much good fellowship and he had soaked in the wonderful warmth and good manners of the people of this still primitive part of the world. He satisfied, at least for a time, his thirst for challenge with peril. His father would have approved.*

After the Balsas trip, Jeff decided to pursue graduate study and in 1963 he enrolled in the Master's Degree program at the University of California at Riverside, the closest campus to Big Bear with an acceptable program of study.

The experience of going back to college in his forties was an interesting one for Jeff. It had both its good and bad points.

Learning was a pleasure for him and he had several very good professors. He found he had nothing in common with any of his fellow students and came away with a rather cynical view of higher education.

He earned his Master's Degree in history in 1968, writing three theses which was the California requirement in those days. One had to be on American history and Jeff's topic was the hypothetical extension of the institution

*NOTE: See: "The Rio Balsas" in *Another Country* by Jeff Cooper.

224

of slavery without the Civil War. One had to be on European history and Jeff's subject was the essential differences between Martin Luther and the later split-offs. The third thesis was on the conquest of Mexico. Jeff went deeply into that subject because he enjoyed it very much and the myriad little-known facts he learned about Cortéz and his people are now part of his extensive memory bank.

Jeff found to his disgust that the other students were not primarily there to learn or to seek truth. They were there to attain that degree as quickly and easily as possible so that they could take the next step, whatever that might be. Jeff enjoyed the give and take of small seminars and delighted in asking difficult questions that would normally confound the other students and bring them up short.

A young woman who sat next to Jeff in class did a paper on the penetration of the hinterland of Brazil by the "bandeirantes", the original military pioneers who penetrated the interior of Brazil from the coast, in large measure to acquire slaves from among the local Indians. They discovered that the Indians did not enslave well. The bandeirantes attempted to bring great numbers of Indians over great distances to reach the coast. Jeff asked the student who had done the paper how this was accomplished? Did they use chains? Who carried them? What were the logistics of a few moving a recalcitrant many over a long distance? She had no idea.

Another young man had written a paper that seemed to Jeff to have as its main purpose getting as many words as possible down in print. When the young man finished his presentation, Jeff asked the class at large if anyone had any idea what the last main point of the paper had been. No one could answer.

Jeff ran into "political correctness" in its early stages. In one class, he made a statement to the effect of "a man armed with a Colt revolver was the equal of many savages." One young woman protested his use of the word "savages". He told her he was quoting directly from a primary source.

The professors and other students probably thought of Jeff as a thorn in their sides for the most part. Only a few professors seemed to welcome his penetrating desire for knowledge and appreciate his ability to engage in wide-ranging conversations on any number of subjects. Dr. Hine was one of these. Another young professor who taught historiography had the reputation of being extremely hard to please and critical. He and Jeff got to tossing around the theory of history—linear vs. cyclical vs. helical—almost to the exclusion of the others in the class. Jeff enjoyed this very much.

Jeff resolved to go on and get a doctorate in Latin American studies. He wanted to do a history of the law enforcement problem in Mexico from colonial times to the present because it interested him, he could speak and read Spanish for research purposes and there was very little written on the subject. Jeff was advised that this was an acceptable topic, but that he could not do it justice except at the University of Arizona at Tucson or the University of

Texas at Austin. This meant he would have to pack up the family and move. Both institutions required two years of residence in addition to study and research and dissertation.

He decided not to do this for two reasons. First, Parry had graduated from Big Bear High School in 1964 and gone on to college, but I was still in high school and he did not want me to have to change schools. Second, he had come to understand that he would probably not make a good university professor. From what he had observed, university professors tended to be envious people. They thought because of their intellect and time and work and study they should make more money and be more revered than they were. Jeff saw this particularly in their writings about each other. He had never known people to be as savage in their written and spoken critiques of each other's work as university professors. Jeff realized it was a passive life in which one does nothing, just observes and criticizes. He knew this was not for him.

What he did do with his new graduate degree was teach. He was taken on by the University of California system and he taught extension courses for all interested students in Big Bear. This supplemented his income and gave him much enjoyment. He could virtually pick any historical topic and if he could get enough students interested, the course was up and away. He taught History of California, History of the Westward Movement and History of the Conquest of Mexico. These courses were not likely to be found in any four-year university because the subjects were considered too specialized for any but graduate students. So a select few in the small town of Big Bear had the unique opportunity to learn a great deal about some fascinating subjects from a master teacher.

Jeff's writings for Petersen led to his correspondence which led to his being asked to come to various places all over the world and teach what he knew. It became apparent to him and to Janelle that there was a need for his kind of expertise coupled with his philosophy. Many people responded to his philosophy of self-reliance and individualism coupled with his teaching of the ability to control one's immediate environment. He embarked on a career as an international consultant in personal protection—firearms handling and mental conditioning. This began with a trip to Guatemala.

Jeff had been contacted by Gene Harshbarger, a Texas expatriate who had lived most of his life in Guatemala. Gene had married a Guatemalteca and established a thriving restaurant business. He had been a shooting enthusiast for years and belonged to a local shooting club. Reading Jeff's work in *Guns & Ammo* had led the members of the group to an interest in hiring Jeff to come down and train the bodyguard of the newly-elected president, Carlos Arana, in practical shooting and mental conditioning for personal protection. The Republic of Guatemala was in the midst of an informal civil war. Gene approached Jeff, who checked out the situation as best he could from a dis-

Jeff and Gene Harshbarger in Guatemala, 1966.

tance to make sure the offer was legitimate and was coming from the right side (anti-Communist, anti-Socialist). A deal was struck and Jeff ended up in Guatemala, training the 26 men of President-elect Arana's personal body-guard.

Of the 26 men, two were too uncoordinated to make it and were dropped right away. Jeff was left with 24, of which two turned out to be very good. Jeff met Carlos Arana, who wore a bullet-proof vest but did not shoot. The mission was accomplished in one visit.

Jeff stayed in a private home during his two weeks there and as he packed up to leave, an anonymous phone call came through to his host informing him that his *"gringo friend"* would not make it through the airport that night. In the eyes of the enemy Jeff was a target, since his work strengthened the resistance of their adversaries.

To Jeff it seemed that a man who is going to strike is not likely to broadcast it, so he did not think the threat had any merit. Nevertheless, his host could not ignore the possibility of action.

He rounded up as many members of the foregoing class as could make it and they all arrived at the airport at about 7 p.m. Jeff sat in the lounge with a man on each side of him, two at his back and two more watching the ticket counters and the doorways.

As a three-hour delay unfolded, the group moved from one point to another, nursing their drinks slowly. A group of Americans became somewhat inebri-

227

ated in the bar and at one point, a large tourist approached Jeff. Jeff's companions adjusted their positions and placed their right hands within easy reach of their pistol butts. The tourist noticed this, stopped and asked, "Anybody here speak English?"

Jeff replied that he did. The tourist looked pleased, and then puzzled when Jeff did not get up to greet him in a more friendly fashion. He started toward Jeff, at which point the two men on either side of Jeff stood up and one of the men in the doorway moved quickly up behind the tourist. He stopped again, looked at Jeff more closely and asked, "What are you, some kind of a senator or something?"

"No. I'm not even a congressman."

Nobody said anything for a few long seconds. Then, "Well, okay. Talk to you later." And he trundled out of the bar and Jeff's group all sat down again. When the plane finally arrived, Jeff boarded and made it home without further incident. As Jeff has pointed out many times, things seldom happen when you are fully prepared for them.

Jeff has returned to Guatemala several more times, once with Janelle, for various other classes and has remained good friends with Gene.

The second invitation came from Salvador and the contact man there was Archie Baldocchi. Archie was another American who had moved to Salvador and married a local girl, Maria Elena Duenas. The Duenas family were wealthy landowners. One of their extended family had been kidnapped and blinded and thrown over the wall into his family compound to be found by his young American wife. Archie had read Jeff's work and thought he was the one to come and teach the landed gentry of Salvador how to defend themselves against terrorism. The Maryknoll priests had a very strong Marxist influence in Salvador and were preaching to the peasants that they should attack the "ricos", kill them and destroy their properties. Some were responding.

Jeff had a touchy moment when he got off the plane in Salvador. He had no real assurance that he had been hired by the right people. It crossed his mind that because of his work in Guatemala, he might have been lured down to Salvador to an ambush, his work being a new thorn in the side of the Communists. His misgivings were dispelled when he met Archie, who was an honest and serious man with great dignity. All the people Jeff has dealt with in Central America are such people. The worst he has ever had to deal with have all been from the United States.

Jeff did what he could. He felt the Salvadoreños were a gentle people—too gentle for their way of life. He does not know how successful his teachings have been. He does know of one failure. One of the young men in one of his classes, Raul, was the son of the Honda distributor for the country. He was a very good shot and a very good horseman. He was murdered.

One night Jeff had dinner with Raúl and his new bride, a beautiful young woman who was the daughter of the president of the airline. Raúl had four bodyguards whom, he told Jeff, he had hired out of the army when they were discharged. Jeff asked him how much he felt he could trust a man who was paid to risk his life and Raúl's reply was, "They would not betray me. They know that if they did they would die." Jeff thinks he was partly right. They did betray him and they did die.

On the day Raúl was murdered, Jeff is almost certain that one of the guards called ahead to give the route. The terrorists had a municipal truck waiting along the road. They rammed Raúl's car and turned him off the road. They shot the four bodyguards instantly. Raúl came out with his .45 and killed one of the terrorists on the spot. When they found Raúl's body later, another of the terrorists was dead with him. Was this a success or a failure? He fought back and did well and exacted a price. The notion we see espoused today that you must not fight back predicates a culture without any concept of dignity. This is one reason Jeff is so highly regarded among so many. He can help those who are interested in maintaining their personal dignity by helping them attain self-reliance in this dangerous and unpredictable world.

Jeff had another brush with danger in Costa Rica during the height of the Sandinista rebellion, when the issue had not yet been decided in favor of the Communists. He was teaching pistolcraft at a cattle ranch in Guanacaste, in the extreme northwest part of the country, and was quartered at a motel only a few miles from the Nicaragua border.

When Jeff came down to breakfast on the fourth morning of his stay he discovered that the motel had been occupied by some sort of security guard for a conference soon to take place. There were men standing around in the yard with AK47s and everywhere Jeff looked there were hard-looking, observant men in civilian clothes filling the doorways.

Feeling conspicuous, Jeff assessed the situation and decided a swift and quiet exit was the best plan. He slipped out a side door and headed down the highway on foot without bothering to check out of his room or retrieve his luggage. After about five miles of walking, checking his back carefully, he met his host's car coming to pick him up. He explained the situation and they turned around and went on with the day's plans. Jeff's host made alternate motel arrangements and managed to take care of the bill and get Jeff's luggage back intact.

That's how Jeff's continuing career as an international consultant started. People in hot spots all over the world would contact Jeff through Petersen Publications and he would check them out as well as he could and travel to all kinds of places to teach defensive pistolcraft.

In 1967, I was graduated from high school and Jeff and Janelle's youngest was off to college. I remember so clearly what my father said to me the night before I left. He said, "You are now officially an adult. Your mother and I will never again have the influence over you that has shaped your character up until now. We have done our best and we have the utmost confidence in you and your good sense. We want you to know that *no matter what you do* we love you and we trust you and we are behind you one hundred percent." That little lecture gave me courage and confidence and also made me a little nostalgic. It was the best possible send-off. On several occasions when I was tempted to do something I knew I would regret, I retreated because the thought of letting my parents down was too much to take.

Things continued to escalate on the international consulting front. Jeff was contacted by Siegfried Hubner, a gun writer from Germany. He arranged for Jeff to come to Europe and teach several times in several places. Jeff taught in Germany, Switzerland and Belgium. Roger Swaelens was his first contact in Belgium and Pal Bakocs was his first contact in Switzerland. Jeff taught three times in England, twice in Sweden and twice in France. Most were one week courses. Wherever he traveled, Jeff would ask his host if they could work in a little hunting. Most people were only too willing to oblige and so he has been able to hunt all manner of game in all manner of places.

In addition, Jeff would take advantage of his travels and contacts to meet and converse with all kinds of people whose personal experiences were of particular interest to him. His thirst for knowledge and intense curiosity had been refined by his graduate studies and now he fully appreciated both the value and the pitfalls of primary source material. He sought out eye witness accounts whenever he could and put them in the context of what else he knew about the subject and the probable point of view of the witness. He was never shy about asking to have meetings set up with anyone he wanted to meet and so has had occasion to discuss endless subjects with some very impressive people. Perhaps the greatest of these was Hans-Ulrich Rudel, the German military aviator of World War II whom Jeff considers perhaps the greatest warrior of all time. Jeff had the profound pleasure of meeting and interviewing Rudel and had the skill to share the experience with his readers.*

In 1972, Paladin Press published Jeff's *Principles of Personal Defense*. This little paperback delineated all Jeff had learned about the mental attitude needed to accompany defensive action, especially the use of weapons. It was the forerunner to the distilled "color code" which later became the standard of mental conditioning as introduced and taught by Jeff and adopted by countless other schools and instructors.

*NOTE: See: "Kriegsoberst!" from *Fireworks* by Jeff Cooper.

Africa, I.P.S.C., Gunsite

O̲ne of Jeff's earliest entertainments had been reading the novels of Edgar Rice Burroughs. Burroughs was the originator of "Tarzan of the Apes" and wrote an entire series of books about Tarzan, all set in Africa. Burroughs never went to Africa and much of what he wrote was fanciful, but nevertheless Jeff was entranced with tales of lions and elephants and jungle trails.

As Jeff grew older, he was introduced by his father to the works of Sir Henry Rider Haggard—*King Solomon's Mines* and *Allan Quatermain*. Rider Haggard had not only been to Africa, he had been very much involved in the formulation of the Transvaal in South Africa so he knew first-hand of what he wrote. So the interest continued with more accurate knowledge.

Jeff read Stuart Edward White, Theodore Roosevelt and then, on his sixteenth birthday, his father gave him Ernest Hemingway's *Green Hills of Africa* and the notion kept building that he wanted to go there and explore.

Jack and Jeff decided to make a hunting trip to Northern Rhodesia and base their operations out of the town of Lusaka. Jeff had his rifle—he bought one of the very first Model 70's in .375—which he still has. He had gone so far as to pack up the rifle and all of the necessary ammunition in waterproof, shockproof boxes for the trip. Pearl Harbor changed their plans. There ensued a hiatus of thirty-two years between Jeff's first serious plan to go to Africa and his first trip there.

> *"I first became aware of Jeff when I read an article written by him for Guns and Ammo magazine. I was the head of the pistol shooting club in South Africa. This was about 1970 or 1971. I wrote to him and he wrote back and then he came to South Africa at our invitation."*
>
> *"He offered us a way forward, a path, and in South Africa we were going through a period when we were under threat from the Com-*

munist world. We had a major terrorist problem in Rhodesia. We were very conscious of the general violent atmosphere and he seemed to offer a very satisfactory path to follow to get ourselves into both a physical and a mental state of preparedness."

"....ostensibly we were talking about pistol shooting, but he includes personal protection and an attitude towards situations and how to save your life. Those issues don't just apply to pistol shooting—they apply to everything—living your life, driving, walking the streets—and it worked and he made it sound so right and it fit. He became the 'Guru'. You can think of him almost as a religious leader. He offered people a way of life. He gave them a sense of security. He gave them a sense of control over their own environments and he taught them pistol shooting....Jeff does not just put across a gun philosophy—he puts across a philosophy of survival. We were under threat for many, many years. I can thank Jeff for (my) still being alive—many times."
– BARRY MILLER

Jeff and Danie Van Graan with Jeff's lion. Taken near Engonyameni in 1992, Jeff stopped this lion's charge at 11 paces. A supreme thrill.

232

Barry was Jeff's first contact on the continent of Africa, the first of many wonderful friends Jeff would make there. Jeff first taught in South Africa and then Rhodesia and began to include various hunting excursions with each trip. From his first farm shoot of blesbok in Natal to his many encounters with one of his favorites, the buffalo, to his lion in 1992 to his yet-to-be-planned try for a hippo on dry land, African hunting for Jeff has been all that he had hoped for and more. For more than twenty years he and Janelle both have learned to love Africa—its people, its flora and fauna, its wildness. They have had the good fortune to share this personally with two of their children and four of their five grandchildren. They have had the pleasure of introducing many friends to the unique and captivating charm of this wonderful part of the world. The African experience has proved addictive and both Jeff and Janelle have vowed to continue to travel there both with and without accompanying family and friends for as long as they are able.

In the early 1970's Jeff and Janelle agreed that it looked as though Jeff's thriving career as international firearms consultant would be best served by his move to a place where he could buy a good piece of land, build his own ranges and set up his own school on his own property and let people come to him. The traveling had become extensive and did not seem to be the most efficient way to make what Jeff had to teach available to the many interested people who clamored for his instruction. They decided to look around for a fairly large piece of land in a good location where the local gun laws would make it easy to operate a shooting school.

They had Arizona in mind from the beginning. Jeff had visited the Prescott area with his father years before and remembered it fondly. The Arizona gun laws were very favorable and the weather near Prescott was not so hot in the summer as to be unbearable nor so cold or so snowy in winter as to prohibit outdoor activity. They decided on Arizona and looked for several years.

In August of 1973 they found their property. A large cattle ranch in the Chino Valley area north of Prescott was being divided and sold and the location was perfect. They acquired as many acres as they could, one hundred and sixty. It was near the small town of Paulden, Arizona, about 25 miles north of Prescott. They put their money down, put the much-loved house in Big Bear up for sale and waited for a buyer.

The housing market in Big Bear was bad in 1973 and 1974, but Jeff and Janelle began to put together their ranch anyway, piece by piece. Their acreage was about four miles off the paved highway, and there was nothing there and nothing between them and the highway but bare land, rolling hills with scrub trees and shrubs, antelope, rattlesnakes, coyotes, rabbits, ground squirrels, quail and an occasional bobcat. There were no telephone lines, no sewer lines, no electrical lines and for the last half mile or so, no road at all. It was truly a pioneering effort of a relatively rigorous sort. Jeff and Janelle were both 54 years old.

The Gunsite gate in winter.

The "Sconce" takes shape.

Janelle points to the big sign welcoming I.P.S.C. members.

Jeff with Ian Smith, last President of Rhodesia.

*Paralee Cooper marries
Bruce Edgar Heath,
June 22, 1968.*

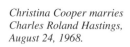
*Christina Cooper marries
Charles Roland Hastings,
August 24, 1968.*

Above: Linda Theresa Cooper marries Joe Bailey Wisdom, January 6, 1973.
Right: Jeff and Janelle were proud parents (shown here at Parry's wedding).

Distinguished competitive shooters made distinguished wedding guests. From left to right: Ray Chapman, Al Nichols, Elden Carl, Jeff.

The house in Big Bear was slow to sell, so Jeff and Janelle put up a double-wide trailer on their land for temporary housing, dug a well, put in a septic tank and a generator, equipped their Volkswagen van with a radio telephone for communication and started to build the ranges Jeff designed.

At this same time, Jeff finished his definitive work on what his field laboratory had taught them all over the last many years about practical pistolcraft. This was *Cooper on Handguns*, published in 1974. This book was a commercial success and became the bible for his students, setting the standard for what came to be known as "The Modern Technique of the Pistol".

In 1975, having finally sold the Big Bear house for something like fifty cents on the dollar, Jeff and Janelle moved to their Arizona ranch permanently. They said goodby to the lake and the mountains and their numerous friends with regret, but entered into their new venture with characteristic enthusiasm and optimism. They named their property "Gunsite" and began their full time efforts to build their school which they named "The American Pistol Institute."

Jeff's international following read about the activities of the Bear Valley Gunslingers and the Southwest Pistol League with great interest. Suggestions to form an international organization came from all over the world. In 1976, interested men from the four corners of the globe met in Columbia, Missouri to discuss these suggestions. The result was the formation of the International Practical Shooting Confederation, known as I.P.S.C. or "*ippsick*".

Jeff was the founder and was named the first president of the organization. As such, he gave up competition. First of all, he had no time for the amount of practice it took to stay in top form. Secondly, he felt that a competitor should not have a serious hand in making the rules of competition. No matter how honest a man is or how much of a distinguished sportsman he may be he will want the rules to favor his particular position. Jeff felt that the man who makes the rules should be above that.

I.P.S.C. lost no time in setting up matches for international competitions and the first one took place in Berndorf, Austria that same year, 1976. The second was in Salisbury, Rhodesia in 1977 and the third in Roodepoort, South Africa in 1979. The organization has continued to grow and the popular international competitions have continued each year since their inception, taking place in all sorts of exotic locales.

So in the mid 1970's, with all three daughters married and starting their own families, Jeff and Janelle built Gunsite ranch and The American Pistol Institute. From a raw and remote piece of land without any sign of civilization in sight to a thriving and successful school, known throughout the world as *the* place to learn defensive pistolcraft and later rifle technique and shotgun as well, they planned and saved and built and saved and planned and built more, piece by piece.

Gunsite

"He's a born teacher. He learns so that he can teach."
        – ELDEN CARL

*"Logic. Looking for answers and tons of knowledge at (his)....
immediate disposal to put....in a framework of others' searches and
conclusions. Add ability to communicate with people and his literary
ability and this curiosity and enthusiasm. That's it. There's nobody
else with this package."*
        – BARRY MILLER

*"The fact that he has become a world authority in his field does not
surprise me. If he is going to do something, he is going to do it right."*
        – CHARLES BRAGG

*"Jeff was the first to articulate a moral attitude toward self-defense
which resonates with many of us: that it is not so much a right as a
positive duty. The fact that he was actively developing and training
others in combat techniques added to his credibility in this area."*
*"I realized when I first went to Gunsite that many of my class-
mates were seeking not only Jeff's instruction, but his judg-
ment....... This attitude that Jeff inspires is very valuable in his role
as teacher....."*
        – PAUL KIRCHNER

*"His ability to see something, grasp what's going on and then write
it down and communicate it to somebody else—nobody else does it
as well."*
        – GILES STOCK

"I want to emphasize the rare nature of Jeff's instruction—a combination of technical ability placed within a moral framework. Jeff was the first instructor I knew of who insisted that mere skill with a weapon was insufficient; the skill and the tool must only be used in a righteous cause....Gunsite became the Camelot of the Great Southwest....(those) who rode away from Gunsite were different men and women from those who had arrived six days before. That is the enduring legacy of my friend Jeff Cooper."

— BARRETT TILLMAN

Jeff's purpose at Gunsite was to establish a center where he could shoot and teach pistol easily and handily within walking distance of his house. (Rifle and shotgun classes were added later when the desire for Jeff's instruction in the use of these weapons became apparent.) They began with what they called "the square range", a rectangular pistol range going back to 50 meters. Then they extended that range out to 500 meters and built a bench rest platform. The next to be built was the "funhouse", an indoor reaction course built like a block house with hallways and rooms and stairs and an entrance and exit.

They built roads and then poured money into maintaining them. Every cloudburst that came along meant a potential outlay of thousands of dollars just to maintain the accessibility of Gunsite from the highway.

Water was supplied by a deep well which operated with a pump attached to the windmill. When several windless days went by in a row, Jeff and Janelle had to concern themselves with their dwindling water supply. The addition of a gas-operated generator supplemented the wind power.

With no electrical lines, they had to supply their own electricity with another windmill which was connected to an entire bank of large black batteries which were kept on several shelves in the barn. Again, when the wind deserted them, electricity had to be produced by a back-up generator. To conserve energy, all electricity was turned off completely every night.

The radio phone in the Volkswagen was interesting. Whenever an incoming call was connected, the horn in the Volkswagen would honk and someone had to run out to the car to answer. Radio communication operates one way at a time and many people could not get used to the fact that they had to state their business, then pause and refrain from speaking until the answer was forthcoming. Jeff and Janelle kept the Volkswagen parked right by the front door of their trailer for convenience, but calls came in when the car was in use too and the horn would honk at the most inconvenient times, startling the drivers of other vehicles or the people in the parking lot at the market.

Jeff turned his attention to the curriculum. He began with pistol only, since this was the area where he had developed the greatest changes. When he first found he needed help in running a class, he turned to Bruce Nelson, a distinguished competitor in the Southwest Pistol League since the age of 17 who had gone on to a career in law enforcement. Bruce was smart, personable and dedicated and had a lot of experience to draw upon in the area of lethal confrontations in police work. He had made a study of police shootings from a number of agencies' files and had put together a presentation on officer survival which was fascinating. He generously shared this with the Gunsite students.

Jeff wanted to make sure that the students he taught at Gunsite were good citizens. He knew that whatever criteria he required could be circumvented by a diligent crook, but he did the best he could. In the beginning, prospective students had to produce at least one of the following credentials:

- current commissioned service in the armed forces of the United States, or, if enlisted, a letter of recommendation from the current commanding officer.
- current active duty in any law enforcement agency of the United States.
- life membership in the National Rifle Association.
- letter of recommendation from the head of the law enforcement agency having jurisdiction over the prospective student.
- letter of recommendation from the head of the prospective student's church.

Prospective students who could not provide any of these were turned away.

Making money was never a goal. Jeff and Janelle set their prices exactly where they thought they would be able to break even, taking into consideration the maintenance of the facilities and the continuous improvements they planned. Each time they had to raise prices, they did so with reluctance. When unforeseen expenses came up, they would use their own money unstintingly. Gunsite was truly a labor of love.

They bought more land, bringing the total to about 240 acres. They added buildings and ranges and a campground. The first lecture sessions were held on the veranda of Jeff and Janelle's trailer. Later they added a large classroom and then a gunsmithy with attached living quarters so that work on guns could be done on the premises.

The early faculty Jeff recruited came from distinguished competitors from the California days. As the school increased in size and more instructors were needed, Jeff would recruit very carefully from the best of the students. He had an eye for both quality in shooting skill and in the ability to teach others. He would invite those he thought could handle the job back for observation. Some made it and some did not. Often students would approach Jeff or Janelle and request a try at teaching. Asking was no guarantee that a trial run would be forthcoming.

Jeff wanted many qualities in his instructors. First, he wanted good shots. They had to be so good that they could do anything they asked the student to

The Teacher.

do easily and quickly, on demand. Second, they had to have the desire to impart knowledge to others. That is a quality one either has or does not. Third, they had to have a thorough knowledge of the theory being taught. Fourth, they had to have what Jeff referred to as "command presence"—a force of personality that generates respect. When Jeff found a man with these four characteristics, he also required that the man be able to get away from his own business for week-long stints at Gunsite. Fortunately, there were many excellent people who could and the faculty at Gunsite developed into the best in the world. (When choosing instructors, Jeff also gave preference to those who had come face to face with an armed enemy and prevailed.)

Jeff was asking no more from his instructors than he was able to deliver himself—in fact less. He had developed the theory himself, had more "command presence" than most and his desire to impart knowledge (of all kinds) never ceased. He is also a very good shot. A combination of fast reflexes, perfect eyesight and physical coordination, keen intellectual interest, practice, competition and the rewards of success honed in Jeff a skill with weapons which began early and has never ceased.

Jeff was never a member of any Olympic team and he never qualified in the military as a "distinguished expert" but his skill can be measured in other ways. He never had any trouble qualifying as expert rifleman in the military and he shot successfully on a number of minor rifle teams. He did not go into competitive pistol shooting until the Big Bear days, and there he cleaned up. He was the overall Annual Champion in 1959, 1960 and 1961, shooting against the full line up of the old masters. This was a relatively small group and they were in the process of inventing a new technique, so assessing the skill of the competitors is difficult. However, years of teaching weaponcraft to countless people, often distinguished military and police marksmen, plus involvement in creating the I.P.S.C. programs which bring together the top competitors from all over the world, is some basis for judging how good one had to be to win Annual Champion in southern California in the early 1960's.

I watched the Leatherslap demonstration of 1965 and although I did not know enough to be impressed at the time, I do now. Jeff always planned a few small feats of skill as crowd-pleasing teasers before the actual Leatherslap began. In 1965, we pinned a regular-sized balloon against a tree trunk 164 yards from the line of fire at a slight incline against the hillside. The balloon waved slightly in the breeze. Jeff invited all the masters to the line to try their luck at hitting that balloon with their pistols—one shot each. Jeff had the first shot and broke the balloon. We heard a small boy ask his father how that was done and the man's explanation was that there was someone hiding up there in the trees with a .22.

As an attention-getter, this part of the demonstration was not as exciting as planned. Jeff had figured that it would take each shooter several tries to hit that balloon and the tension would build accordingly. No such luck!

We moved on to the second part of the demonstration involving an ax blade. Jeff had seen a similar feat at a side show when he was a boy and adapted the idea. It involved mounting two clay pigeons about five feet apart to a backstop of metal, and then placing an ax, blade forward, between the two. The bullet only had to hit the backstop in order for the lead splash to break both targets, but the audience did not know that and would think that the bullet had to be split exactly in half upon the blade. Jeff practiced until he could be sure to hit the metal backstop every time, unsighted, from seven yards distance, drawing and shooting as quickly as possible. Colonel Bud Reynolds gave the appropriate buildup over the microphone. At the signal, Jeff pulled a very fast draw from a competition holster and the entire crowd saw that ax blade move backward. When Bud retrieved the ax, we could all see the bright new lead splash on each side of the blade!

Jeff had intended to explain to the crowd exactly what they had seen as opposed to what the feat looked like, with appropriate admonitions regarding not believing everything one sees. His shot took the edge right off his little speech so he gave up the explanation.

That crowd never knew how amazing those two shots were, and neither did I until much later. The competitors all knew however, and those shots were the subject of much discussion and admiration for years.

These were one-time "trick" shots and don't say much for consistency. For those who have taken Jeff's rifle instruction, he can consistently go clean on the proscribed course on snap shots. Up until just a few years ago (when running became difficult), he could consistently break forty points out of fifty in less than two minutes on the "Rifle 10" course. He has several times broken twenty seconds on the "Rifle Bounce" and he has over the years demonstrated such things on demand.

Just before the Gulf War, Jeff was invited to Fort Benning to shoot the twenty-five millimeter automatic cannon which constitutes the main battery of the Bradley infantry fighting vehicle. Due to a fortuitous administrative glitch, Jeff was able to fire the weapon extensively—much more than the usual V.I.P. allowance. The gun is easy to shoot and Jeff had a marvelous time shooting it at all sorts of targets at various ranges, both moving and stationary.

When the shooting was over Jeff inadvertently overhead a bit of conversation between two staff instructors on the far side of the vehicle:

"Who is that old guy?"

"Don't worry about it. He does that for a living."

Of course that is not exactly true, but if it shoots, Jeff will be happy to try it out, will enjoy doing so and will score well. (He did so with the great, one-twenty smooth-bore of the Abrams tank on an earlier occasion.)

Just the other day, a ground squirrel (considered a common nuisance around Gunsite) ran across the porch of the Sconce, stealing a crust and scar-

The Shooter.

ing away all the quail. When Janelle commented on it, Jeff picked up his old .22 rifle, slid the door open and hit that running squirrel squarely with one offhand shot from a distance of about 10 yards. He was and is an excellent shot.

At Gunsite, Jeff found that he was able to produce a very capable practitioner in 28 hours of instruction and the expenditure of about 500 rounds of ammunition. This was predicated on the student being there because he or she wished to learn. Students sent to school by someone else, whose tuition was paid by someone else, never did as well as the self-motivated individual who paid his own way. This was a real economic accomplishment on the part of the school. Governments all over the world think that the more shooting a student does the better the school is. This proved to be untrue.

Gunsite set four grades of achievement. The first was a Certificate of Completion, which meant you had attended and been exposed to it, but did not get it. There were very few of those because of the dedication of the staff, but they did have some. Jeff did not want people who did not measure up walking away from Gunsite with a bonafide grade.

The next level was Marksman. This meant you were okay. Then there was Marksman First Class or M1. This was good and meant you were a good shot. Then there were the Expert or E tickets. For about 15 years, an E ticket from Gunsite meant the highest level that could be achieved anywhere in the world for competence with a handgun in a defensive sense. This is no longer true and may never be true again. There are a few hundred of those E tickets around.

The school expanded into rifles, putting carbines into a class by themselves. The combat shotgun program was developed and was very effective, particularly for law enforcement. Pistol developed into three levels, general, remedial and advanced. Rifle developed into two levels, general and advanced. Tutorials could be had if necessary, but were discouraged for costs' sake. Jeff continued to teach around the world wherever there was a need that could not be met in Arizona.

Gunsite under Jeff was always dedicated to excellence and nothing else. Many people who graduated from classes there have said innumerable times that they owe their lives to Jeff and the lessons he taught them. This is a very satisfying accomplishment that gives both Jeff and Janelle much pleasure. The snowball effect of Jeff's teachings is hard to estimate, but many of his students were and are instructors in their own right and spread the word all over the world. This also is worth contemplating on a snowy evening in front of the fire.

"I was surprised to learn, many years after my first API class (in 1978), that Jeff did not maintain a file of after-action reports from his students. At one time it seems that a few dozen Gunsite grads

had saved their lives by applying the lessons learned—not all of whom did so by shooting, which is further proof of the quality of their training."

– BARRETT TILLMAN

In 1977, my husband Joe and I made a decision to leave our jobs in Florida and move back out West. Joe had been born in Arizona and wanted to be closer to his parents who were getting older. I also wanted to be back in the West and thought Arizona sounded just fine, especially since both my parents and one of my sisters and her family had moved there. When Joe wrote of our intentions to my parents, they asked us to come to Gunsite and see if helping them build their school was agreeable to us. We talked it over and moved in with Mom and Dad in their trailer in May of 1977.

They had held their first class, which was highly experimental, before we arrived and were gearing up to begin regularly scheduled classes. There was a great deal to do all the time and it was all inspiring and exciting. Joe and I jumped in with both feet. We both took the general pistol class and settled in to doing what needed to be done. I took over secretarial work and student coordination while Joe took over range maintenance and minor construction and also later helped instruct. (He had been six years in the Marine Corps,

Jeff instructs Lindy in rifle technique while Joe looks on.

achieving the rank of Captain.) We worked closely with Bruce Nelson in those days and I was delighted to be able to see Bruce on a regular basis, having first met him in Big Bear when I was 15.

We left in May of 1978. It was just not in the cards for this father-in-law to work side by side with this son-in-law. Others have commented that similar situations normally do not work well. In any case, my husband and my father have much in common, but are totally different in many important ways. The break was not amiable and is the greatest regret of my life. The Gunsite experience with the great people and the wonderful bonding which took place amongst the students and the healthy atmosphere and the sense of accomplishment we all felt was something I look back on with the greatest of pleasure. I wish it could have continued.

I know that my parents also wanted very much for our involvement to work out and they also regret that it did not.

The school did continue and it flourished. When a student finished a week-long class at Gunsite he came away with a new (or improved) skill with his weapon, a thorough understanding of what he would need to do to improve his chances of prevailing in a lethal situation, numerous new friends who shared at least that interest and often many more, and a membership in the Gunsite "family". He (or she) felt a new self-confidence and calm sense of self-worth in the knowledge that he had much better control over whatever dangerous situation might present itself, if it ever should. Gunsite built better people and every graduate knew it.

Hunting and war stories

Prior to the development of Gunsite and all through its development and progress, Jeff continued to travel and teach and hunt all over the world whenever the opportunities arose. He developed his deep and abiding love for Africa and he racked up numerous noteworthy and memorable experiences in various other interesting locales.

To Barry Miller of Durban, South Africa, Jeff feels he owes a debt which can never be repaid. Barry introduced Jeff to the black buffalo of Africa—*Syncerus caffer*. To Jeff, as well as to numerous other outdoorsmen of both the past and the present, the "joined-horn infidel" is the world's grandest game animal. The buffalo is today the quarry most likely to bring his pursuer to grief. If a hunter is properly armed, well-schooled on bovine anatomy, and capable of maintaining his concentration under conditions of extreme excitement, he is unlikely to be brought down by a buffalo. However, the chance is always there, and the list of celebrities killed by the African buffalo is a long one. Robert Ruark once said that the buffalo was the only thing on earth that scared him, and it is thus that the buffalo hunter partakes of an experience not available to others.

When Barry first met Jeff he saw at once that Jeff needed to meet the African buffalo face-to-face in order to round out his hunting experiences. On the occasion of the world pistol championship in Rhodesia in 1977, Barry introduced Jeff to Tony Weeks, who was primarily an airline pilot, but who was also a passionate backwoodsman. Tony knew of a ranch down on the Lundi River that was supposed to contain a shootable bunch of buffalo and a party was quickly organized to go down there and look into the situation. Tony and Barry and Jeff were accompanied by Ray Chapman, the renowned pistol champion, and Alex du Plessis, a shooting enthusiast and resident of Salisbury. The expedition was an informal one, and they picked up local trackers on the way.

The drive down from Salisbury to the ranch took most of a day. Not more than a quarter mile outside the ranch fence Barry shot a prime warthog boar with his .44 Magnum pistol. The field dressing of this animal occupied the party long enough so that when they arrived at their proposed campsite it was full dark. They made themselves as comfortable as they could. About fifty paces off in the thorn, the trackers had built a roaring fire over which they had hung a large pot. They proceeded to sing and improvise a percussion section with more pots. This was great ambiance for Jeff's first night sleeping out in the African bush.

In the years following this first experience, Jeff came to discover that there are four basic necessities to an African hunting trip, as follows:

1. A good camp cook. Any experienced outdoorsman is capable of preparing his own meals, but the necessity for doing so cuts into his hunting time, which is always limited. It is also vastly more pleasant to come into camp after a hard day's hunting to find a meal waiting, rather than to be faced with the chore of meal preparation. One can survive on cold corned beef and beans from a can, but a well-prepared hot meal does wonders to improve the adventure.

2. A good tracker. Much of the game encountered in Africa is apprehended by tracking, and this is especially true of lion and buffalo. Jeff's experience is that any country black asked will claim to be an excellent tracker, but these claims are mostly untrue. A really good tracker is rare and will only be located through connections with people who know the country. Watching a good tracker work is a delight as he moves rapidly through terrain which shows no evidence of traffic to the unpracticed eye.Without a really good tracker the African hunt is not likely to be fully productive.

3. Warm bedding. In the more than twenty years Jeff has hunted in Africa he has never slept hot, but has often been cold. There are certainly places on the continent where heat is a problem, but Jeff has not been to them. Moreover, most of the material written by the early explorers and hunters was the product of Englishmen, who originated in a cold, damp island and to whom any temperature over 70 degrees is uncomfortable. On this first trip, the best Jeff's party could do was scrape up a few cotton sleeping bags which were both skimpy and short. Since that first trip, he has been much better prepared.

4. Enough beer. The Africans Jeff knows are enthusiastic beer drinkers and one must not skimp on this portion of the provisions.

On this first trip on the Lundi the only one of the four essentials they had was plenty of beer.

Jeff settled down for a not very comfortable night, made distinctly more pleasant by the snorting of the hippos in the river below the bluff on which they were camped. To him, the snort of a hippo a hundred yards away sounded exactly like the snort of a horse at arm's length.

They were up and out early the next morning and while Jeff did no shooting that day, he hardly missed it. He reveled in the new sights and sounds and smells of Africa. He caught a glimpse of a leopard flashing across the dirt track ahead of them in the headlights of the car. He saw a lordly eland bull clear an 8-foot game fence without so much as a running start. He saw an elfin bushbuck bark at him through the trees, but he did not take it for fear of spooking the primary target. He later learned that buffalo do not spook much. They do not like to run and they are not particularly alarmed by gunfire.

They were back at camp by mid-afternoon and Tony proposed that they go down along the river to "shoot something to eat". Jeff was astonished. The warthog Barry had shot the previous evening was big and should have provided enough meat for the entire party for at least one full day. "What about that pig?", Jeff asked Tony. Tony grinned at him and said, "That's gone."

That was Jeff's first experience with the legendary meat hunger of the Bantu people, which is based upon the perennial fear of protein deficiency, called *kwashiorkor* or "second-child disease". The story is that when the first child is weaned to make room for the second, he is placed upon a grain diet and often develops the unpleasant symptoms of the swollen belly, runny nose and spindly legs. The Bantu people revere fresh meat as the staff of life. The word throughout most of the various tribes is *nyama*, and it is never heard pronounced without explosive enthusiasm. This is why it is possible for any hunting party to fill its ranks with enthusiastic helpers, paid or not. They crave *nyama*, and money is incidental. There seems to be no limit to what they can consume and the hunter's rifle is in effect a wizard's wand.

Ray and his trackers finally ran across the elusive bunch of buffalo on the third day, but it was not large and did not seem to contain any trophy bulls. No contact was made.

On the fourth day they decided to break camp and set forth for the home of a forest ranger Tony knew up near the borders of Wankie Park to the northwest. This was Kerry Finn, a native Rhodesian of Scottish ancestry. He received the group with traditional Rhodesian hospitality and the following morning they set out in cars. Contact was quick and it became clear that a good-sized herd had just crossed the road at right angles.

The party set out in a line, walking some twenty paces apart. In no more than 15 minutes, Jeff began to notice the unmistakable odor of cattle—not that of manure, but of warm, living beef. To Jeff, suddenly finding himself standing within smelling distance of a bunch of wild African buffalo was a powerful shock. Suddenly, a black, armored head snapped up above the grass just ahead and a little to the right. Then another directly to the right. Then a third to the left front. Then more. They were right in amongst them. At a range of perhaps 25 paces Jeff placed the crosswire a hand's breadth under the chin on the central bull and gently squeezed the trigger. At the sound of the shot the animal lowered his nose and swung to his left, and just as he turned broadside Kerry let go with his double 470 slightly to Jeff's left and rear.

The buffalo ran to their right front and they both took off after him. Jeff remembers seeing Kerry's empty case fly through the air as he snapped another

Jeff's first buffalo, Rhodesia, 1977.

round into the chamber without taking his eyes off his target.

The bull was almost immediately out of sight in the thorn bush but Kerry and Jeff attempted to keep him in view. Kerry prevailed and Jeff saw him race to a stop, raise his rifle and fire. As Jeff cleared a thorn bush he saw the bull some 35 paces ahead, on the ground and facing them with a trickle of blood running from a 50-caliber hole in his frontal bone.

That was one of the greatest shots Jeff has ever witnessed. From a dead run under extreme pressure, Kerry was able to stop himself and place the round from his heavy rifle exactly where he intended. Kerry was later killed in action in the Rhodesian War, but Jeff has the buffalo's skull displayed today on the terrace of his home as a memorial to an outstanding warrior. When people admire the trophy Jeff is quick to tell them the story.

As they were dressing out the buffalo, they attracted the attention of a passing herd of elephant, one of whom was disturbed by the smell of blood. The rest of the herd did not seem to mind, but one young bull, probably anxious to display his bravery, turned and advanced upon the hunters, flapping his ears and screaming. None of Jeff's party was authorized to shoot an elephant, but they had to recognize the threat. Kerry pointed to a bush about 10 paces out and told them that if the bull advanced past that they were to kill him, shooting for third wrinkle in the forehead, dead center. They stood there at the ready while the young bull demonstrated in a fury. In due course he decided to drop the display and moved off to join the herd. Jeff has since been told that when an elephant demonstrates like that he is not actually charging, but rather attempting to intimidate. When he comes in to kill he

Jeff and Ray chat at the I.P.S.C. shoot in South Africa before taking off to go buffalo hunting in Rhodesia, 1979.

keeps his ears flat back and points his trunk straight forward, reaching. This is the theory and it most certainly has basis in fact, but anyone who makes "always" or "never" statements about wildlife behavior shows he does not know much about wildlife behavior.

From this point on, Jeff was absolutely hooked on hunting the black buffalo of Africa. As soon as he could arrange it, he went again, this time in 1979 and again in Rhodesia. The Rhodesian government treated him to an organized hunt up in the Kariba area on the Zambezi River. Besides Jeff, the party consisted of Dave Westerhout, Regional Director of IPSC, Ray Chapman, Raul Walters, Dick Thomas, and Dr. Albert Pauckner of Ansbach, Germany. This was a semi-official occasion under the direction of the renowned professional hunter Paul Coetzee, and they were allotted three elephants, including one big one, a buffalo apiece, and a mixed assortment of lesser game. ("Coetzee" is a good example of Afrikaaner pronunciation. Paul told them that to get it right one had to imagine saying, "I can't make it today, but I *could see ya* tomorrow", the double e being pronounced ee ah.)

On his first buffalo hunt, Jeff had used a 350 Remington Magnum with factory 250-grain ammunition. The performance of this combination on the buffalo was unsatisfactory. The bullet struck the forward area of the neck, ripped diagonally through some six inches of hide, proceeded 18 inches more, mushrooming perfectly, and stopped in the base of the neck short of the body cavity. This was good bullet performance and would have been perfectly satisfactory on elk, moose, lion or kudu—but not on buffalo. There is simply too much of a buffalo and he frequently shows almost no effect from gunfire.

On his second try for buffalo, Jeff used the 460 G&A Special, which projects a 458 caliber, 500-grain bullet at about 2400 f/s from a short barrel. It proved totally reliable and the second buffalo hunt was entirely successful as were many subsequent hunts for *Syncerus caffer*.

The Kariba hunt in 1979 occurred at a time when the Rhodesian war was in full cry. The organization now down in history as the "Selous Scouts" was fully active. This outfit is now legendary and almost any story told about irregular war has been applied to them. Jeff's party ran across a bunch one day mounted in trucks and the two groups stopped to exchange views. The organization was entirely racially mixed, there being no difference in rank, position, uniform or armament between black and white. They were very tired and very dirty, but the thing that struck Jeff most was their singing. All members of the command knew all the songs of all the tribal groups involved, with the whites singing Sindebele, and when the tunes were changed, the blacks singing in English, Portuguese and Afrikaans. The morale of the Selous Scouts was based upon individual excellence rather than group thinking.

During the hunt, either in vehicles or on foot, Jeff's party had to maintain a continuous military alert in all directions at all times. Brian, their chief of security, habitually carried an FN 30-caliber assault rifle with the stock folded, and he kept his piece on fully automatic. When Jeff asked him if he thought he could hit anything with it, he replied that it was not necessary since, if the enemy ambushed them, they would do so from very short range and in superior numbers. He said that if they opened fire it would be from a distance of feet rather than yards, and that he would respond by emptying his entire 20-round magazine in the general direction of the attackers. "I probably won't hit any of them," he said, "but I will scare them to death and ordinarily they will put down their weapons and run."

Jeff thought about this and suggested a partner system. He was carrying a borrowed Czech 30-06 rifle mounted with an excellent German telescope sight. He had checked it out and knew where it hit. He suggested to Brian that on the occasion of an ambush he proceed normally and Jeff would wait until the ambushers were running away at which time he would pick them off one at a time. Brian agreed to this concept. As may be supposed, it never became necessary.

While encamped at Kariba, a plan was made to go down onto the Chirundu flats bordering the Zambezi where the prospects for good elephants were better. The fact that they were in a war zone was brought home when the host came in with several bottles of iodine and asked if they would please mark their blood types carefully in iodine on the inside of each forearm. The flats below the escarpment were heavily mined and everyone needed to prepare for the possibilities.

The Hunter.

As they approached the Chirundu Bridge from the rear, they passed a battery of six 25-pound field pieces pointing northward where they could reach across the river. They were heavily camouflaged, but there is no doubt the enemy knew where they were. When they got to the infantry camp they dismounted, and Brian and Jeff went skulking up over a small knoll where they could see the bridge and its approaches from both sides. There was no visible installation on the southern or Rhodesian side, but across the water, perhaps 400 meters away, there was a sentry box manned by the enemy. From Jeff's position in the bushes he could see a man walking back and forth carrying his AK47 which Jeff could just barely identify through his 6x sight.

Jeff squirmed into a solid prone position using the loop sling and analyzed the shot. He estimated that at that range, his bullet would probably drop 20 inches below the line of sight. His hold was rock solid and the next time the sentry stopped to look around Jeff placed the horizontal wire a handbreadth above the top of his head. There was no tremor in the rifle and everything seemed perfect.

"What are you up to Mr. Cooper?" asked Brian.

"I'm going to take that sportsman from here. Is that okay?"

"No, no, no, certainly not! Put that rifle down!"

"Why can't I take him?"

"It would jolly well cause an incident!"

"What's wrong with that? I suppose those 122's they threw into Kariba Village night before last was not an incident? If I deck that bird they will fling a lot of mortar shells into the camp behind us, and at that point the 25-pounders can let go and flatten that base across the river. That's the sort of incident we could really enjoy!"

"NO! Don't do it. I am telling you, don't do it!"

"Okay, it's your war, but let me do this, let me take the shell out of the chamber and squeeze-in on that lad just to prove to myself that I could have done it."

"No, Mr. Cooper, don't do that either!"

"What's the matter? Don't you trust me?"

"No!"

So they did not get into any action up near Kariba, though they expected and anticipated it. The Rhodesians seemed more concerned about their guests' skins than their own and they did not push their luck. Still, there was a special thrill about hunting in a war zone. One slept with one's shoes on. As they rode out through the wire in an advanced post up near Centenary, a large sign in red letters ordered, "Make Ready." The opposite side of that sign, which they saw as they came back in, was, "Unload." Jeff was careful to observe the sign on the way out, but displayed uncharacteristic bad manners on the way in.

Back home, Jeff continued writing and teaching and building and improving his school. When asked for assistance by those who could not arrange to come to Gunsite for instruction, he took his expertise to them. In 1982, at the time of the invasion of Lebanon, he was invited to Israel by Israeli Military Industries to test and evaluate a new heavy-weight pistol design they wished to introduce to the world market. He asked that he be permitted to carry his own pistol.

"No. That is forbidden," they exclaimed.

"Make an exception."

"You won't need a pistol. We will protect you."

"I don't want to be protected. I want to carry my own pistol."

"We will give you an Uzi."

"I don't want an Uzi, I want my own pistol. I don't need this job anyway." Pause. "You'd make a good Jew."

"Thank you."

Jeff carried his own pistol and at the conclusion of the trip he was made informally an honorary Rabbi.

The Israeli pistol exhibited one design flaw right away and Jeff was impressed with the speed with which the engineers corrected the problem. They made rapid progress.

During a lull in the work, the head of the operation told Jeff he had arranged a visit to the Holy City with car and driver provided by the company. This venture proved to be quite overwhelming, despite the fact that Jeff has never been a religious man. The immediate presence of the concrete memorials of the traditions of Western civilization were moving.

They visited the wall where it is possible to speak directly to God simply by slipping your written word into the cracks. They visited the Church of the Nativity in Bethlehem where alone, rather than with a crowd, Jeff was shown the exact spot upon which Jesus Christ was born, together with the manger in which he was laid. Just opposite is the shelf upon which the gifts of the Magi were placed. Obviously the authenticity of these wonderful sites is open to some question since the events took place a very long time ago. This does not detract from the experience in any way.

They visited the tomb of King David, just Jeff and his guide. The Rabbi in charge approached and asked Jeff for his name. Jeff replied that he was not one of the chosen people, but rather a *goy*. The Rabbi said it did not matter since he was obviously a warrior and David was a patron of warriors. Jeff told the Rabbi that his name was *Iohanna*, Hebrew for John. The Rabbi wrote it on a piece of paper, wrapped it around a candle, lit the candle and placed it upon the breast of the sarcophagus. Very heady feeling.

They did not visit the Tomb of the Rock for it was Ramadan and the Arabs were in a bad mood. Just across the canyon there rose the mountain from which Mary ascended bodily into Heaven. Jeff and his guide traced the Via

Dolorosa along which Christ made his way to Golgotha, and they stood on the spot where he was crucified. For Jeff, these experiences were very effective and he understood why his host had arranged the trip.

Throughout his visit, Jeff inquired about the possibility of going to see the war. The Israeli army had pushed north through Lebanon to Beirut. Jeff's hosts deflected his requests until they could think of no more excuses and one day Jeff was handed the uniform of the Israeli Defense Force (Zahal) and told to be dressed and ready the following morning at 4 a.m. When he came down to the lobby in the uniform and wearing his pistol openly, the woman behind the counter was obviously delighted, saying, "Oh, you are with Zahal!" Jeff answered, "*Ken*," this being one of the dozen Hebrew words he had picked up.

Jeff's guide was an Israeli major who spoke perfect English, as Jeff found most Israelis did. They traveled in a Landrover which mounted a belt-fed light machinegun in the back seat. The trip was a long one and they stopped for a mid-morning snack on the causeway at Tyre.

The high-rise buildings along the waterfront had been greatly damaged and the amount of broken glass was imposing. They were only a couple of days behind the leading edge of the Israeli forces and Jeff noticed especially that their sanitation was outstanding. As they approached the southern limits of Beirut, Jeff could smell battle, but he saw not one abandoned body. The smell of battle was highly evocative to Jeff, it being a combination of burning rubber, high explosives and spoiled flesh. As he traveled forward, his mind said, "Ah, yes, that's how it was. I remember now."

As they moved into the center of Beirut they entered the zone of confusion immediately behind the front lines. Many things impressed themselves upon Jeff. Israeli soldiers standing in line with soap and towel for a wash. Endless columns of 155 field guns streaming over the horizon. A Russian T-34 tank left over from World War II, still in action, and a long line of tank transporters carrying captured Russian T-55 tanks back to the rear for repair.

They drove on down into west Beirut, which was not yet subdued. Jeff had no accurate way of telling who was on what side since the usual signature, which was the curved magazine of the AK47, was not reliable. Jeff asked the major how to tell friends from enemies and he replied with a grin, "If they shoot at us, they're enemies."

On the way back they stopped for a moment by the building in which David Adan, the brilliant young Israeli general, whom Jeff had met in the United States, had been killed. It had been a pistol situation and from what Jeff could gather, proper pistol technique might have saved his life.

Jeff thoroughly enjoyed the whole experience. While he did not learn a great deal of Hebrew, he came away with a good feel for the Israeli attitude. He was delighted at the verification of Heinlein's dictum that an armed society is a polite society. Almost all the young people he saw were carrying

Uzis, and it amused Jeff to see them drop into an ice cream parlor and clank their machine pistols down on the tables amidst their banana splits.

Israel at that time was a nation at war and everybody was in the army. Jeff saw none of the famed women soldiers at the front line. Those in uniform he saw were in support positions as drivers, nurses, communicators and such. Jeff was impressed with the cheerful toughness of the Israelis and saw them do everything right—except shoot. His impression was that they do not as a group understand marksmanship and their justified cockiness did not admit of any desire to learn. In Jeff's opinion, this was unfortunate, but by no means confined to the Israelis alone. He has encountered it in all sorts of places throughout the world.

Jeff had another brush with war in 1987. This was a good many years after the fall of Rhodesia. Jeff and Barry had joined Ian Macfarlane for a buffalo hunt in the northern part of Botswana in the Tamafuta country which adjoins the western frontier of Wankie Park. The legal boundary between "Zimbabwe" and Botswana was at that point a straight line cut through the thorn with a bulldozer.

One day, they wound up with a wounded buffalo on their hands which, as they followed, cut left across the line into forbidden territory. Barry had hit the buffalo very hard and Jeff was quite sure the animal was down just a little further on. No hunter can accept the loss of a wounded beast, so they went after him, two trackers, Ian, Barry and Jeff. Following a wounded buffalo is one of life's supreme thrills and they were all keyed up like harp strings.

As they proceeded, the trackers began to look nervous and Ian suggested that they abandon the pursuit and get back across the border. Jeff asked how often that section of the border was patrolled and the answer was usually once a day, sometimes twice. Jeff asked, "With what?" And the answer was, a Landrover. "How many men?" The answer was, usually three, sometimes four.

Jeff thought for a moment and then said to Ian, "We've got three rifles here and we can clean them up before they know they're in trouble." Ian looked at Jeff sadly. "Jeff," he said, "I live in this country, you don't. Let's get out of here." So they got out. As Kipling put it:

> "Go, stalk the red deer o'er the heather.
> Follow the fox, if you can.
> But for pleasure and profit together,
> Allow me the hunting of man."

273

A Partnership

Gunsite and The American Pistol Institute flourished all through the decade of the 1980's and into the early 1990's. Jeff and Janelle poured their hearts and souls and money into their school, and it showed. They built their permanent home, "The Sconce" (a word whose several meanings include small fort), on the point of land overlooking the first rifle range with a beautiful view of the Chino Valley and the distant San Francisco Peaks. The house was designed by Jeff, with unique architectural features intended for security and defensibility. They continued to add buildings and ranges and refinements to existing structures and ranges.

The number of graduates increased and they spread the word. Other schools sprang up, encouraged by the success of Gunsite, but Gunsite remained the first and the best. The demand for additional classes increased for several reasons. First, as the word spread, more and more people wanted to attend, including entire groups from both law enforcement agencies and the military. Second, graduates had such wonderful experiences they wanted to come back. Since it was not cost effective to take the same class over and over again, they suggested remedial and refresher and advanced classes be added. Third, graduates felt the instruction in handguns was so good, Jeff should create classes teaching every weapon he knew. Since Jeff had been a rifleman first, rifle classes were easy to develop, although rifle technique has never been revolutionized in the way practical shooting revolutionized handguns. Although Jeff had never been a dedicated shotgunner, he knew the principles and could easily adapt what he knew to his practical outlook and method of teaching.

The idea of using all the instructors on a part-time basis kept the faculty in top-notch condition. First, they came when they could and viewed each of the weeks they could get away to teach a class at Gunsite as a vacation—a

The Sconce before. . .

. . .and after.

I. All guns are always loaded.
II. Never let the muzzle cover anything you are not willing to destroy.
III. Keep your finger **off** the trigger until your sights are on the target.
IV. Be sure of your target.

Above: Safety rules—simple, effective.
Below: Range rules.

1. Toe the line.
2. Check your piece, make ready, and holster.
3. Protect your eyes.
4. Protect your ears.
5. Set condition Orange.
6. Think about the front sight.
7. Wait for "GO!"

vacation with pay and a sense of accomplishment as icing on the cake. Second, if an instructor proved not quite up to the standard Jeff wanted, he did not have to be fired. Jeff could simply not ask him to return. That kept all the instructors on their toes and motivated to do well, keep their skills up and please Jeff. What better characteristics could an employer ask for?

Jeff and Janelle employed a secretary and a gunsmith and various people to work on range maintenance. The singular position they had trouble with was that of Operations Manager, the position Joe had held first. Jeff wanted someone with all the credentials asked of an instructor, but the Operations Manager was full time and was required to live on the premises. Jeff also wanted a family man and this meant a degree of isolation that meant quite an adjustment for most people.

Perhaps the biggest impediments to having a good man in that position long-term were two things. First, Jeff was not inclined toward participatory management. Gunsite was his and he was in charge. He expected a strict obedience to orders (which were often couched in mild terms as "suggestions" but were never to be taken lightly) and was not open to discussion about them. Second, he had an aversion to discussing anyone's shortcomings directly to his face. This led him to air whatever displeasure he might be feeling with anyone's performance with others, mostly Janelle. None of the high-quality men Jeff and Janelle hired for the position of Operations Manager was able to perform his best under those conditions and, to everyone's regret, the position was held and vacated by a number of good people over the years. The school did not seem to suffer very much because of this.

For many people, Jeff is not easy to be around. He has no small talk and does not suffer fools. He has no time for what he considers to be trivia, and that includes most of what the average person finds himself concerned with on a day-to-day basis. He is concerned with accomplishment and excellence and holds himself to that single concern. That offends some people and causes them to characterize Jeff as arrogant and elitist.

"Jeff never liked or was comfortable at large parties where all one does is make small talk. He would rather have one-on-one conversations. That was his pleasure and enjoyment. If I did not have time to really sit down and talk with him, there was no small talk. He has tried to become better at this through the years, but it doesn't come naturally. You really have to pay attention. If you know nothing about anything, you could not have a conversation with him at all. I think maybe Jeff feels that there is so little time to impart knowledge and there is so much to know and there is so much he wants to share, he doesn't want to waste time. Small talk is a waste of time. He's happiest when he has one's undivided attention."

"I don't think Jeff would ever intentionally demean another. I

don't think he has that kind of mean streak in him at all. He's just on a different plane. His feminine, intuitive side got the short shrift."

— VIRGINIA DEAN ARTHUR

"I think Jeff is completely objective. He has never been in a position where he was required to have any small talk. He's never been a salesman and he has almost never been anyone's employee. He's never been forced into a position where he had to come up with miscellaneous conversation......Making excuses is absolutely contrary to Jeff's approach.....He certainly is completely outspoken."

— CHARLES BRAGG

"He's very demanding and difficult to work for. He is difficult to approach at times. You don't always get enough time to ask your question or to put your idea across. When he renders a decision on your question or conclusion, that's it. Quite frequently there is no discussion and no explanation. At times he is a little overbearing."

— GILES STOCK

"As is often the case with strong personalities, the man's faults tend to be manifestations of his virtues. Certainly that's true in Jeff's case, as he holds extraordinarily strong beliefs—to the point that I would include him among the three or four most opinionated people I've ever known."

— BARRETT TILLMAN

"I think most of the people who don't like him just can't cut it because he's too sure of himself. He's sure of himself to the point of arrogance, although I don't really consider him arrogant. I've heard people say that about him. But if you know what you know and you know more than other people do that's a hell of a burden to carry. I don't suffer fools and neither does Jeff so I have no problem with that."

"If you are not daunted by his seeming overconfidence then he is more than happy to impart anything he knows and if you are willing to learn than you can learn a lot of things."

"I have talked to guys who say Jeff is smart and accomplished but a tough guy to get along with. I ask why and they say he is just a hard guy. I guess some people can't stand hard, tough people....

I suppose there is an element of jealousy and resentment for what he has accomplished. Jeff has no time for this stuff."

"He is not a snob. He would never draw the line at ignoring some-

body just because of their status. What they have to contribute is the only question. A snob would never operate that way and subsequently would learn less."

– ELDEN CARL

"Jeff has no small talk. He thinks only about big subjects and he simply ignores social amenities. Just a few years ago in Denver I brought up an old friend of mine for whom I have a great deal of respect and affection and introduced him to Jeff because he was eager to meet Jeff. He had heard so much about him. Jeff said, 'How do you do,' and then simply turned around and walked off. I was rather saddened by the fact that he would so ignore my good friend. Of course, Jeff did not know that he was such a good friend of mine and that he thought very highly of Jeff and had raised two sons very much in the image of Jeff Cooper disciples. My friend has hardly spoken to me since. I was a little disappointed in that but that is Jeff. You just have to take him the way he is. You have to respect him for that tremendous reservoir of knowledge that he has but you had better not expect him to kowtow to social graces."

"He would never deliberately insult anyone, but by his manner he would ignore him. People understand this and forgive this for the other things that they get from him. This has to be their attitude or else they are insulted and go away."

– JAY MARKS

"....many people thought Jeff was conceited—which would translate as they thought Jeff thought he was better then they....To me, Jeff was judging himself against his ideals rather than against his neighbors. And he was very humble when comparing himself against his ideals. Maybe others thought it was conceited for his standards to be ideals rather than simply his neighbors'. I do not know. But I never got a feeling of conceit from Jeff—only of confidence from what he had done, and humility for what he had been unable to do. This seemed to me to be as a person should be."

– CLIFFORD DOUGLAS

Jeff has been more successful in his dealings with people than anyone with such a distinct lack of "good old boy" charm has any right to be. This is due to Janelle. As in the best partnerships, their individual strengths complement each other and meld into a whole that is greater than the two parts.

"To an extent unusual in even the best marriages, (Janelle) and Jeff

Jeff and Janelle, like Currier and Ives, Lewis and Clark, Gilbert and Sullivan.

are bound together. I think that the pride of winning and keeping such an extraordinary woman must have given Jeff great strength."

— PAUL KIRCHNER

"He's very military and very much of a strong bearing and Janelle was the soft side. Janelle was polite, gracious—an exceptional host. Jeff rarely if ever compliments. If he does, you have to ask Janelle if you have been complimented."

— GILES STOCK

"I think she has been an absolutely ideal wife for Jeff. When I think of all the people I know who might have married Jeff, the unions might have lasted ten minutes. Janelle is the detail person in that union. She is the ideal spouse for Jeff."

— CHARLES BRAGG

"His feminine, intuitive side got the short shrift. That's one reason Janelle is so valuable to him in their marriage. I'm sure she has smoothed over innumerable social situations. All of his friends are just crazy about her. They meet her and she is very special. Jeff knows this."

— VIRGINIA DEAN ARTHUR

"In terms of Jeff and Janelle as a couple, the two of them together make a powerful and effective couple. Jeff has some rough edges that Janelle rounds off completely. Janelle often excuses weaknesses in people that Jeff points out and treats very roughly. The two of them get along so well together because I'm sure each realized that the other fills the gaps."

— JAY MARKS

Throughout the period of Gunsite's growth, Jeff continued to write. In 1980 *Fireworks* was published by The Janus Press. This was subtitled "A Gunsite Anthology" and included short autobiographical essays on a variety of subjects.

In 1981, the student coordinator at Gunsite proposed that they publish a newsletter for former students. *Gunsite Gossip* was born. Written by Jeff, with quotes and stories from many other sources, the newsletter was put out whenever Jeff had several pages worth of information he felt was worth sharing. This turned out to be at least monthly, and more often 15 to 20 times a year. Tom Siatos at *Guns & Ammo* proposed that excerpts from the *Gunsite Gossip* form a regular column in that magazine. Jeff had his doubts about this and told Tom that he felt his observations to be too pungent for general distribution. Tom's reply was, "Let me worry about that." This became "Cooper's Corner". People often tell Jeff that the only reason they buy the magazine is to read "Cooper's Corner". In due course, a compilation of the best from the newsletter was published in 1990 by Gunsite Press as *The Gargantuan Gunsite Gossip.*

Also in 1981, Jeff published a very small collection of "seventeen points to ponder" in booklet form and titled it *Quoth The Raven.* Genealogical research of Janelle's family had revealed an ancestor named Turgar, first Earl of Picheslei. He was a viking and as such his symbol was the symbol of Odin—a raven. Jeff adopted this for the symbol of Gunsite. This inspired the title of his booklet, a collection of notable quotes from authors, statesmen, warriors, philosophers and friends. This collection reveals the essence of Jeff's philosophy.

In 1988, Gunsite Press published *To Ride, Shoot Straight, and Speak the Truth,* the second collection of autobiographical essays. This was followed in 1992 with the third in the series, *Another Country.*

> *"One of the things that really impressed me about Jeff was in reading <u>Another Country</u>. In reading his writings I knew a part of him better than I ever had through all the years I have known him. He reveals himself through his writings. The two things that really impressed me were his joy of living and his appreciation of the moment."*
>
> *– VIRGINIA DEAN ARTHUR*

Life after Gunsite

J eff and Janelle turned 70 in 1990. Their efforts to build and maintain Gunsite had been monumental and the work showed no signs of becoming less arduous. To keep the school and the ranch in good repair and the excellence of the instruction intact required full time vigilance and enormous effort. Each wanted the other to slow down and take life a little more easily. They wanted to take more leisure trips together and spend more time with their children and grandchildren. They discussed the future of the school and decided to seek a buyer.

To their intense disappointment, none of their sons-in-law wanted to step in and take over. Each had his own established career. Jeff and Janelle quietly put out the word that they would consider selling to the right person. The right person meant someone who would continue to maintain and improve the school in the manner Jeff and Janelle would desire; someone who was also dedicated to the theories taught there and the pursuit of excellence above all else; someone to whom the perpetuation of Jeff's vision was paramount.

In 1992 they found a buyer and sold. They were anxious to insure the future of the school and so they made the purchase agreement ridiculously easy and entered into negotiations with little more than understandings and handshake terms. The buyer reiterated his dedication to maintaining Jeff's vision and Jeff himself as head of instruction and curriculum. Jeff and Janelle continued to live in the Sconce, right in the middle of the property.

Incident upon unfortunate incident turned what began as an amiable relationship into an intolerable clash of wills and intent. In 1993, the new buyer banned Jeff from the ranges he had planned and built and told him his services were no longer needed in the area of instruction—in fact no longer needed anywhere at all in the operation of the school.

This was a disaster for Jeff and Janelle. They were suddenly cut off from

The grandchildren then. . .

what had become their life's work, the culmination of years of dedicated research and effort, the achievement of a lifetime. They were virtually cut off from the staff and the instructors and the students in an instant and effectively isolated in their house in the middle of what had now become "enemy territory". It was a shock to them both. For all their education and sophistication, they were both naive in a business sense and inclined to trust people and take them at their word.

As word of the situation at Gunsite spread, many people came forward with the benefit of hindsight, offering solace and advice and shaking their heads at the fact that Jeff and Janelle had not entertained more offers, asked a higher price, signed a tighter contract and generally been more cautious. Such support was appreciated but not encouraged. It was not productive. Jeff and Janelle watched the deterioration of their school and its standards painfully over the months following the sale, but there was nothing to be done. The immortal words of Rudyard Kipling's *If*, one of Jeff's favorite poems, had come close:

> *"If you can meet with Triumph and Disaster*
> > *And treat those two impostors just the same:*
> *If you can bear to hear the truth you've spoken*
> > *Twisted by knaves to make a trap for fools,*
> *Or watch the things you gave your life to, broken,*
> > *And stoop and build 'em up with worn-out tools."*

. . .and now. From left to right, Vicky Hastings Carruthers, Tyler Heath, Amy Heath, Tess Hastings Jones, Lisa Heath Altevogt.

> *"It has amazed me that the reverses at Gunsite did not send him into a funk. His whole lifetime of building up what culminated in Gunsite is down the tube, but this has not thrown him. He still is enjoying life to the fullest and appreciating everything moment by moment."*
>
> *– VIRGINIA DEAN ARTHUR*

Jeff refused to allow the situation to dampen his spirits for long. He continued to teach and travel and write, and continues to do so today. In 1994, he and Janelle hosted a month-long tour of South Africa for a group of shooters who had all taken the rifle class from Jeff—a trip which included ten days of hunting. His enthusiasm for sharing "the Golden Joys" was catching and the trip was a marvelous learning experience for all involved. He and Janelle returned to Africa in 1996 for another memorable month.

Jeff is a member of the Board of Directors of the National Rifle Association and meetings, board business and correspondence keep him occupied. He continues to produce a monthly column for *Guns & Ammo* magazine, as well as the more-than-monthly newsletter called *Jeff Cooper's Commentaries*. He remains a participant in the activities of the International Practical Shooting Confederation. He continues to teach shooting classes outside Arizona whenever the demand presents itself. His volume of correspondence from all over the world continues unabated. He and Janelle don't have time for regret.

Jeff in an official N.R.A. photo.

Each year Jeff and Janelle host a "Gunsite Reunion and Theodore Roosevelt Memorial" confabulation at the NRA's Whittington Center near Raton, New Mexico. Participants (all graduates of one or more of Jeff's classes) meet, shoot, gab far into the night and gather in the evening for "declamations". This consists mostly of poetry recitations, both original and borrowed, of a sort consistent with the patriotic and adventurous spirit of Theodore Roosevelt. We also have songs and stories and other readings. We all come away from the weekend refreshed and renewed. As author, illustrator, Gunsite grad and friend Paul Kirchner put it, "Only Jeff Cooper could concoct such an event!"

As the years have gone by, Jeff has received awards and tributes and accolades too numerous to list. Janelle keeps a file of all the written tributes he has received from students, readers, fans, friends and acquaintances. To reproduce them all would take an entire book. His impact has been and continues to be wide and far-reaching.

> *"As I reflect back over the last 30 years or so, it occurs to me to say something on the order of 'Thank God for Jeff Cooper'.....You are the Last American Hero to more of us than you may imagine. If a better future is to be built, it will be upon your legacy of honor, manliness and integrity.....We owe you a debt we cannot repay."*
> *– W. FRANK WARREN*

> *"I know you will not be offended when I say I place you with my favorite 19th century writers.....The waning days of a curious century are made better by writings such as yours."*
> *– HOWARD MCCORD*

> *"...he is truly the father of the modern technique of the pistol.....No one since Samuel Colt has had a greater impact on practical pistolcraft than Jeff Cooper."*
> *– FINN AAGAARD*

"He'll be remembered for being a teacher—but he's more than a teacher. He's one of those people you meet, not very damned often, that you'd like to call a friend."

– JOHN GANNAWAY

"He is a man I hold in high regard, and whose acquaintance I value. Somebody I would one day point out to my son as an example of what he should use as a role model."

– PIERRE VAN DER WALT

"....I have to tell you that if I were to win a gold medal in the Olympics it would not mean as much to me as receiving (this award) from your father. When I was growing up I was surrounded by indifferent stepfathers and weakness. I craved masculinity and strength but there was no real man around to help me. I discovered your father's writing and consumed all of it I could get my hands on. Being the man God would have me be is of utmost importance in my life, and your father has helped me so much in this. I so respect and appreciate him....."

– TOM RUSSELL

"I would like to see Jeff remembered as a complete man. A man of thought, of wisdom, of historical appreciation, of timeless values, and yet of direct physical courage and action. A man of action who knew the Classics and applied them to his own life. A man who saw an important problem—the preservation of individual liberty—and through thought as well as experiment made a great contribution to this important value. A man who tried to live the values of the classic gentleman warrior, and won the hand and love of a great lady in so doing."

"I would like to see it thought that his values and conduct are the right way to live."

– CLIFFORD DOUGLAS

Changes at Gunsite

On the afternoon of September 30, 1999, four very welcome visitors came to the Sconce with a big bottle of champagne and some good news. Gunsite had at last been sold. Rumors of a sale had been floating around for several months with various buyers named, but at last a contract had been signed and the new owner came by for a celebration. Owen "Buz" Mills, his wife Sonja, his father-in-law David Pedwell and his friend Coulbourn "Bud" Dykes were welcomed by Jeff and Janelle with open arms. Buz, a successful businessman, had been a Gunsite student years ago and had entered into negotiations to buy the school when it became available the second time. My husband Joe and I were there as well to meet them and it was a happy scene after years of what had become an uncomfortable situation at best.

The deterioration of the physical plant was worse than any of us knew, but Buz immediately set out to repair, upgrade, and add to the ranges, offices, classrooms, pro-shop and other facilities with a fervor that energized everyone. He was determined to bring Gunsite back to its former glory and to cement its place as the pre-eminent small arms shooting school in the world. He had recruited Bud to be his General Manager. A decorated Army veteran who had seen extensive combat in Vietnam, and a retired police chief from Maryland, Bud was capable as well as amiable and an excellent choice to run the day-to-day operations of the school. One month after the sale, Bud was killed in the crash of a light plane while on a hunting trip. This was a great loss to everyone, especially to Buz who had specifically gone ahead with the purchase of the school because Bud had agreed to come aboard as his right-hand man. Nevertheless, Buz forged ahead, spending enormous amounts of time and money to accomplish his goal. In time, he hired retired Marine Colonel Bob Young, who had been one of Jeffs instructors, to manage the school, and the work went on.

Jeff was welcomed back in a consultant capacity with the added duty of teaching the Masters Series classes each year. These are basic pistol and rifle classes where Jeff recruits the best of his most senior instructors to assist with the teaching. Only a few of these classes are set up each year, but if one wants to receive weapons training directly from this legendary teacher and master of the skill, it is still possible at Gunsite today.

> *"To say that Jeff Cooper is the greatest living teacher of personal defense with fire arms is only to begin the description. He is also the most articulate and intellectual living American proponent of the characteristics of personal honor that founded the United States and have kept her free for over two hundred years.*
>
> *"Even now at nearly 82 years of age, Colonel Cooper pursues a full schedule of writing, hunting and professional events—and still finds time to provide instruction in the use of pistol or rifle to about 100 students each year."*
>
> — *DR. ART ROBINSON*

Books

Jeff has written and had published two new books in the last few years. *The Art of the Rifle* came out in 1997, and *Gargantuan Gunsite Gossip 2* in 2001.

The Art of the Rifle includes almost everything Jeff has learned about shooting rifles. If one reads it, studies it and puts it into play, marksmanship with a rifle will not be a problem. Jeff is very pleased with the book because he feels that all one needs to know about shooting rifles is encapsulated there on the book shelf. It is condensed reading, with no extraneous words, and one finds that there is no room for less than full attention to every detail. A second printing in full color is also available.

Gargantuan Gunsite Gossip 2 is the second compilation of Jeffs extracted writings from his newsletter, formerly titled *Gunsite Gossip* and now titled *Jeff Cooper's Commentaries.* Jeff's newsletter writings were designed to be read by Gunsite graduates. They range widely afield from the subjects of guns and shooting to include many comments upon life in general, politically and socially. The newsletter is both a technical and a philosophical commentary. He writes what occurs to him when it occurs to him, and if he likes the way it comes out, he includes it in his newsletter. These various observations make it into book form if they are true or significant for longer than the moment. Jeff has been criticized for not "sticking to what he knows" but this criticism comes from those who do not know Jeff. He is not a specialist and his excellent education, intellectual curiosity, extraordinary memory, voracious reading habits and ability to plow through the chaff to get to the wheat make him someone worth listening to on any subject at all.

Honors and Events

Jeff has always maintained that life should be measured not in days but in events. In the last few years, events of significance have not slowed at all. Four of these deserve elucidation. 1) At long last, his all-purpose rifle concept found concrete form in the introduction of the Steyr Scout from Steyr-Mannlicher of Austria. 2) He traveled to Italy to be presented an honorary medal as a member of the San Gabriel Possenti Society. 3) After four terms as a member of the Board of Directors of the National Rifle Association, he received a lifetime appointment to the Executive Council. 4) He had a mountain named after him!

1) For perhaps thirty years or more Jeff had conceived and been perfecting the concept of an all-purpose rifle, one that would excel in nearly every situation in which a rifle would be the weapon of choice. As the years went on, the concept was refined in Jeff's mind by observation of rifle classes and competitions and practical experience in the field. Several times Jeff approached different rifle manufacturers with the idea, but none took him up on it until Steyr-Mannlicher of Austria said yes. More specifically, it was Heinz Hambrusch, then president of the company,

Heinz Hambrusch presents Jeff with a special model of the Steyr Scout at the SHOT Show in Las Vegas in 1997.

who said yes and took the concept from idea to product. With the help of excellent designers and engineers within the company, the Steyr Scout was introduced in the fall of 1997. In .308 because of the relatively universal availability of ammunition, the rifle features the following:

—light weight
—box magazine with interchangeable additional magazine in butt
—forward-mounted scope for quick target acquisition
—detente magazine position to provide for ease of practice and/or "catch and release"
—sling mounts
—retractable bipod
—spacers at rear to add or subtract to overall length
—light, crisp trigger
—three-stage safety with lock-down travel mode

In addition to the features that Jeff had conceived, the engineers at Steyr added two things. First, in order to make the light weight limit Jeff insisted upon, they hit upon the idea of fluting the barrel. This had a beneficial side effect which no one anticipated. The fluted barrel not only makes the rifle lighter, but it has the effect of making the barrel stronger as well as causing it to cool faster because of the added surface. Second, the comfortable curved configuration of the composite stock is entirely Steyr's design. It seems to be pleasing to most everyone who picks up a Steyr Scout, making it the ultimate in "user friendliness".

The Steyr Scout is not 100% of what Jeff had conceived, but it comes close and he is generally very pleased with it. He is aware that the entire life's blood of the gun manufacturing industry is newness and change to keep selling guns to gun buyers. Producing a rifle that does it all so that one does not need another rifle ever again is anathema to gun makers. However, Steyr does not market it that way and gun buyers keep on buying the latest thing and the world keeps turning. The fact that the Steyr Scout exists at all pleases Jeff.

The Steyr Scout and friend.

2) Francesco Possenti was an Italian born in Assisi in 1838. The eleventh of thirteen children, it is said that he was accomplished with handgun, rifle and shotgun before he entered the Passionist monastery near the town of Isola del Gran Sasso in central Italy. There he was given the name Gabriele of the Sorrowful One (or Sorrowful Mother). The story is that in 1860, 20 militant renegades (probably Garibaldinis) stormed into the town of Isola following a battle at Pesaro. They began to set fires, steal people's possessions and molest the women. Possenti asked his rector for permission to try to do something to protect the Isolans. The rector agreed and Possenti hurried into town. He managed to disarm two soldiers, taking their pistols. As the other soldiers approached, a lizard ran across the road in front of Possenti. He took aim, fired, and the lizard was shot dead. The marauders were so impressed by this feat that when Possenti ordered the soldiers to put out the fires, return the stolen items and leave town, they did. The grateful people of Isola escorted Possenti back to his monastery in a triumphant procession. Thus, at age 22, Possenti became known as the "Savior of Isola".

St. GABRIEL POSSENTI (1838-1862).
Patron of marksmen.

Possenti died two years later, most likely of tuberculosis, and was canonized in 1920 by Pope Benedict XV. The St. Gabriel Possenti Society was founded by its current president, Mr. John Michael Snyder of Arlington, Virginia. This Society, which emphasizes the historical, philosophical and theological bases for the doctrine of legitimate self-defense, promotes public recognition of Possenti and of his firearms marksmanship. Among its many functions, the Society lobbies the Vatican to have St. Gabriel Possenti declared the Patron of Handgunners.

So, February 27th being St. Gabriel Possenti's Feast Day, the Society held a conference in his memory in Rome in 2001 and among the activities was the presentation of engraved commemorative medallions to selected persons who had demonstrated a commitment to the principles upon which the Society is based. Selected persons must be nominated by

From left to right: Francesco Possenti, Jeff, Archbishop Pereira and John Michael Snyder.

Dad and Mom and I in front of the bust of Pope Pius XI in the Vatican.

members of the Society. Jeff was nominated by his friend and long-time correspondent, Count Antonio Randaccio-Lodi of Rome and received his medallion in the shadow of St. Peter's Basilica. Other recipients on that day included Most Reverend Archbishop Custodio Alvim Pereira (Vice President of the Chapter of St. Peter's Basilica), the current Francesco Possenti (great grandnephew of St. Gabriel Possenti, and three Italian authors. Accompanied by Janelle, myself and the Marc Heim family of Comano, Switzerland, Jeff enjoyed this splendid occasion with his usual gusto. We were able to include a tour of the Vatican, where we made a special stop to take photos of Jeff standing beside a bust of Pope Pius XI— the one who blessed him on that long-ago day in Rome when he was eight years old. It was a momentous visit indeed.

3) Jeff has served six terms as a member of the Board of the National Rifle Association of America. He managed to win his place on each ballot, even once when the Nominating Committee of the NRA did not place his name there. In 2001, he was elected to the Executive Council by unanimous vote of the Board. This is a lifetime position. His current membership on the Board will expire when his term runs out.

This new membership is quite an honor. All other members of the Executive Council save one are former Presidents of the NRA. Mr. Warren Cheek, who served for many years as Secretary of the NRA is the other non-Presidential member. The position involves attendance at meetings, but not voting status. The role is rather like that which Jeff holds at Gunsite—a contributing consultant.

Janelle, Jeff and NRA President Charlton Heston on the occasion of Jeff's election to the Executive Council of the National Rifle Association (2002).

Pik Jeff Cooper

天
山

The Chinese characters for Tien Shan, "Mountains of heaven."

David Bowden at the summit of Pik Jeff Cooper.

4) In September of 2000, a former student of Jeff's traveled to Central Asia as a member of a Russian survey team of cartographers. In Kyrgyzstan they were called upon to chart a very remote and mountainous region in the Tien Shan Range. Most of the peaks had never been surveyed and thus never named. David Bowden was offered the chance to climb and name several of the rugged peaks in the area and one he chose to name Pik Jeff Cooper. If one wishes to look up the location, it is Latitude 42° 4' 50" by Longitude 78° 42' 10". David named another mountain Pik Ulrich Rudel after Hans Ulrich Rudel whom Jeff considers to be the greatest flyer and marksman of all time. Jeff is flattered to be in such company, as well as immensely flattered by the singular honor of having a mountain named after him.

Reflections

When I first set out to write this book, I very much wanted to gain as clear an understanding of my father as an individual as I could, given my unavoidable perspective. I am generally pleased with the result, yet more cognizant than ever that it is difficult at best to "know" another human being. We humans are ever-evolving and constrained by our own viewpoints, some of which, in turn, are also ever-evolving. In an effort to lift the lid just a little more, I hit upon the idea of asking my father to list those people he most admires and why. The following is his very telling reply:

Last week our number three child handed me a daunting assignment. She asked me to prepare a list of individuals I deemed particularly worthy of admiration—to be of either sex, of any age, and of any historic period. This set me to thinking to the extent that I am at present in danger of overheating my bearings. Lindy asked me not only to list these people, but to add a very short statement of why I thought each to be worthy of admiration. A proper response to this demand might take many years to complete and more research than is available at any source of which I am aware. The fact that a task is difficult seldom diminishes its zest—often to the contrary—however, I realize that I cannot give this job the effort it deserves, but I feel obliged to take a swing at it anyway. Herewith, therefore, "the list"—incomplete and unjust as it may be. In no order.

LES ADMIRABLES

JANE ELLEN MARKS COOPER, my bride of 60 years. I have lightly termed her "The Countess," as that is the only title I may apply to the consort of a "guru". The Countess is the only person I have ever encountered, either in person or by reputation, who is without flaw. Life has handed her its full share of tribulation, fulfillment and adventure, and she has met each successive year with unmatched wisdom, courage and pleasure—in equal measure. The Countess is one of God's best handworks. I must have led a truly exemplary life in my previous incarnation if I deserve her in this one.

SOCRATES. Thought is what raises man above the level of the beast, and Socrates taught us how to think.

BILL BUCKLEY. Here is one who has combined the stylistic challenges of life with its physical enjoyment in truly outstanding style.

WADE HAMPTON of Carolina. According to legend, General Hampton was the best horseman, the finest shot, the best dancer, the richest man, the strongest man, the handsomest man, and the best at everything else that myth could create. When the war broke out, Wade Hampton, without a whisper of military training or experience, recruited, equipped, trained, and organized his own "Hampton Legion," and marched off to fight superbly for his state and for the Confederacy.

MERRILL TWINING, Lieutenant General, USMC. According to three different generals, Merrill Twining was the finest mind that the Marine Corps ever produced. He also was the first Marine (subsequent to those who fought separately at Pearl Harbor) to kill a Japanese soldier in personal combat.

CARLOS WIDMANN, my diversified host in Guatemala. Carlos is a generalized big shot who runs his own plantations, directs his own banks, flies his own aircraft (fixed wing and rotary), is father to six successful children, is a frequently suggested candidate for president of the republic (a job which he always turns down), an honor graduate of Orange Gunsite, and a very fine shot.

HANNIBAL. He was not only a self-made military genius, but a conspicuously charming individual. He peculiarly inspired love in the men who fought for him and repeatedly defeated the might of Rome—not with the Carthaginian army but with a motley crew that he largely recruited and inspired himself. This was a man that it would be a pleasure to have to dinner, assuming that the host could speak Punic, Latin, Celt-Iberian, Etruscan, and Greek, the last of which he preferred.

GEORGE PATTON. He was the quintessential American soldier, a West Pointer who rose to the occasion when at last it fell his way. Patton was raised for the part, trained for the part, looked the part, acted the part, and was the part. And just by the way, he was an outstanding horseman, an Olympic swordsman and a very fine shot. There is the role model for the American soldier.

CORTÉZ. Hernando Cortéz, adventurer and missionary, was "the Grand Conquistador." Here was the man who accomplished everything with nothing. With a force of 400 "gentlemen/adventurers" and 200 beached mariners, he set forth into an unknown world to conquer an empire of between six and sixteen million people, and he brought it off. Eyewitness chroniclers assert that his two most striking personal characteristics were magnificent horsemanship and an almost unbelievable plausibility. One historian claims that Cortéz "could talk anybody into or out of anything." As with the other Conquistadors, Cortéz came "to the New World to serve God and to become rich." He did very well at both tasks.

CLIFTON BLEDSOE CATES, General, USMC. Cliff Cates was my first boss as Commandant of the Basic School. He went on up as Commander of the First Marines at Guadalcanal, and finally as Commandant of the Marine Corps. He won the French Croix de Guerre at Belleau Wood. He commanded at Tinian, the only perfectly executed battle of World War II. As Commanding General of Marine Corps Schools at Quantico, he constituted the nerve center of the Marine Corps for four years. Typically he always regarded himself as, first of all, a rifleman, certainly an endangered species today.

ALKIBIADES. Here is a man of such brilliance that even the Greeks of the Golden Age regarded him as an exaggeration. At one time during the Peloponnesian War, Alkibiades was under sentence of death in both Athens and Sparta at the same time. He was artistically talented (producing his own plays), extremely rich, largely unprincipled and, according to eyewitnesses, the handsomest man anybody ever saw. Quite a combination.

THOMAS SOWELL, currently the outstanding intellect of our time. Sowell stands as the incarnate rebuttal of the principle of affirmative action.

JULIUS CAESAR. This was the man who was "too good." From childhood he was better at everything he tried than anybody else who tried it. He is known as a warrior, but he was also an explorer, an historian, a naturalist, and a noteworthy lecher. He not only introduced the Roman short sword (gladius hispaniensis) to the Roman army, but he explicitly defined the Latin language. He was, in all respects, "too good," and the Roman politicians could not put up with that. When a man stands that tall, other men will eventually jerk the rug from under him.

HERMAN HANNEKEN, Brigadier General, USMC. Hanneken, in 1918, was the Sergeant of Marines who pulled off what is possibly the most artistic spook shot of all time. As an acting captain of Haitian Constabulary, Hanneken was given an impossible task which he carried out brilliantly. He was the man we needed when Osama bin Laden declared holy war against Western civilization. He was not only the perfect "tool for the task", but he looked the part. I know, because I met him personally.

FINN AAGAARD (pronounced "auger"). Finn was a Norseman relocated in Africa during its great hunting days. He was a professional hunter (PH) of the old breed such as extolled by Dinesen, Roosevelt, Bell, and Hemingway. When East Africa bit the dust, Finn moved to the United States and settled in Texas, where we knew him. He was first of all a hunter and he excelled at every sort of hunting. He was a good organizer, a fine naturalist and an excellent shot. He was notable for his outstanding modesty, and he was a man who did not have all that much to be modest about. Independently, he and I resolved never to "press trigger" on a leopard, as he put it. Long ago

298

I decided that I would never shoot a leopard (barring emergencies), since the beast is simply too beautiful to shoot. Some years thereafter I discovered that Finn felt the same way. Neither of us condemns the leopard hunter, if the hunt is conducted in properly sporting fashion, but neither of us would ever hunt a leopard.

VON LETOW-VORBECK. Von Letow began World War I as a German major in East Africa. Since Britannia ruled the waves, he was cut off from his homeland at once and stayed out of contact until the war was over, four years later. Here is another man who accomplished a great deal with almost nothing. He had no supplies, no communication, no reinforcements, and little in the way of popular support, yet he fought with what he had for four years, taking what he needed in both equipment and supplies from his enemies on the spot. He was contacted only twice by the Kaiser, the first time to be told that he was promoted from Major to Major General, and the second to tell him that he had been awarded the Blue Max. His great setback, by his own account, was the breakage of his eyeglasses which forced him to read maps remotely by means of an aide.

CLINT ANCKER, Colonel, U.S. Army. A personal friend, Colonel Ancker is a fine example of that perfect man, the scholar/warrior. The list is small, including as it does Xenophon, Caesar, Marcus Aurelius, Einhard, Clausewitz, Mahon, and only a few others. Colonel Ancker is a West Pointer who did a full job in Viet Nam and spent years with the armored forces of the United States along the Iron Curtain in Germany. He also got quickly into the Gulf War, where he served as S3 with the 11th Armored Cavalry. The wind slipped out of his sails during the disastrous Clinton years, during which Colonel Ancker would doubtless have gone on up to high command in the military service which the Clinton clique so disgracefully despised. Great men are not common, but we do sometimes find them. This happens, however, only when there is a slot for them to fill. If the circumstances had not been just right, no one would ever have heard of Genghis Khan, for example. Clint Ancker is, in my opinion, a significant American soldier. He is a Charter Member of the Gunsite African Rifles.

DENIS EARP, Lieutenant General, South African Air Force. It has been our great good fortune to have been the guest of General Earp on several visits to South Africa, where we had occasion to discuss the conduct of the Angolan War to the north. General Earp is a highly cultivated man, one of the few now alive who has flown a Spitfire in combat, and he is also an experienced hunter of African big game. Through the good offices of Denis Earp, I have been able to discuss operations in that rather obscure war in more detail than most, and I have learned many things which would never have come to my attention, either from textbooks or from the popular press. I know, for example, how the South Africans used the French Mirage fighter to the dismay of the East German pilots who flew from the Communist side, and I also know the details of the employment of the outstanding South African artillery. General Earp has led a very full military life, in the course of which he tragically lost his only son, killed in action. He is a distinguished man in whose acquaintance I take great pleasure.

DENYS REITZ was conspicuously active as a youth in the second Boer War, and described his adventures therein most expertly in the notable account "Commando." Since he was underage at the start of the war, he requested special permission from Paul Kruger to sign up and bear arms. According to legend, Kruger told him that the English outnumbered the Boers 3-to-1 and asked if he thought he could handle that problem. Reitz responded, "Sir, if I can get three in a row, I can take them all out with one shot." As it turned out, he fought a most impressive war, and his account of it is required reading for anyone who seeks an understanding of irregular warfare.

MARC HEIM. Marc Heim is another personal friend whom I admire very much. He is a Swiss now living in the Ticino, though he travels extensively in Taiwan, Israel, South Africa, and the United States. He is an extraordinarily good shot with both pistol and rifle, and has established several records which are unlikely to be surpassed (among which is the breaking of four flying clay birds out of five, with a sporting rifle). Marc is fluent in "all the necessary languages." He is several times a graduate of Orange Gunsite who acquired E tickets with both rifle and pistol. As such he is a Charter Member of the Gunsite African Rifles.

THEODORE ROOSEVELT. Too little can be set forth to characterize Roosevelt I, who stands as one of the two great American presidents. As with most great men, TR was especially outstanding for his versatility, being as he was a scholar, historian, explorer, rancher, soldier, and politician. One does not pick flaws with such a man, but if Roosevelt I had a weakness it was that he was a rather poor marksman. To put it bluntly, he did not shoot well. But we can forgive him that, since his career not only does credit to the man, but also to the country which he served. He may be properly termed "Roosevelt the Great."

HANS-ULRICH RUDEL, Oberst, Luftwaffe. Rudel was one of those greats who goes by one name only, encompassing in one man probably the greatest marksman and the greatest flyer who ever lived. Here is the man who destroyed 519 armored vehicles, personally, one at a time, from the air. Here is the man who destroyed the Battleship Marat with one bomb. Here is the man who shot down sixteen fighter planes with a bomber. Here is the man

300

Jeff met with Hans-Ulrich Rudel in Germany in 1978.

who combined skill, hardihood and valor in a way that would not be believed as fiction. It was my privilege to spend a day with him at Sonthofen in Bavaria. It was a curious feeling to shake the deadliest hand heretofore known to man.

WINSTON CHURCHILL. Churchill is another great man who cannot be characterized in capsule form; scholar, warrior, author, philosopher, historian, and politician. As it was said of him by Field Marshal Montgomery, "He was the greatest man of the twentieth century and the greatest Englishman of all time."

JOHN GANNAWAY. John is the gunman to define the breed, but he is more than that. Not only a true master of smallarms, he is one of very few master teachers of the art. He knows all that needs knowing about both shooting and hunting—an incarnate encyclopedia of weaponcraft. He is also a Charter Member of the Gunsite African Rifles.

ERIK VON KUEHNELT-LEDDIHN was the most erudite man of our age. The scope of his learning was staggering to Bill Buckley, whose grasp of things in general fairly staggers me. A true polymath, *K.L. was qualified in all fields—fluent in eleven languages, among other things. In this depressing age of ignorance, it is inspiring to know that people like K.L. can exist. It gives us confidence in God's expertise.*

The foregoing material was prepared in answer to a request from daughter Lindy as described. I was startled at the request since it asked for a massive effort in historical biography, which would involve many years work at the library at a major university. I undertook the task with trepidation, so large that I cannot possibly do justice to it. But Lindy wants it, and here it is, "warts and all." There are many names not included whose absence will distress me when I call them to mind, but I cannot wait until I think of everyone. So I offer the list with full apologies. (How can I put in Hannibal but not Alexander? How can I put in Hampton and exclude Lee? How can I leave out Tolkien and Kipling and Edgar Rice Burroughs? My mind is not big enough and my life is not long enough. Oh, rue the day! Let us play anyway.)

One may draw any number of conclusions as to my father's character from the list he compiled in response to my request. He values excellence above all. He admires warriors, intellectuals, achievers, copers. He has a special admiration for those who accomplish much with very little. He definitely has a soft spot for those who achieve with style and, ever the aesthete, those who look good while doing so. It may not be obvious from what he has written, but he especially admires a cheerful spirit and a good sense of humor.

One of the most enlightening aspects to me is the fact that he responded willingly, quickly and with relish. How many people do you know who would not think this was a massive chore, to be put off until the requester grew tired of asking? His enthusiasm for intellectual exercises is one of his most unique characteristics.

More Reflections

My father has been pleased with this book—both with the fact that I undertook the task at all and with the final product. Its very existence has afforded us the opportunity to spend more time together and that has been most pleasurable as well as educational for me. One cannot spend time with my dad without learning—it is his passion and he pulls his companions along with him.

Dad is at a point in his life where he fully realizes that most of his life is behind him. He contemplates this without trepidation and has spent a certain

Jeff was the keynote speaker at an NRA banquet in Prescott in February of 2001.

amount of time discussing with me what he hopes his life and achievements have meant. I believe the most satisfying moments for him are in contemplation of the letters he receives from people whose lives have been saved (or who have been able to save the lives of others) because of something they have learned from him. In addition, those letters from doubters who later write to tell him, "You were right!", give him a great deal of gratification.

In any case, Dad continues to teach and travel and write and learn and enjoy the good things in life to the fullest. Age has not diminished his capacity or enthusiasm to pass along his wisdom to those who are willing to listen, and learn.

I ran across this verse from Rudyard Kipling and it struck me as being applicable to my father as well:

The Appeal

"If I have given you delight by aught that I have done

Let me lie quiet in that night which shall be yours anon

And for the little, little span the dead are bourn in mind

Seek not to question other than the books I leave behind."

The upcoming occasion of their 60th wedding anniversary prompted a toast by friends at the NRA meeting in January of 2002.

Epilogue

So there you have it—my exploration of the man who is my father—an attempt to discover who he is, what made him that way and why who he is has engendered such admiration and devotion from so many people all over the world. He believes that excellence in individual human achievement is worth striving for and that those who choose to do so are living as they should and will be therefore fulfilled. He believes in those systems which support the individual in his efforts and decries those which do not. My mother put it very well when she said, "He is wise and has always been sure of his moral and spiritual values, from whence they came and what backs them up historically. He has never hesitated to express not only how he feels about something but why it is a good idea. Jeff does not mince words and he won't put up with people who try to dilute what he says. I can't help but agree that that very firmness is the key to his attraction."

As a child, your father is simply that and you cannot conceive of any other. As you mature, you meet other fathers and watch them interact with their children and still, the unique character of your own father is elusive, obscured by its very proximity.

In my life, it was not until I had been away from home for years that I began to encounter fans of my dad's in the most unusual places who talked to me about him and let me know how much what he said and wrote and taught meant to them—in some instances changed their lives profoundly. No one else in my acquaintance had a father with so strong and wide an impact.

And then came the Africa trip in 1994, where I met people for the first time whose names I had heard for years. Their warmth and intelligence and accomplishment shone. Here were outstanding individuals who looked to my father as a beacon. These were highly successful and personable people whose regard for Jeff was enormous. The little bar called "Cooper's Corner" at the game farm in the Eastern Transvaal was the epitome of a journey that opened my eyes to my father's legacy.

As I researched and wrote this book, my relationship with my parents changed. They became less distant and more human. I came to admire them less because they are my parents and more because of who they are and what they have accomplished. I admire them for better reason than I did before.

I know my father is not without fault. I am not blind to the fact that he snubs people when he has decided he has no time for them. He sometimes speaks harshly before he considers deeply what impact his words might have. He speaks his mind with not much thought to people's sensitivities and feelings. He dismisses the interests of others when he thinks they have no merit and makes no attempt to hide his feelings for the sake of diplomacy. I find it interesting that he knows so little of the personal lives of his closest friends. He "knows" people only by their accomplishments.

He is also enormously generous in a uniquely discriminating way. He follows his highly developed sense of what is fitting and what is not. For instance, he is unsparing with his time and his knowledge. What he knows is available to everyone who shows an interest because he feels that seeking after knowledge is a noble effort. With his material possessions he is never aimless in his giving. I have known him to lend highly-prized possessions to persons he does not know really well because they showed a particular aptitude and seemed to appreciate the loan. He has put all five of his grandchildren (and me) through the High Performance Driving course at Bondurant's school because he thinks this is a skill we should not be without. He does not push weaponcraft instruction on anyone, but the three grandchildren who expressed an interest not only received his instruction in rifle technique, but they all got to travel to Africa with Jeff and Janelle and hunt for their first trophies under his expert tutelage (as did I).

In 1986, he and Janelle hosted twenty-four guests to a weekend at the wonderful Hotel Heinz in Vianden, Luxembourg. This was an expression of appreciation to all their friends on the continent who had hosted them over the years in various ways. His generosity is never without thought—never without the purpose to uplift or instruct.

He is also enthusiastic and fun and demanding in the very best sense of the word. As friend Marti Tueller puts it, "Jeff creates this wonderful atmosphere where one is required to be civilized and use one's brain." To me he is kind and loving and the best father in the world. I share the sentiments of my Uncle Jay when he said, "I certainly have a great deal of respect and admiration and a little feeling that I hoped I would never disappoint Jeff."

If this book has turned out to be an unabashed tribute, so be it. That was not my intention when I began, but the story unfolded by itself and there are no skeletons hiding in the closet. The result lies here for you to judge. My hope is to have enlightened and perhaps entertained. If my father's story is also inspirational, that would be the best legacy I could hope to leave.

My father and I, 1994.

Acknowledgements

I could not have written this book without the unstinting support of my husband, Joe, and my mother and father. They encouraged me to tackle this project in my own way and in my own time and so allowed the final product to emerge.

Special thanks to Clifford Douglas, without whose initial suggestion I would not have attempted the book.

Special thanks to Nancy Tappan, who encouraged me and helped with everything.

Special thanks to Paul Kirchner, who designed the jacket cover.

Thanks to all the people I interviewed for information and insights. Many of them are quoted throughout the text and many are not. They all took time to write to me or speak into my tape recorder and share their experiences for my dissection and use. I am grateful to them all.

One special person who would have added so much to my story died before I made the appointment to see him. This was my friend, Bruce Nelson. He lived close by and was just two years older than I, so I thought I could always see him and I put off our interview while I tackled the more distant subjects. He died unexpectedly and entirely too soon on February 15, 1995. His passing was a shock and a great loss to us all. I missed the opportunity to explore what I know would have been his thoughtful insight into the life and contribution of my father. I miss him. We all do.

There are many others whose encouragement and support helped me greatly. I thank them all and hope they will not miss being named directly. I consider myself supremely lucky to have friends and family so ready to assist me in my efforts.

COOPER — PATERNAL

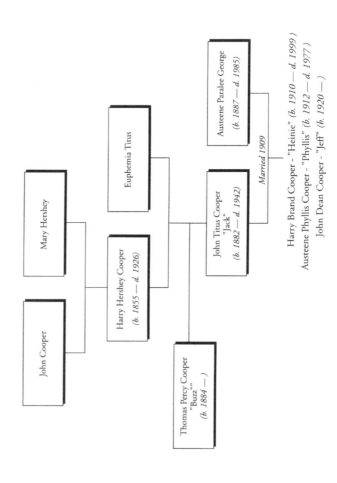

John Cooper

Mary Hershey

Harry Hershey Cooper
(b. 1855 — d. 1926)

Euphemia Titus

Thomas Percy Cooper
"Buzz"
(b. 1884 —)

John Titus Cooper
"Jack"
(b. 1882 — d. 1942)

Austeene Paralee George
(b. 1887 — d. 1985)

Married 1909

Harry Brand Cooper - "Heinie" (b. 1910 — d. 1999)
Austeene Phyllis Cooper - "Phyllis" (b. 1912 — d. 1977)
John Dean Cooper - "Jeff" (b. 1920 —)

COOPER — MATERNAL

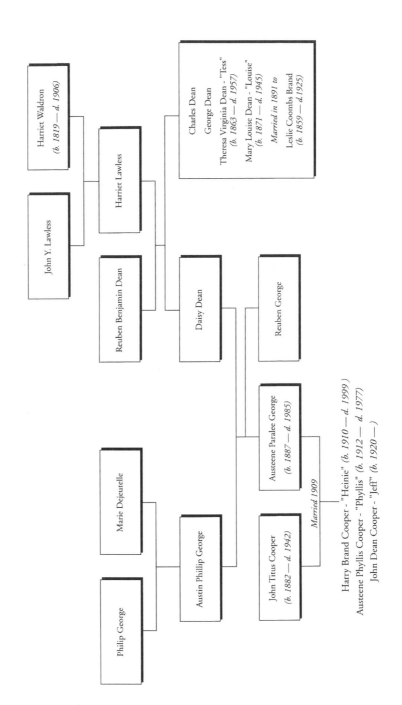

Harriet Waldron
(b. 1819 — d. 1906)

John Y. Lawless

Harriet Lawless

Reuben Benjamin Dean

Charles Dean
George Dean
Theresa Virginia Dean - "Tess"
(b. 1863 — d. 1957)
Mary Louise Dean - "Louise"
(b. 1871 — d. 1945)
Married in 1891 to
Leslie Coombs Brand
(b. 1859 — d. 1925)

Daisy Dean

Reuben George

Marie Dejeuelle

Philip George

Austin Phillip George

Austeene Paralee George
(b. 1887 — d. 1985)

John Titus Cooper
(b. 1882 — d. 1942)

Married 1909

Harry Brand Cooper - "Heinie" (b. 1910 — d. 1999)
Austeene Phyllis Cooper - "Phyllis" (b. 1912 — d. 1977)
John Dean Cooper - "Jeff" (b. 1920 —)

MARKS — PATERNAL

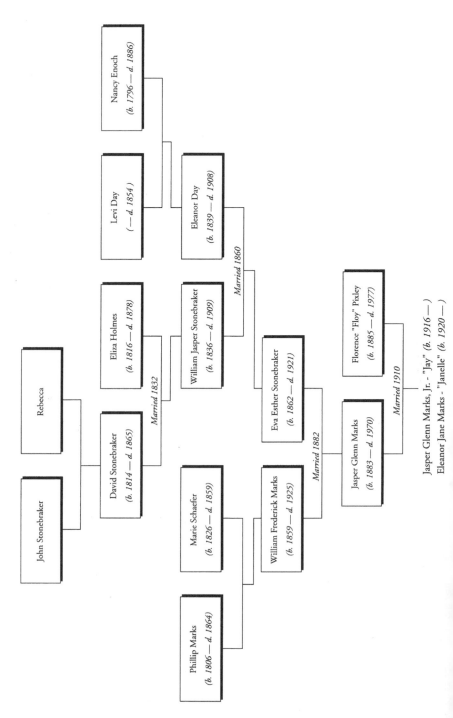

John Stonebraker

Rebecca

David Stonebraker
(b. 1814 — d. 1865)

Eliza Holmes
(b. 1816 — d. 1878)

Married 1832

Levi Day
(— d. 1854)

Nancy Enoch
(b. 1796 — d. 1886)

William Jasper Stonebraker
(b. 1836 — d. 1909)

Eleanor Day
(b. 1839 — d. 1908)

Married 1860

Phillip Marks
(b. 1806 — d. 1864)

Marie Schaefer
(b. 1826 — d. 1859)

William Frederick Marks
(b. 1859 — d. 1925)

Eva Esther Stonebraker
(b. 1862 — d. 1921)

Married 1882

Jasper Glenn Marks
(b. 1883 — d. 1970)

Florence "Floy" Pixley
(b. 1885 — d. 1977)

Married 1910

Jasper Glenn Marks, Jr. - "Jay" *(b. 1916 —)*
Eleanor Jane Marks - "Janelle" *(b. 1920 —)*

MARKS — MATERNAL
(PIXLEY)

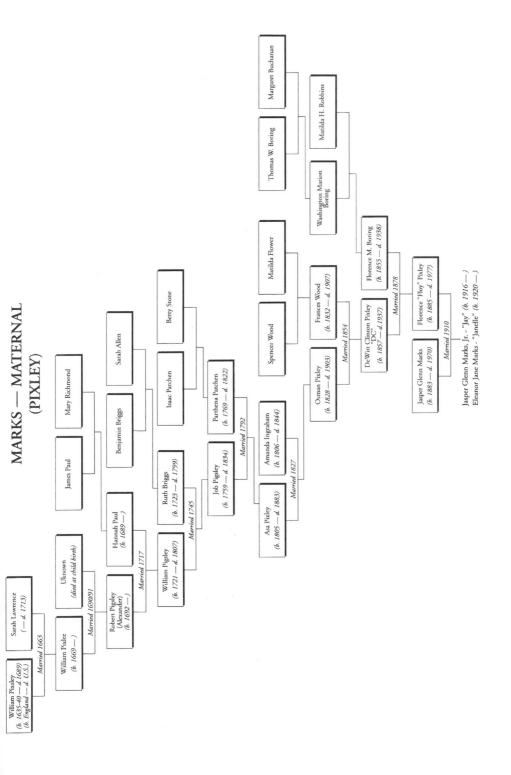

William Pixley
(b. 1635–40 — d. 1689)
(b. England — d. U.S.)

Sarah Lawrence
(— d. 1713)

Married 1663

William Pixlee
(b. 1669 —)

Uknown
(died at child birth)

Married 169091

James Paul

Mary Richmond

Robert Pigsley
(Alexander)
(b. 1692 —)

Hannah Paul
(b. 1689 —)

Married 1717

Benjamin Briggs

Sarah Allen

William Pigsley
(b. 1721 — d. 1807)

Ruth Briggs
(b. 1723 — d. 1799)

Married 1745

Isaac Patchen

Betty Stone

Job Pigsley
(b. 1759 — d. 1834)

Parthena Patchen
(b. 1769 — d. 1822)

Married 1792

Asa Pixley
(b. 1805 — d. 1883)

Amanda Ingraham
(b. 1806 — d. 1844)

Married 1827

Spencer Wood

Matilda Flower

Osman Pixley
(b. 1828 — d. 1903)

Frances Wood
(b. 1832 — d. 1907)

Married 1854

Thomas W. Boring

Margaret Buchanan

Washington Marion
Boring

Matilda H. Robbins

DeWitt Clinton Pixley
"DC"
(b. 1857 — d. 1937)

Florence M. Boring
(b. 1855 — d. 1938)

Married 1878

Jasper Glenn Marks
(b. 1883 — d. 1970)

Florence "Floy" Pixley
(b. 1885 — d. 1977)

Married 1910

Jasper Glenn Marks, Jr. - "Jay" (b. 1916 —)
Eleanor Jane Marks - "Janelle" (b. 1920 —)